Lectures on Rhetoric and Oratory

Delivered to the Classes of Senior and Junior Sophisters in Harvard University – A History of Public Speaking

Vol. 1 of 2

By John Quincy Adams

Late Boylston Professor of Rhetoric and Oratory

Published by Pantianos Classics

ISBN-13: 978-1-78987-346-7

First published in 1810

Contents

Advertisement

THE literary institutions of our country are under many obligations to the mercantile profession. The enlarged and liberal views of opulent individuals, in this class of the community, have frequently prompted them to laudable and munificent appropriations for the promotion of science and the means of education. Among men of this description the benevolent founder of the professorship, under which the following lectures were delivered, is highly distinguished.

Nicholas Boylston esq. was an eminent merchant of Boston. He died August 18, 1771, aged fifty six. In the gazette notices of his death, he is characterized as "a man of good understanding and sound judgment, diligent in his business, though not a slave to it, upright in his dealings, honest and sincere in all his professions, and a stranger to dissimulation." [1] By his last will, made a few weeks before his decease, among other judicious dispositions of his property, he bequeathed fifteen hundred pounds lawful money, as a foundation for a professorship of rhetoric and oratory in Harvard College. This sum was paid to the college treasurer in February 1772, by his executors, and was placed at interest, for the purpose expressed by the donor.

The progressive accumulation of the fund was in a degree impeded, in the course of the revolutionary war; and it was not until the year 1804, that the amount was considered adequate to the object. In the summer of that year, the "rules, directions, and statutes of the *Boylston professorship of rhetoric and oratory* in Harvard college," which had previously been prepared and adopted by the corporation, were approved by the board of overseers.

In June 1805 the honorable *John Quincy Adams* was chosen, by the corporation, the first professor on this foundation. This choice was confirmed by the overseers on the twenty fifth of July. Mr. Adams accepted the appointment with a reservation, which should leave him at liberty to attend on his public duties in congress; he being at that time a senator of the United States
from Massachusetts. At subsequent meetings of the corporation and overseers, a dispensation was assented to in this particular, and some alterations were made in the statutes.

He was installed June 12, 1806; and on that occasion pronounced the inaugural discourse, which was soon after published, at the unanimous request of the students; and which is now prefixed to his lectures.

The professor immediately after his induction entered on the duties of his office; but, in consequence of his public engagements, and as permitted by the terms of his acceptance, confined his attention to a course of public lectures to the resident graduates, and to the two senior classes of under-graduates, and to presiding at the declamations of the two senior classes. His public lectures were continued weekly, in term time, as required by the statutes, excepting such intermissions, as were occasioned by his attendance on confess.

On the twelfth of August 1808 he completed his course, comprising thirty six lectures, and had advanced nearly through a repetition of it, when, early in July last, he announced, by a letter to the corporation, the resignation of his office, "on account of a call in the foreign service of the country." He took leave of the students in his lecture, delivered on the twenty eighth of July, and soon afterward embarked for Russia, being appointed minister plenipotentiary to the court of St. Petersburg. Previously to his departure, he was respectfully requested, by the two senior classes in the college, to consent to a publication of his lectures. He yielded to this request, though not without hesitation, as his approaching departure and various incidental occupations would render a revisal of the work impracticable; and especially as the whole subject, belonging to the professorship, had not been discussed. These lectures however comprehend what, in his estimation, belongs to rhetoric; and contain the theory of his branch. The practical part, or what belonged to *oratory*, he intended to treat at a future period; and to give, under that head, a detailed analysis of the productions of the most distinguished orators, ancient and modern.

However the author may have regretted, that these lectures were thus destined to appear before the world without his deliberate revisal, they will, it is believed, be considered as a valuable acquisition to the public, in their present form. The multiplied stores, derived from extensive reading, the energies of a strong and discriminating mind, and the results of much experience and observation, are therein exhibited. To relieve and animate the discussions, appertaining to his subject, he thought proper frequently to indulge in figurative expression to a degree, which some may not entirely approve. This however was not less the result of deliberation, than of taste. He considered his auditory; that impression was indispensable; and regarded the intimation of Quinctilian, *Studium discendi voluntate constat.* It is certain that his success, in securing the fixed and habitual attention of his auditors, was complete. It will be found that they were not excited without an adequate and interesting object. In addition to the mass of information and ingenious discussion on his appropriate topic, those great and essential principles, on which the true dignity and beauty of the human character depend, will be found, on every fit occasion, to be forcibly inculcated. Like his admired *Milton,* it was his constant aim to point out "the right path of a virtuous and noble education." In concurrence with the habitual genius of our Alma Mater, he consulted the best good of the pupils, and "sought to temper them such lectures and explanations upon every opportunity," as might "lead and draw them in willing obedience, inflamed with the study of learning and the admiration of virtue; stirred up with high hopes of living to be brave men, and worthy patriots, dear to God, and famous to all ages."

The corporation lost no time in supplying the vacancy, occasioned by Mr. Adams' resignation. On the twenty fifth of August last, they made choice of the Rev. *Joseph McKean* for that office. His election was confirmed by the overseers. Mr. *McKean,* having accepted the appointment, was installed, in the usual academical form, on the thirty first of October; and on that occasion delivered an appropriate Latin address. He entered immediately on the duties of his office.

February 26, 1810.

[1] In the philosophy chamber, at Cambridge, is an excellent portrait of this gentleman, painted by *Copley.* It is in a style of ease and amenity, which renders it singularly prepossessing. The expression of the countenance is admirable. *Lavater* would have said, *I see there the genuine indications of intelligence, rectitude, and benevolence. That man must have been the delight of his friends.*

Inaugural Oration, Delivered at the Author's Installation, as Boylston Professor of Rhetoric and Oratory

IT is the fortune of some opinions, as well as of some individual characters, to have been, during a long succession of ages, subjects of continual controversy among mankind. In forming an estimate of the moral or intellectual merits of many a person, whose name is recorded in the volumes of history, their virtues and vices are so nearly balanced, that their station in the ranks of fame has never been precisely assigned, and their reputation, even after death, vibrates upon the hinges of events, with which they have little or no perceptible connexion. Such too has been the destiny of the arts and sciences in general, and of the art of rhetoric in particular. Their advancement and decline have been alternate in the annals of the world. At one period they have been cherished, admired, and cultivated; at another neglected, despised, and oppressed. Like the favorites of princes, they have had their turns of unbounded influence and of excessive degradation. Now the enthusiasm of their votaries has raised them to the pinnacle of greatness; now a turn of the wheel has hurled them prostrate in the dust. Nor have these great and sudden revolutions always resulted from causes seemingly capable of producing such effects. At one period the barbarian conqueror destroys, at another he adopts, the arts of the vanquished people. The Grecian muses were led captive and in chains to Rome. Once there, they not only burst asunder their own fetters, but soon, mounting the triumphal car, rode with supreme ascendency over their victors. More than once have the Tartars, after carrying conquest and desolation over the empire of China, been subdued in turn by the arts of the nation, they had enslaved. As if by a wise and equitable retribution of nature the authors of violence were doomed to be overpowered by their own prosperity, and to find in every victory the seeds of defeat.

On the other hand the arts and sciences, at the hour of their highest exaltation, have been often reproached and insulted by those, on whom, they had bestowed their choicest favors, and most cruelly assaulted by the weapons, which themselves had conferred. At the zenith of modern civilization the palm of unanswered eloquence was awarded to the writer, who maintained, that the sciences had always promoted rather the misery, than the happiness of mankind; and in the age and nation, which heard the voice of Demosthenes, Socrates has been represented as triumphantly demonstrating, that rhetoric cannot be dignified with the name of an art; that it is but a pernicious practice...the mere counterfeit of justice. This opinion has had its followers from the days of Socrates to our own; and it still remains an inquiry among men, as in the age of Plato, and in that of Cicero, whether eloquence is an art, worthy of the cultivation of a wise and virtuous man. To assist us in bringing the mind to a satisfactory result of this inquiry, it is proper to consider the art, as well in its nature, as in its effects; to derive our inferences, not merely from the uses, which have been made of it, but from the purposes, to which it ought to be applied, and the end, which it is destined to answer.

The peculiar and highest characteristic, which distinguishes man from the rest of the animal creation, is reason. It is by this attribute, that our species is constituted the great link between the physical and intellectual world. By our passions and appetites we are placed on a level with the herds of the forest; by our reason we participate of the divine nature itself. Formed of clay, and compounded of dust, we are, in the scale of creation, little higher than the clod of the valley; endowed with reason, we are little lower than the angels. It is by the gift of reason, that the human species enjoys the exclusive and inestimable privilege of progressive improvement, and is enabled to avail itself of the advantages of individual discovery. As the necessary adjunct and vehicle of reason, the faculty of speech was also bestowed as an exclusive privilege upon man; not the mere utterance of articulate sounds; not the mere cries of passion, which he has in common with the lower orders of animated nature; but as the conveyance of thought; as the means of rational intercourse with his fellow-creature, and of humble communion with his God. It is by the means of reason, clothed with speech, that the most precious blessings of social life are communicated from man to man, and that supplication, thanksgiving, and praise, are addressed to the Author of the universe. How justly then, with the great dramatic poet, may we exclaim,

"Sure, he that made us with such large discourse,
Looking before and after, gave us not
That capability and God-like reason,
To rust in us, unus'd."

A faculty thus elevated, given us for so sublime a purpose, and destined to an end so excellent, was not intended by the supreme Creator to be buried in the grave of neglect. As the source of all human improvements, it was itself susceptible of improvement by industry and application, by observation and experience. Hence, wherever man has been found in a social state, and wherever he has been sensible of his dependence upon a supreme disposer of events, the value and the power of public speaking, if not universally acknowledged, has at least been universally felt.

For the truth of these remarks, let me appeal to the testimony of history, sacred and profane. We shall find it equally clear and conclusive from the earliest of her records, which have escaped the ravages of time. When the people of God were groaning under the insupportable oppressions of Egyptian bondage, and the Lord of Hosts condescended, by miraculous interposition, to raise them up a deliverer, the want of eloquence was pleaded, by the chosen object of his ministry, as an argument of his incompetency for the high commission, with which he was to be charged. To supply this deficiency, which, even in the communication of more than human powers. Eternal Wisdom had not seen fit to remove, another favored servant of the Most High was united in the exalted trust of deliverance, and specially appointed, for the purpose of declaring the divine will to the oppressor and the oppressed; to the monarch of Egypt and the children of Israel. "Is not Aaron, the Levite, thy brother? I know that he can speak well. And he shall be thy spokesman unto the people; and he shall be, even he shall be to thee instead of a mouth, and thou shalt be to him instead of God."

It was not sufficient for the beneficent purposes of divine Providence, that the shepherd of his flock should be invested with the power of performing signs and wonders to authenticate his mission, and command obedience to his words. The appropriate instrument to appall the heart of the tyrant upon his throne, and to control the wayward dispositions of the people, was an eloquent speaker; and the importance of the duty is apparent in the distinction, which separated it from all the other transcendent gifts, with which the inspired leader was endowed, and committed it, as a special charge, to his associate. Nor will it escape your observation, that, when the first great object of their joint mission was accomplished, and the sacred system of laws and polity for the emancipated nation was delivered by the voice of heaven from the holy mountain, the same eloquent SPEAKER was Separated from among the children of Israel, to minister in the priest's office; to bear the iniquity of their holy things; to offer up to God, their creator and preserver, the public tribute of their social adoration.

In the fables of Greece and Egypt the importance of eloquence is attested by the belief, that the art of public speaking was of celestial origin, ascribed to the invention of a God, who, from the possession of this faculty, was supposed to be the messenger and interpreter of Olympus. It is attested by the solicitude, with which the art was cultivated, at a period of the remotest antiquity.

With the first glimpse of historical truth, which bursts from the oriental regions of mythological romance, in that feeble and dubious twilight, which scarcely discerns the distinction between the fictions of pagan superstition and the narrative of real events, a school of rhetoric and oratory, established in the Peloponnesus, dawns upon our view. After the lapse of a thousand years from that time, Pausanias, a Grecian geographer and historian, explicitly asserts, that he had read a treatise upon the art, composed by the founder of this school, a contemporary and relative of Theseus, in the age preceding that of the Trojan war. The poems of Homer abound with still more decisive proofs of the estimation, in which the powers of oratory were held, and of the attention, with which it was honored, as an essential object of instruction in the education of youth.

From that era, through the long series of Greek and Roman history down to the gloom of universal night, in which the glories of the Roman empire expired, the triumphs and the splendor of eloquence are multiplied and conspicuous. Then it was, that the practice of the art attained a perfection, ever

9

since unrivalled, and to which in succeeding times have listened with admiration and despair. At Athens and Rome a town meeting could scarcely be held, without being destined to immortality; a question of property between individual citizens could scarcely be litigated, without occupying the attention, and engaging the studies of the remotest nations and the most distant posterity.

There is always a certain correspondence and proportion between the estimation, in which an art is held, and the effects, which it produces. In the flourishing periods of Athens and Rome, eloquence was power. It was at once the instrument and the spur to ambition. The talent of public speaking was the key to the highest dignities; the passport to the supreme dominion of the state. The rod of Hermes was the sceptre of empire; the voice of oratory was the thunder of Jupiter. The most powerful of human passions was enlisted in the cause of eloquence, and eloquence in return was the most effectual auxiliary to the passion. In proportion to the wonders, she achieved, was the eagerness to acquire the faculties of this mighty magician. Oratory was taught, as the occupation of a life. The course of instruction commenced with the infant in the cradle, and continued to the meridian of manhood. It was made the fundamental object of education, and every other part of instruction for childhood, and of discipline for youth, was bent to its accommodation. Arts, science, letters, were to be thoroughly studied and investigated upon the maxim, that an orator must be a man of universal knowledge. Moral duties were inculcated, because none but a good man could be an orator. Wisdom, learning, virtue herself, were estimated by their subserviency to the purposes of eloquence, and the whole duty of man consisted in making himself an accomplished public speaker.

With the dissolution of Roman liberty, and the decline of Roman taste, the reputation and the excellency of the oratorical art fell alike into decay. Under the despotism of the Caesars, the end of eloquence was perverted from persuasion to panegyric, and all her faculties were soon palsied by the touch of corruption, or enervated by the impotence of servitude. Then succeeded the midnight of the monkish ages, when with the other liberal arts she slumbered in the profound darkness of the cloister.

At the revival of letters in modern Europe, eloquence, together with her sister muses, awoke, and shook the poppies from her brow. But their torpors still tingled in her veins. In the interval her voice was gone; her favorite languages were extinct; her organs were no longer attuned to harmony, and her hearers could no longer understand her speech. The discordant jargon of feudal anarchy had banished the musical dialects, in which she had always delighted. The theatres of her former triumphs were either deserted, or they were filled with the babblers of sophistry and chicane. She shrunk intuitively from the forum, for the last object she remembered to have seen there was the head of her darling Cicero, planted upon the rostrum. She ascended the tribunals of justice; there she found her child. Persuasion, manacled and pinioned by the letter of the law; there she beheld an image of herself, stammering in barbarous Latin, and staggering under the lumber of a thousand volumes. Her heart fainted within her. She lost all confidence in herself. Together with her irresistible powers, she lost proportionably the consideration of the world, until, instead of comprising the whole system of public education, she found herself excluded from the circle of sciences, and declared an outlaw from the realms of learning. She was not however doomed to eternal silence. With the progress of freedom and of liberal science, in various parts of modern Europe, she obtained access to mingle in the deliberations of their parliaments. With labor and difficulty she learned their languages, and lent her aid in giving them form and polish. But she has never recovered the graces of her former beauty, nor the energies of her ancient vigor.

The immeasurable superiority of ancient over modern oratory is one of the most remarkable circumstances, which offer themselves to the scrutiny of reflecting minds, and it is in the languages, the institutions, and the manners of modern Europe, that the solution of a phenomenon, so extraordinary, must be sought. The assemblies of the people, of the select councils, or of the senate in Athens and Rome, were held for the purpose of real deliberation. The fate of measures was not decided before they were proposed. Eloquence produced a powerful effect, not only upon the minds of the hearers, but upon the issue of the deliberation. In the only countries of modern Europe, where the semblance of deliberative assemblies has been preserved, corruption, here in the form of executive influence, there in the guise of party spirit, by introducing a more compendious mode of securing decisions, has crippled the sublimest efforts of oratory, and the votes upon questions of magnitude to the interest of nations are all told, long before the questions themselves are submitted to discussion. Hence those nations, which for ages have gloried in the devotion to literature, science, and the arts, have never been able to exhibit a specimen of deliberative oratory, that can bear a comparison with those, transmitted down to us from antiquity.

Religion indeed has opened one new avenue to the career of eloquence. Amidst the sacrifices of paganism to her three hundred thousand gods, amidst her sagacious and solemn consultations in the entrails of slaughtered brutes, in the flight of birds, and the feeding of fowls, it had never entered her imagination to call upon the pontiff, the haruspex, or the augur, for discourses to the people, on the nature of their duties to their Maker, their fellow-mortals, and themselves. This was an idea, too august to be mingled with the absurd and ridiculous, or profligate and barbarous rites of her deplorable superstition. It is an institution, for which mankind are indebted to Christianity; introduced by the Founder himself of this divine religion, and in every point of view worthy of its high original. Its effects have been to soften the tempers and purify the morals of mankind; not in so high a degree, as benevolence could wish, but enough to call forth our strains of warmest gratitude to that good being, who provides us with the means of promoting our own felicity, and gives us power to stand, though leaving us free to fall. Here then is an unbounded and inexhaustible field for eloquence, never explored by the ancient orators; and here alone have the modern Europeans cultivated the art with much success. In vain should we enter the halls of justice, in vain should we listen to the debates of senates for strains of oratory, worthy of remembrance, beyond the duration of the occasion, which called them forth. The art of embalming thought by oratory, like that of embalming bodies by aromatics, would have perished, but for the exercises of religion. These alone have in the latter ages furnished discourses, which remind us, that eloquence is yet a faculty of the human mind.

Among the causes, which have contributed thus to depress the oratory of modern times, must be numbered the indifference, with which it has been treated, as an article of education. The ancients had fostered an opinion, that this talent was in a more than usual degree the creature of discipline; and it is one of the maxims, handed down to us, as the result of their experience, that men must be born to poetry, and bred to eloquence; that the bard is always the child of nature, and the orator always the issue of instruction. The doctrine seems to be not entirely without foundation, but was by them carried in both its parts to an extravagant excess.

The foundations for the oratorical talent, as well as those of the poetical faculty, must be laid in the bounties of nature; and as the muse in Homer, impartial in her distribution of good and evil, struck the bard with blindness, when she gave him the powers of song, her sister not unfrequently, by a like mixture of tenderness and rigor, bestows the blessing of wisdom, while she refuses the readiness of utterance. Without entering however into a disquisition, which would lead me far beyond the limits of this occasion, I may remark, that the modern Europeans have run into the adverse extreme, and appear, during a considerable period, in their system of public education, to have passed upon eloquence a sentence of proscription. Even when they studied rhetoric, as a theory, they neglected oratory, as an art; and while assiduously unfolding to their pupils the bright displays of Greek and Roman eloquence, they never attempted to make them eloquent themselves. Of the prevailing indifference to this department of human learning no stronger evidence could be offered, than the circumstances, under which we are assembled.

Nearly two centuries have elapsed since the foundation of this university. There never existed a people more anxious to bestow upon their children the advantages of education, than our venerable forefathers; and the name of Harvard is coeval with the first settlement of New England. Their immediate and remote descendants down to this day have inherited and transmitted the same laudable ardor, and numerous foundations of various kinds attest their attachment to science and literature; yet so far have rhetoric and oratory been from enjoying a preeminence in their system of education, that they are now, for the first time, made a separate branch of instruction; and I stand here to assume the duties of the first instructor. The establishment of an institution for the purpose was reserved to the name of Boylston; a name, which, if public benefits can impart a title to remembrance, New England will not easily forget; a name, to the benevolence, public spirit, and genuine patriotism of which, this university, the neighboring metropolis, and this whole nation have long had, and still have many reasons to attest; a name, less distinguished by stations of splendor, than by deeds of virtue; and better known to this people by blessings enjoyed, than by favors granted; a name, in fine, which, if not encircled with the external radiance of popularity, beams, brightly beams, with the inward lustre of beneficence. The institution itself is not of a recent date. One generation of mankind, according to the usual estimates of human life, has gone by, since the donation of Nicholas Boylston constituted the fund for the support of this professorship. The misfortunes, which befell the university, unavoidably consequent upon our revolution, and other causes, have concurred in delaying the execution of his intentions until the present time; and even now they have the prospect of little more than honest zeal for their accomplishment.

In reflecting upon the nature of the duties I undertake, a consciousness of deficiency for the task of their performance dwells upon my mind; which, however ungraciously it may come from my lips, after accepting the appointment, with which I am honored, I yet cannot forbear to express. Though the course of my life has led me to witness the practice of this art in various forms, and though its theory has sometimes attracted my attention, yet my acquaintance with both has been of a general nature; and I can presume neither to a profound investigation of the one, nor an extensive experience of the other. The habits of instruction too are not familiar to me; and they constitute an art of little less difficulty and delicacy, than that of oratory itself; yet, as the career must necessarily be new, by whomsoever it should here be explored, and as it leads to a course of pleasing speculations and studies, I shall rely upon the indulgence of the friends and patrons to this seminary towards well-meant endeavors, and assume with diffidence the discharge of the functions, allotted to the institution. In the theory of the art, and the principles of exposition, novelty will not be expected; nor is it perhaps to be desired. A subject, which has exhausted the genius of Aristotle, Cicero, and Quinctilian, can neither require nor admit much additional illustration. To select, combine, and apply their precepts, is the only duty left for their followers of all succeeding times, and to obtain a perfect familiarity with their instructions is to arrive at the mastery of the art. For effecting this purpose, the teacher can do little more, than second the ardor and assiduity of the scholar. In the generous thirst for useful knowledge, in the honorable emulation of excellence, which distinguishes the students of this university, I trust to find an apology for the deficiencies of the lecturer. The richness of the soil will compensate for the unskilfulness of the tillage.

Sons of Harvard! You, who are ascending with painful step and persevering toil the eminence of science, to prepare yourselves for the various functions and employments of the world before you, it cannot be necessary to urge upon you the importance of the art, concerning which I am speaking. Is it the purpose of your future life to minister in the temples of Almighty God, to be the messenger of heaven upon earth, to enlighten with the torch of eternal truth the path of your fellow-mortals to brighter worlds? Remember the reason, assigned for the appointment of Aaron to that ministry, which you purpose to assume upon yourself. **I know, that he can speak well;** and, in this testimonial of Omnipotence, receive the injunction of your duty. Is your intention to devote the labors of your maturity to the cause of justice; to defend the persons, the property, and the fame of your fellow citizens from the open assaults of violence, and the secret encroachments of fraud? Fill the fountains of your eloquence from inexhaustible sources, that their streams, when they shall begin to flow, may themselves prove inexhaustible. Is there among you a youth, whose bosom burns with the fires of honorable ambition; who aspires to immortalize his name by the extent and importance of his services to his country; whose visions of futurity glow with the hope of presiding in her councils, of directing her affairs, of appearing to future ages on the rolls of fame, as her ornament and pride? Let him catch from the relics of ancient oratory those unresisted powers, which mould the mind of man to the will of the speaker, and yield the guidance of a nation to the dominion of the voice.

Under governments purely republican, where every citizen has a deep interest in the affairs of the nation, and, in some form of public assembly or other, has the means and opportunity of delivering his opinions, and of communicating his sentiments by speech; where government itself has no arms but those of persuasion; where prejudice has not acquired an uncontroled ascendency, and faction is yet confined within the barriers of peace; the voice of eloquence will not be heard in vain. March then with firm, with steady, with undeviating step, to the prize of your high calling. Gather fragrance from the whole paradise of science, and learn to distil from your lips all the honies of persuasion. Consecrate, above all, the faculties of your life to the cause of truth, of freedom, and of humanity. So shall your country ever gladden at the sound of your voice, and every talent, added to your accomplishments, become another blessing to mankind.

Lecture One - General View of Rhetoric and Oratory

IN entering upon a course of lectures on subjects, which have not hitherto been treated, as separate branches of instruction at this place, and which must in some sort bear the characters of novelty, it will be proper to take a general view of the nature and extent of the field before us. Although, until this time, no specific and peculiar establishment, confined to rhetoric and oratory, has existed, yet the pupils of this seminary have not been destitute of instruction upon its most essential parts, under the direction of teachers in the kindred arts of grammar, or language in general, and of logic. As these departments of study still remain, and the institution, under which I appear, has been superadded to them, by embracing a part of their duties, a preliminary consideration requires, that we should ascertain precisely what is the compass and extent of this art, and where are the lines, by which it is separated from the study of language in general, without which it cannot exist at all; and from the art of reasoning, without which that of oratory would be destitute of all solid foundation.

The subjects, upon which it is my province to discourse, are rhetoric and oratory; terms, which in ordinary language are often used, as synonymous in their meaning; but which are to be distinguished, as properly applying, the former to the theory, and the latter to the practice of the art. This distinction will become the more obvious from the consideration, that the terms are, even in common understanding, no longer convertible, when modified to designate the persons, professing them; and the difference between the rhetorician and the orator, is instantly perceived and distinctly conveyed, by the mere use of these respective appellations. This distinction it will be proper constantly to bear in mind. It is always useful to mark the difference, as well as the relation between the cause and its effect; and in the progress of our discussion we shall have frequent occasion separately and distinctly to examine as well the principles of the rhetorician, as the performances of the orator.

The definitions of rhetoric, by the ancient writers upon the art, are so numerous and so various, not only in the selection of their terms, but in the ideas, which they embrace, that Quinctilian, after recapitulating and submitting to the test of critical examination a great number of them, declares, that every new author seemed possessed with the foolish ambition of discarding all definitions, before adopted by any other, and determined at all events to give one of his own. Among the many imperfect, redundant, and affected forms, which this rage for novelty of expression, and this studied indocility to the toils of preceding laborers, have occasioned, I shall present to your consideration only those of the three great masters, from whom every thing of real importance to the art has been derived, Aristotle, Cicero, and Quinctilian himself. Rhetoric, says Aristotle, is the power of inventing whatsoever is persuasive in discourse.

This is liable to two objections. First, as it includes only one part of the art, invention, omitting the essential requisites of disposition and elocution. And secondly, though persuasion be one of the principal ends of rhetoric, it is not exclusively so. Of a very important and extensive class of discourses, styled by Aristotle himself, and by all the other ancient rhetoricians, demonstrative orations, persuasion is not even the principal end; and, even in the fields of deliberative and judicial eloquence, all the arts of rhetoric have often been employed without producing persuasion.

This difficulty stands yet more conspicuously in the way of Cicero's definition, the art of persuasion; a definition, appearing indeed only in the rhetorical compilations of his youth, of which he himself afterwards entertained a very indifferent opinion. To say, that rhetoric is the art of persuasion, is to make success the only criterion of eloquence. Persuasion must in a great measure depend upon the will, the temper, and the disposition of the hearer. If the adder will turn away his ear, what persuasion is there in the voice of the charmer? Persuasion then is not the infallible test of the rhetorical art; neither is rhetoric exclusively in possession of persuasion. To enumerate all the instruments of persuasion, would be to give a catalogue of all the passions and motives. which can, without the exercise of force, be made to operate upon the human mind.

Persuasive speech, and more persuasive sighs.
Silence, that speaks, and eloquence of eyes.

Pope's Iliad, xi. 250.

To this it has been justly replied, that persuasion, being so nearly identified with the ultimate purpose of all oratorical art, may without danger be admitted, as the same in every case, where philosophical precision is unnecessary. Of deliberative and judicial eloquence persuasion is the great and fundamental object; and the public speaker, in composing or pronouncing his discourse, should never lose sight of this principle. There is no better test for the correctness of any precept in the science of rhetoric, nor for the excellence of any example in the practice of oratory, than its aptitude to persuasion. But as the object of a scientific definition is to comprise in the fewest words the whole substance of the term defined, and nothing more, it must be allowed, that those of Aristotle and Cicero are not absolutely unexceptionable.

The definition, adopted by Quinctilian from some former writer, whom he does not name, is more correct, more precise, and comprehensive. Rhetoric in his judgment is the science of speaking well. The principal reason, which he assigns for preferring this definition to all the rest, may perhaps be controverted, for he contends, that it includes the moral character of the speaker, as well as the excellence of speech; because none but an honest man can speak well. I shall on a future occasion examine impartially, and endeavor to ascertain precisely the true value of this opinion, which is so warmly advocated by all the great orators of antiquity. At present I shall only remark, that admitting the maxim in its fullest latitude, it does not appear to me to be necessarily implied in this definition; nor can I admit the argument, as decisive for giving it the preference.

The reasons, which I deem far more conclusive for adopting it, are its comprehensive simplicity, and its remarkable coincidence with that virtual definition of the art, contained in the holy scriptures. The art of speaking well embraces in the fewest possible words the whole compass of the subject. You can imagine no species of rhetorical excellence, which would not be included in the idea, and the idea involves nothing beyond the boundaries of the art. It is full without redundance, and capacious without obscurity.

It has also the sanction of holy writ. Observe the force of the expressions, used in the solemn interview between the supreme Creator and

"That shepherd, who first taught the chosen seed,
"In the beginning, how the heavens and earth
"Rose out of chaos."

And Moses said unto the Lord, O my Lord, I am not eloquent, neither heretofore, nor since thou hast spoken unto thy servant. What is the eventual reply? Is not Aaron the Levite thy brother? I know that he can speak well. In the language of sacred inspiration itself, to speak well is precisely equivalent to the art of eloquence, and in this definition the words of Quinctilian are ratified by the voice of heaven.

His approbation of another definition, which includes in the idea of rhetoric the art of thinking, together with that of speaking well, is not warranted by the same infallible authority. The connexion between genuine rhetoric and sound logic is indeed indissoluble. All good speaking must necessarily rest upon the basis of accurate thinking. But to form a precise idea of the two arts, we must carefully distinguish them from each other, and confine them to their respective peculiar departments; logic to the operations of the mind, within itself; rhetoric to the communication of their results to the minds of others. In this view logic is the store house, from which the instruments of rhetoric are to be drawn. Logic is the arsenal, and rhetoric the artillery, which it preserves. Both have their utility; both contribute to the same purposes. But the arts themselves are as distinct, as those of the architect, who erects the building, and of the armorer, who fabricates the weapons. Thus Aristotle, who perceived as well the clear distinction, as the necessary relation between these faculties, has treated of them in two distinct works; and unfolded their mysteries with all the energies of his profound, comprehensive, and discriminating genius.

Equally proper and necessary will it be to separate in our minds the science of rhetoric, or of speaking well, from that of grammar, or the science of speaking correctly. Grammar stands in the same relation to rhetoric, that arithmetic bears to geometry. Rhetoric is not essential to grammar, but grammar is indispensable to rhetoric. The one teaches an art of mere necessity; the Other, an art of superadded ornament. Without a system of grammatical construction, the power of speech itself would be of no avail, and language would be a mere intellectual chaos; a perpetual Babel of confusion. But the powers of grammar extend no farther, than to the communication of ideas. To delight the imagination, or to move the passions, you must have recourse to rhetoric. Grammar clothes the shadowy tribes of mind in the plain, substantial attire of a Quaker; rhetoric arrays them in the glories of princely magnificence. Grammar is sufficient to conduct you over the boundless plains of thought; but rhetoric alone has access to the lofty regions of fancy. Rhetoric alone can penetrate to the secret chambers of the heart.

If then we adopt the definition of Quinctilian, that rhetoric is the science of speaking well, we may apply the same terms to define oratory, substituting only the word art, instead of science. In this respect our language offers a facility, which neither the Greek nor the Latin possessed. The Greeks had no term to designate the art, as distinguished from the theory. Their science was rhetoric, and their speaker was a rhetor. The Romans adopted the first of these words. as they received the science from Greece. To signify the speaker they used the word orator, derived from their own language. Some attempts were made to put in circulation the term oratoria, but they were resisted by their philological critics, and it is expressly censured and rejected by Quinctilian, as irreconcilable with their etymological analogies. The want of the proper word is most strikingly discovered in the titles of Cicero's rhetorical works. At one time it led him to the necessity of assuming a part for the whole, and of styling four books of rhetoric a treatise upon invention. At another it compelled him to embody the talent itself in the person of the speaker, and denominate his system of oratory, the orator. The English language however has been less scrupulous in its adherence to the niceties of etymology. It has admitted the term oratory, which the Romans so fastidiously excluded, and annexes to it a modification of idea, distinct from that of the Grecian term, which has also been made English by adoption. Thus accumulating our riches from the united funds of Grecian genius and of Roman industry, we call rhetoric the science, and oratory the art of speaking, well.

But to avoid misapprehension, a further explanation of the sense, in which the words are to be understood, appears to be necessary. Speech as the most ordinary vehicle of communication between men, in all their relations with one another, whether of a public or private nature. By the art or science of speaking well, it is not intended to give rules for a system of private conversation in the domestic intercourse of a family, or in the ordinary associations of business or of friendship. There are doubtless frequent occasions, when the means of oratorical persuasion may be used, as seasonably and as usefully in private, as in public; between two individuals, as before a numerous audience.

Talk logic with acquaintance, that you have,
And practise rhetoric in your common talk,

TAM. SHR.

says one of the characters in Shakespeare to his collegiate friend; and the advice is good. But it is not for this, that an artificial system of eloquence was ever constructed, or ought ever to be taught. A musician of taste and skill will habitually give to his voice, even in ordinary conversation, more melodious and variegated inflexions, than a person, ignorant of his art; yet this is no reason for him to modulate his voice in conversation by the scale of his gamut. It is unquestionably true, that those move easiest, who have learnt to dance; but this is no reason for entering a room with the steps of a minuet, or walking the streets in a hornpipe. Equally absurd would it be to exercise in the familiar converse of life the practices of an orator by system; and we must be always understood, as having reference to public speaking, when we define oratory, as the art of speaking well.

Oratory then is an art. This point has not been seriously controverted in modern times; though among the ancients it was debated with great warmth and ingenuity. A more important question however, which has been agitated in all ages, and will perhaps never be placed altogether beyond the reach of controversy, is, whether oratory can be numbered among the useful arts? Whether its tendencies are not as strong to the perversion, as to the improvement of men? Whether it has not more frequently been made an engine of evil, than of good to the world? Or whether at best it is not one of those frivolous arts, which consists more in arbitrary, multifarious subdivisions and hard words, than in any real, practical utility. The question is to you, my friends, of so much importance, that in justice to you, to myself, and to the institution, under which I address you, I think a more ample consideration of its merits proper and necessary. Your time and your talents are precious, not only to yourselves, but to your connexions, and to your country. They ought therefore not to be wasted upon any trifling or unprofitable, and much less to be misspent upon any mischievous pursuit. In the observations, which I shall now submit to you, it is my intention to suggest the peculiar utility of the art, in the situation of this country, and adapted to the circumstances, which may probably call upon many of you for its exercise, in the progress of your future lives.

In the state of society, which exists among us, some professional occupation is, to almost every man in the community, the requisition of necessity, as well as of duty. None of us liveth to himself; and as we live to our families, by the several relations and employments of domestic life, to our friends, by the intercourse of more intimate society and mutual good offices, so we live to our country and to mankind in general, by the performance of those services, and by the discharge of those labors, which belong to the profession we have chosen, as the occupation of our lives. Whatsoever it is incumbent upon a man to do, it is surely expedient to do well. Now of the three learned profes-

19

sions, which more especially demand the preparatory discipline of a learned education, there are two, whose most important occupations consist in the act of public speaking. And who can doubt, but that in the sacred desk, or at the bar, the man, who speaks well, will enjoy a larger share of reputation, and be more useful to his fellow creatures, than the divine or the lawyer of equal learning and integrity, but unblest with the talent of oratory?

But the pulpit is especially the throne of modern eloquence. There it is, that speech is summoned to realize the fabled wonders of the Orphean lyre. The preacher has no control over the will of his audience, other than the influence of his discourse. Yet, as the ambassador of Christ, it is his great and awful duty to call sinners to repentance. His only weapon is the voice; and with this he is to appall the guilty, and to reclaim the infidel; to rouse the indifferent, and to shame the scorner. He is to inflame the lukewarm, to encourage the timid, and to cheer the desponding; believer. He is to pour the healing balm of consolation into the bleeding heart of sorrow, and to sooth with celestial hope the very agonies of death. Now tell me who it is, that will best possess and most effectually exercise these more than magic powers? Who is it, that will most effectually stem the torrent of human passions, and calm the raging waves of human vice and folly? Who is it, that, with the voice of a Joshua, shall control the course of nature herself in the perverted heart, and arrest the luminaries of wisdom and virtue in their rapid revolutions round this little world of man? Is it the cold and languid speaker, whose words fall in such sluggish and drowsy motion from his lips, that they can promote nothing but the slumbers of his auditory, and administer opiates to the body, rather than stimulants to the soul? Is it the unlettered fanatic, without method, without reason; with incoherent raving, and vociferous ignorance, calculated to fit his hearers, not for the kingdom of heaven, but for a hospital of lunatics? Is it even the learned, ingenious, and pious minister of Christ, who, by neglect or contempt of the oratorical art, has contracted a whining, monotonous sing-song of delivery to exercise the patience of his flock, at the expense of their other Christian graces? Or is it the genuine orator of heaven, with a heart sincere, upright, and fervent; a mind stored with that universal knowledge, required as the foundation of the art; with a genius for the invention, a skill for the disposition, and a voice for the elocution of every argument to convince and of every sentiment to persuade? If then we admit, that the art of oratory qualifies the minister of the gospel to perform in higher perfection the duties of his station, we can no longer question, whether it be proper for his cultivation. It is more than proper; it is one of his most solemn and indispensable duties.   If

> Nature never lends
> The smallest scruple of her excellence,
> But like a thrifty goddess, she determines
> Herself the glory of a creditor,
> Both thanks and use,

more especially is the obligation of exerting every talent, of improving every faculty incumbent upon him, who undertakes the task of instructing, of reforming, and of guiding in the paths of virtue and religion, his fellow mortals.

The practitioner at the bar, having a just idea of his professional duties, will consider himself as the minister of justice among men, and feel it his obligation to maintain and protect the rights of those, who entrust their affairs to his charge, whether they are rights of person or of property; whether public or private; whether of civil or of criminal jurisdiction. The litigation of these rights in the courts of justice often requires the exertion of the most exalted intellectual powers; and it is by public speaking alone, that they can be exerted. For the knowledge of the law the learning of the closet may suffice; for its application to the circumstances of the individual case, correct reasoning and a sound judgment will be competent. But when an intricate controversy must be unfolded in a perspicuous manner to the mind of the judge, or a tangled tissue of blended facts and law must be familiarly unravelled to a jury; that is, at the very crisis, when the contest is to be decided by the authority of the land, learning and judgment are of no avail to the client or his counsel without the assistance of an eloquent voice to make them known. Then it is, that all the arts of the orator are called into action, and that every part of a rhetorical discourse finds its place for the success of the cause. The diamond in the mine is no brighter, than the pebble upon the beach. From the hand of the lapidary must it learn to sparkle in the solar beam, and to glitter in the imperial crown. The crowd of clients, the profits of practice, and the honors of reputation, will all inevitably fly to him, who is known to possess, not only the precious treasures of legal learning, but the keys, which alone can open them to the public eye. Hence if personal utility, the acquisition of wealth, of honor, and of fame, is the pursuit of the lawyer, the impulse of eloquence can alone speed him in his course. If relative utility, the faculty of discharging in the utmost perfection the duties of his station, and the means of being most serviceable to his fellow creatures, is the nobler object of his ambition, still he can soar to that elevated aim only upon the pinions of eloquence.

But besides these two professions, of which oratory may be called the vital principle, a free republic, like that, in which an indulgent providence has cast our lot, bestows importance upon the powers of eloquence, to every class and description of citizens. An estimate of this, and of some specific objections against the art, will form the subject of my next lecture.

Lecture Two - Objections against Eloquence Considered

WE have hitherto considered the importance and utility of the oratorical art, only with regard to its influence upon the private relations of life; and pointed out the inducements, which recommend its cultivation to the lawyer and the divine. These considerations have their weight in all civilized countries, favored with the light of the gospel, and enjoying a regular administration of government. Under all the forms of polity, prevailing among the European nations, considerable scope is allowed to the eloquence of the bar and of the pulpit; under all, the inducements I have suggested for coveting these splendid and useful talents must have their force. There are others, which, if not exclusively applicable to our native country, and our present state of society, are at least of more than ordinary magnitude to us. But before I enter upon a survey of these local and occasional objects, which give so much adventitious cumulation to the arguments of universal application in favor of eloquence, it may be proper to examine with candor the objections, which often have been and still are occasionally urged against it.

These objections are three. First, that rhetoric is a pedantic science, overcharged with scholastic subtleties, and innumerable divisions and subdivisions, burdensome to the memory, oppressive to genius, and never applicable to any valuable purpose in the business of the world. Second, that it is a frivolous science, substituting childish declamation instead of manly sense, and adapted rather to the pageantry of a public festival, than to the sober concerns of real life. And third, that it is a pernicious science; the purpose of which is to mislead the judgment by fascinating the imagination. That its tendencies are to subject the reason of men to the control of their passions; to pervert private justice, and to destroy public liberty. These are formidable objections, and unless a sound and satisfactory answer can be given to them all, both your time and mine, my friends, is at this moment very ill-employed, and the call I am obliged to make upon your attention is a trespass upon something more than your patience.

Let me first remark, that the last of these difficulties is not barely at variance with, but in direct hostility to the other two. If rhetoric be a pedantic science, consisting of nothing but a tedious and affected enumeration of the figures of speech, or if it be a frivolous science, teaching only the process of beating up a frothy declamation into seeming consistency, at least it cannot be that deadly weapon, the possession of which is so pernicious, that the affection of a parent, studious of the learning and virtue of his son, dares not entrust it to his hand. If rhetoric be no more than the Babylonish dialect of the schools, if oratory be no more than the sounding emptiness of the scholar they are at least not those dangerous and destructive engines, which pollute the fountains of justice, and batter down the liberties of nations. These objections are still more at strife with each other, than with the science, against which they are pointed. Were they urged by one and the same disputant, we might be content to array them against each other. We might oppose the argument of insignificance against the argument of danger; and enjoy the triumph of beholding our adversary refute himself. But inasmuch as they spring from different sources, they are entitled to a distinct consideration. From their mutual opposition, the only conclusive inference we can draw against them is, that they cannot all be well founded. Let us endeavour to prove the same against each of them separately, beginning with those, which affect only the usefulness, and not the moral character of our profession.

The first assault then, which we are called upon to repel, comes from the shaft of wit; always a formidable, but not always a fair antagonist. A poet of real genius and original humor, in a couplet, which goes farther to discredit all systems of rhetoric, than volumes of sober argument can effect in promoting them, has told the world, that

> All a rhetorician's rules
> Teach nothing but to name his tools.

But happily the doctrine, that ridicule is the test of truth, has never obtained the assent of the rational part of mankind. Wit, like the ancient Parthian, flies while it fights; or like the modern Indian, shoots from behind trees and hedges. The arrow comes winged from an invisible hand. It rankles in your side, and you look in vain for the archer. Wit is the unjust judge, who often decides wrong; and even when right, often from a wrong motive. From his decisions however, after paying the forfeit, there is always an appeal to the more even balance of common sense. On this review we shall find the poet's position not exactly conformable to truth; and even so far as true, by no means decisive against the study of the science. For what can be more necessary to the artist, than to know the names, as well as the uses of his tools? Rhetoric alone can never constitute an orator. No human art can be acquired by the mere knowledge of the principles, upon which it is founded. But the artist, who understands its principles, will exercise his art in the highest perfection. The profoundest study of the writers upon architecture, the most laborious contemplation of its magnificent monuments will never make a mason. But the mason, thoroughly acquainted with the writers, and familiar to the construction of those monuments, will surely be an abler artist, than the mere mechanic, ignorant of the mysteries of his trade, and even of the names of his tools. A celebrated French comic writer, Moliere, has represented one of his characters,, learning with great astonishment and self-admiration, at the age of forty, that he had been all his life time speaking prose without knowing it. And this bright discovery comes from the information he then first receives from his teacher of grammar, that whatsoever is not prose is verse, and whatsoever is not verse is prose.

But the names of the rhetorician's rules are not the only objects of his precepts. They are not even essential to the science. Figurative and ornamented language indeed is one of the important properties of oratory, and when the art came to be reduced into a system among the ancient Greeks, some of the subordinate writers, unable to produce any thing of their own upon the general subject, exercised their subtlety to discriminate, and their ingenuity to name the innumerably variety of forms, in which language may be diverted from the direct into the figurative channel. Pursuing this object with more penetration than discernment, they ransacked all their celebrated authors for figures of speech, to give them names; and often finding in their search some incorrect expression, which the inattention of the writer had over-looked, they concluded it was a figure of speech, because it was not conform-able to grammatical construction; and very gravely turning a blunder into a trope, invested it with the dignity of a learned name. A succession of these rhetorical nomenclators were continually improving upon one another, until the catalogue of figures grew to a lexicon, and the natural shape of rhetoric was distended to a dropsy.

This excessive importance, given to one of the branches of the science, led to the absurd notion, that all rhetoric was comprised in the denomination of figurative expressions, and finally provoked the lash of Butler's ridicule. But he must have a partial and contracted idea indeed of rhetoric, who can be-lieve, that by the art of persuasion is meant no more than the art of distin-guishing between a metonymy and a metaphor, or of settling the boundary between synecdoche and antonomasia. So far is this from being true, that Aristotle, the great father of the science, though he treats in general terms of metaphorical language, bestows very little consideration upon it, and cau-tions the orator, perhaps too rigorously, against its use. Cicero, though from the natural turn of his genius more liberal of these seductive graces, allows them only a very moderate station in his estimate of the art; and Quinctilian appropriates to them only part of two, out of his twelve books of institutes.

The idea, that the purpose of rhetoric is only to teach the art of making and. delivering a holiday declamation, proceeds from a view of the subject equally erroneous and superficial. Were this its only or even its principal ob-ject, its acquisition might rationally occupy a few moments of your leisure, but could not claim that assiduous study and persevering application, with-out which no man will ever be an orator. It would stand in the rank of elegant accomplishments, but could not aspire to that of useful talents. Perhaps one of the causes of this mistaken estimate of the art is the usual process, by which it is learnt. The exercises of the student are necessarily confined to this lowest department of the science. Your weekly declamation, your occa-sional themes, and forensic disputes and the dialogues, conferences, and ora-tions of the public exhibitions, from the nature of things, must relate merely to speculative subjects. Here is no issue for trial, in which the life or fortune of an individual may be involved. Here is no vote to be taken, upon which the destinies of a nation may be suspended. Here is no immortal soul, whose fu-ture blessedness or misery may hinge upon your powers of eloquence to car-ry conviction to the heart. But here it is, that you must prepare yourselves to act your part in those great realities of life. To consider the lessons or the practices, by which the art of oratory can be learnt, as the substance of the art itself, is to mistake the means for the end. It is to measure the military merits of a general by the gold threads of his epaulette, or to appreciate the valor of the soldier by the burning of powder upon a parade. The eloquence of the college is like the discipline of a review. The art of war, we are all sen-sible, docs not consist in the manoeuvres of a training day; nor the steadfast-

24

ness of the soldier at the hour of battle, in the drilling of his orderly serjeant. Yet the superior excellence of the veteran army is exemplified in nothing more forcibly, than in the perfection of its discipline. It is in the heat of action, upon the field of blood, that the fortune of the day may be decided by the exactness of the manual exercise; and the art of displaying a column, or directing a charge, may turn the balance of victory and change the history of the world. The application of these observations is as direct to the art of oratory, as to that of war. The exercises, to which you are here accustomed, are not intended merely for the display of the talents, you have acquired. They are instruments, put into your hands for future use. Their object is not barely to prepare you for the composition and delivery of an oration to amuse an idle hour on some public anniversary. It is to give you a clue for the labyrinth of legislation in the public councils; a spear for the conflict of judicial war in the public tribunals; a sword for the field of religious and moral victory in the pulpit.

In the endeavour to refute these petty cavils against rhetoric, which have no higher foundation, than a superficial misconception of its real character and object, I have perhaps consumed too much of your time. A more serious obstacle remains to be removed. An obstacle, arising, not from a mistaken estimate of its value, but from too keen a sense of its abuses. An objection, which admits, nay, exaggerates the immensity of its powers, but harps upon their perversion to evil ends; which beholds in oratory, not the sovereign, but the usurper of the soul; which, far from exposing the science to the sneer of contempt, aims at inflaming against it the rancour of jealousy.

Eloquence, we are told by these eloquent detractors, is the purveyor of fraud, and the pander of delusion. Her tongue drops manna, but to make the worse appear the better reason; to perplex and dash maturest counsels. She fills the trump of glory with the venal blast of adulation, and binds the wreath of honor around the brows of infamy. Her voice is ever ready to rescue the culprit from punishment, and to turn the bolt of public vengeance upon innocence. Upon every breeze her breath wings the pestilence of sedition, or kindles the flames of unextinguishable war. Her most splendid victories are but triumphs over reason, and the basis of her temple is erected upon the ruins of truth.

To this tempest of inculpation what reply can we oppose? If we dispute the correctness of the assertions, our adversaries appeal with confidence to the testimony of historical fact. If we assure them upon the word of Cicero and Quinctilian, that none but a good man can possibly be an orator, they disconcert us by calling for our examples of orators, who have been good men.

Let us then tell them, that their objection in this instance is rather against the constitution of human nature, the dispensations of Providence, and the moral government of the universe, than against rhetoric and oratory. It applies with equal force against every faculty, which exalts the human character, virtue alone excepted. Strength of body, vigor of mind, beauty, valor, genius, whatever we admire and love in the character of man; how often are

25

they perverted to his shame and corruption! It applies with equal force against the laws of physical nature. Observe the phenomena of the universe, in which we dwell. The very beams of that glorious sun, the source of genial heat, of heavenly light, of vegetable growth, and of animal life, how often does their radiance blind the eyes, and their fervor parch the plains! How often do they shed pernicious plagues, and kindle consuming fires! The very atmosphere we breathe, unless perpetually purified by the accession of oxygen, is it not the most deadly poison? Virtue, my young friends, is the oxygen, the vital air of the moral world. Immutable and incorruptible itself, like that being, of whom it is the purest emanation, in proportion as it intermingles with and pervades every other particle of. intellectual nature, it inspires the salutiferous gale, the principle of life, and health, and happiness. But this is the peculiar privilege of virtue. Like all the other gifts of Providence, eloquence is, according to the manner, in which it is applied, a blessing or a curse; the pest of nations, or the benefactress of human kind.

Here then we might rest our defence. We might rely on the trite and undisputed maxim, that arguments, drawn from the abuse of any thing, are not admissible against its use. But we must proceed one step further, and say, that in this case the argument from the abuse is conclusive in favor of the use. Since eloquence is in itself so powerful a weapon, and since by the depravity of mankind this weapon must, and often will be brandished for guilty purposes, its exercise, with equal or superior skill, becomes but the more indispensable to the cause of virtue. To forbid the sincere Christian, the honest advocate, the genuine patriot, the practice of oratorical arts, would be like a modern nation, which should deny to itself the use of gunpowder, and march, with nothing but bows and arrows, to meet the thunder of an invader's artillery. If the venal orators of Athens would have sold their country to the crafty tyrant of Macedon, what could baffle their detested bargains, but the incorruptible eloquence of Demosthenes? If the incestuous Clodius and the incendiary Catiline had eloquence enough for the destruction of imperial Rome, what but the immortal voice of Cicero could have operated her salvation? Or to bring the issue closer home to your own hearts, when would you so anxiously desire, and so eagerly hail this irresistible power of words, as at the very moment after hearing it perverted by cruelty, hypocrisy, or infidelity, for the purposes of violence or of fraud?

In these objections then, the most plausible of those, which ever have been advanced against rhetoric and oratory, there is nothing, which ought to deter an honest and a generous mind from their assiduous cultivation. Of the arguments I have urged to convince you, that the study is at once useful and honorable, your own minds will judge. You will perhaps think, that I have dwelt with more earnestness, than the occasion required, upon topics, concerning which your hearts were already; with me. That I have been over anxious in demonstrating what was to you before sufficiently proved. That, under the blaze of a meridian sun, I have been sweating with the toll of making daylight visible to your eyes. And is it truly so? Are you convinced beyond a

26

doubt, that the powers of eloquence are a wise, an honorable, a virtuous pursuit? A pursuit, to which justice, patriotism, and piety, with equal energy stimulate your souls? Then go with me but one step further; draw with me the only valuable inference, which can result from this long dissertation; the practical inference, which alone can make it of any use to you. Invert the advice of Timotheus to Alexander, and say to yourselves,

If the world be worth enjoying.
Think! Oh! think it worth thy winning.

I will conclude with urging upon your reflections the last great consideration, which I mentioned, as giving its keenest edge to the argument for devoting every faculty of the mind to the acquisition of eloquence; a consideration, arising from the peculiar situation and circumstances of our own country, and naturally connecting my present subject, the vindication of the science, with that, which will next claim your attention; I mean its origin and history.

Should a philosophical theorist, reasoning a priori, undertake to point out the state of things, and of human society, which must naturally produce the highest exertions of the power of speech, he would recur to those important particulars, which actually existed in the Grecian commonwealths. The most strenuous energies of the human mind, would he say, are always employed, where they are instigated by the stimulus of the highest rewards. The art of speaking must be most eagerly sought, where it is found to be most useful. It must be most useful, where it is capable of producing the greatest effects; and that can be in no other state of things, than where the power of persuasion operates upon the will, and prompts the actions of other men. The only birth place of eloquence therefore must be a free state. Under arbitrary governments, where the lot is cast upon one man to command, and upon all the rest to obey; where the despot, like the Roman centurion, has only to say to one man, go, and he goeth, and to another, come, and he cometh; persuasion is of no avail. Between authority and obedience there can be no deliberation; and wheresoever submission is the principle of government in a nation, eloquence can never arise. Eloquence is the child of liberty, and can descend from no other stock. And where will she find her most instructive school? Will it not be in a country, where the same spirit of liberty, which marks the relations between the individuals of the same community, is diffused over those more complicated and important relations between different communities? Where the independence of the man is corroborated and invigorated by the independence of the state? Where the same power of persuasion, which influences the will of the citizens at home, has the means of operating upon the will and the conduct of sovereign societies? Should it happen then, that a number of independent communities, founded upon the principles of civil and political liberty, were so reciprocally situated, as to have a great and continual intercourse with each other, and many momentous common interests, occasional as well as permanent, there above all others will be the spot,

27

where eloquence will spring to light; will flourish; will rise to the highest perfection, of which human art or science is susceptible.

The experience of mankind has proved exactly conformable to this theory.
The Grecian commonwealths furnish the earliest examples in history of confederated states with free governments; and there also the art of oratory was
first practised, the science of rhetoric first invented; and both were raised to
a pitch of unrivalled excellence and glory.

From this powerful concurrence of philosophical speculation with historical proof, there are several important inferences, which ought to be pressed
with peculiar energy upon the consideration of all youthful Americans; and
more especially of those, who are distinguished by the liberal discipline of a
classical education, and enjoy the advantages of intellectual cultivation. They
cannot fail to remark, that their own nation is at this time precisely under the
same circumstances, which were so propitious to the advancement of rhetoric and oratory among the Greeks. Like them, we are divided into a number
of separate commonwealths, all founded upon the principles of the most enlarged social and civil liberty. Like them, we are united in certain great national interests, and connected by a confederation, differing indeed in many
essential particulars from theirs, but perhaps in a still higher degree favorable to the influence and exertion of eloquence. Our institutions, from the
smallest municipal associations to the great national bond, which links this
continent in union, are republican. Their vital principle is liberty. Persuasion,
or the influence of reason and of feeling, is the great if not the only instrument, whose operation can affect the acts of all our corporate bodies; of
towns, cities, counties, states, and of the whole confederated empire. Here
then eloquence is recommended by the most elevated usefulness, and encouraged by the promise of the most precious rewards.

Finally, let us observe how much it tends to exalt and ennoble our ideas of
this art, to find it both in speculation and experience, thus grappled, as with
hooks of steel, to the soul of liberty. So dear, and so justly dear to us are the
blessings of freedom, that if no other advantage could be ascribed to the
powers of speech, than that they are her inseparable companions, that alone
would be an unanswerable argument for us to cherish them with more than
a mother's affection. Let then the frosty rigor of the logician tell you, that eloquence is an insidious appeal to the passions of men. Let the ghastly form of
despotism groan from his hollow lungs and bloodless heart, that eloquence is
the instrument of turbulence and the weapon of faction. Nay, let the severe
and honest moralist himself pronounce in the dream of abstraction, that
truth and virtue need not the aid of foreign ornament. Answer; silence them
all. Answer; silence them forever, by recurring to this great and overpowering truth. Say, that by the eternal constitution of things it was ordained, that
liberty should be the parent of eloquence; that eloquence should be the last
stay and support of liberty; that with her she is ever destined to live, to flourish, and to die. Call up the shades of Demosthenes and Cicero to vouch your
words; point to their immortal works, and say, these are not only the sub-

limest strains of oratory, that ever issued from the uninspired lips of mortal men; they are at the same time the expiring accents of liberty, in the nations, which have shed the brightest lustre on the name of man.

Lecture Three - Origin of Oratory

HAVING endeavoured in my former lectures to define with precision the objects, upon which I am in future to discourse, and attempted to vindicate their utility, I shall now proceed to give you some account of their history; in doing which I shall, for the sake of perspicuity, continue to preserve the distinction, which I first laid down, between the science of rhetoric and the art of oratory.

The origin of oratory has undoubtedly the priority in point of time. Such must obviously be the case with all the arts. Many a house must have been built, before a system of architecture could be formed; many a poem composed, before an art of poetry could be written. The practice must in the nature of things precede the theory. All didactic treatises must consist of rules, resulting from experience; and that experience can have no foundation, other than previous practice. Now the practice of oratory must in all probability be coeval with the faculty of speech. Philosophical inquirers into the origin of language have, with some appearance of reason, affirmed, that the first sounds, which men uttered, must have been exclamations, prompted by some pressing want or vehement passion. These, by the constitution of human nature, would be best calculated to excite the first sympathies of the fellow savage, and thus afford the first instance of an influence, exercised by man over man, through the medium of speech. The character, derived from this original, it has preserved through all its progress, and to a certain degree must forever retain; so that even at this day eloquence and the language of passion are sometimes used, as synonymous terms. But however the practice of oratory may have existed in the early ages of the world, and among those civilized nations, whose career of splendor preceded that of the Grecian states, we have no monuments, either written or traditionary, from which we can infer, that the art of speaking was ever reduced into a system, or used for the purposes, to which eloquence has since been employed. In the sacred scriptures indeed we have numerous examples of occasions, upon which the powers of oratory were exercised, and many specimens of the sublimest eloquence. But these were of a peculiar nature, arising from the interpositions of providence in the history and affairs of the Jewish people. There we learn, that the faculty of speech was among the special powers, bestowed by immediate communication of the Creator to our first parents. Thus if the first cries of passion were instigated by physical nature, the first accents of reason were suggested by the father of spirits. But of the history of profane eloquence there is no trace or record remaining earlier, than the flourishing periods of the Grecian states.

There were three circumstances in their constitution, which concurred to produce their extraordinary attachment to this art, and with it to so many others, which have immortalized their fame. Their origin is involved in such a tissue of fables, that it is impossible to rely upon any particulars of their early history. Thus much however may be considered as certain, that the Assyrian, Persian, and Egyptian states, whose national existence was earlier than theirs, were all single governments, and all unlimited monarchies; while from the remotest ages Greece was divided into a number of separate sovereignties, each independent of all the others, but all occasionally connected together upon certain objects and enterprizes, which concerned their common interests. Such were the expedition of the Argonauts under the conduct of Jason; the war of Thebes by the confederacy of seven princes against Eteocles; and finally the Trojan war; that war, the memory of which the energies of one poor, blind, vagrant poet have rendered as imperishable, as the human mind.

With all their great and shining qualities, the Greeks were ever notorious for a propensity to the marvellous; and a Roman poet has applied to the whole nation an epithet, which St. Paul tells us had been justly appropriated to the Cretans. Thus, of these three great expeditions, the causes, and almost all the story, as related by the Greeks, were undoubtedly fabulous. Some ingenious modern writers have taken occasion from these manifest falsehoods of detail, to raise doubts concerning the reality of the whole history, and even to contend, that no such city as Troy ever existed. But the great outlines of the narrative are so connected with unquestionable events, that it requires at least as large a share of credulity to believe in the accuracy of the modern systems, as in the fidelity of the ancient tales. For my own part I find it as hard to credit, that there never was such a city as Troy, as that it was built by the hands of Neptune and Apollo, or destroyed by the resentments of Juno. The link in the chain between real and fabulous history is so indistinct, that we cannot precisely ascertain where it lies; but in general we must admit some foundation for events, which have left indelible traces behind them, though we know the particulars of the narrative to be fictitious. Long after we have lost sight of land, a bottom may still be found by the plummet.

The original separation of the Greeks into a number of independent states, their associations for certain national purposes, and the spirit of liberty, which pervaded them, are circumstances as firmly established, as any part of the history of mankind. And each of these circumstances essentially contributed, first, to produce, and then to promote that extraordinary attachment to the art of speech, for which they have ever been famed. The narrow bounds, within which the territories of many states were circumscribed, made it practicable for the whole people to assemble within the compass of a single voice. Their independence of each other, and the common objects, which concerned them all, rendered a frequent intercourse of embassies and negotiations among them necessary; and above all their liberty, which made their public actions dependent upon their own will, and their will susceptible of influence by the power of reason, could not fail to create the art of oratory, and to prepare the triumph of eloquence.

From a passage in the Corinthiacs of Pausanias, which I have noticed, it appears that Pittheus, the uncle of Theseus, about half a century before the Trojan war, opened a school of rhetoric at the city of Troezene; and wrote a book upon the subject, which Pausanias declares he had read. Some doubts have indeed been started, whether Pausanias had not been deceived by an Epidaurian, from whom he procured the manuscript; and there is no other evidence extant, confirming the existence of such a treatise, or leading to a conjecture of its contents. There is otherwise nothing improbable in the story; for the time, when Pittheus is alleged to have lived, is contemporary with the age of Solomon; at which time we have the most indisputable proof in the sacred scriptures, that the art of literary composition, so intimately connected with that of oratory, had been carried to a high pitch of perfection. All the books of Moses, including probably that of Job, must have been written live hundred years before that time; and the Grecian Peloponnesus appears to have been first settled by a colony from Egypt, the same country, whence the Israelites issued to make the conquest of the promised land, and the same where Moses had received his education and acquired his learning. Be this as it may, innumerable passages in the Iliad and Odyssey leave no doubt, that rhetoric was taught, and oratory practised, in high refinement, during, and before the war of Troy. We are there told, that Phoenix was sent with Achilles to teach him eloquence, as well as heroism;

Μύθων τε ῥητῆζ ἔιεγαι, πζημτζά τε ἔζγων.

IΛ. I. 443.

or, as Pope has translated it,

To shine in councils, and in camps to dare.

IL. IX. 571.

And in the Odyssey, Minerva herself is said to have performed the same office to Telemachus. Both these poems are full of speeches, exhibiting all the excellencies and all the varieties of practical eloquence. In the third Iliad Antenor gives a minute and contrasted character of the style of eloquence, for which Menelaus and Ulysses were respectively distinguished. The one concise, correct, and plain; the other artful to that last degree of perfection, which consists in concealing art, copious and astonishing by unexpected and irresistible arguments; while in another passage the eloquence of Nestor, mild, insinuating, and diffuse, is discriminated with clear accuracy from both the others. Nor need I tell you, who are so well acquainted with Homer, that the speeches, attributed to these three personages in the Iliad and Odyssey,

31

all exactly correspond with the character, thus appropriated by the poet to each of them.

From this time however for the space of about four hundred years, no other traces of the science are to be found; and its first reappearance is in the island of Sicily, where a school of rhetoric is said to have been held, about five hundred years before Christ; and the first teacher of which was Empedocles. He was soon succeeded in the same country by Corax and Tisias. One of his pupils also was Gorgias of Leontium, whose reputation has fluctuated from the extreme of admiration to that of debasement.

Gorgias lived to the extraordinary age of one hundred and nine years. He had a great number of contemporary rhetoricians; among whom were Thrasymachus of Chalcedon; Prodicus of the island of Ceos, and the original author of that beautiful and instructive fable of the choice of Hercules; Protagoras of Abdera; Hippias of Elis; Alcidamus of Elea; Antiphon, who first published a rhetorical treatise, and a judicial oration together; Policrates, damned to fame, as one of the advocates against Socrates upon his trial; and Theodore of Byzantium. All these writers are included by Plato under the contemptuous denomination of word weavers.

Gorgias was the first, who extended so far the principles of his art, that he professed to prepare his pupils for extemporaneous declamation upon any subject whatsoever. His fame was spread far and wide. His country, being at war with the Syracusans, sent an embassy, at the head of which they placed him, to solicit the alliance of the Athenians. His eloquence was admired at

Athens no less, than in his own city. It secured successful issue to his mission; and some of his orations have received the approbation of Aristotle and Quinctilian. It is said by Cicero, that a golden statue of him was erected in the temple of Delphi, by the united offering of all Greece; an honor, never shown to any other man.

Unfortunately however for Gorgias, he found in Socrates, or rather in his disciple, Plato, a rival and antagonist, whose works and reputation have stood the test of ages, better than his own; which have sunk under the weight of his adversary's superiority. Among the dialogues of Plato is one, entitled Gorgias, from the name of this rhetorician, and upon the subject of the art. He is there represented in a very ridiculous light; first, undertaking to make an orator eloquent upon every topic whatsoever; and yet, when required by Socrates, unable to speak with common sense upon the first elements of his art. In the hands of Plato Gorgias is a driveller so despicable, that Socrates appears disgraced by a victory over him. It is however well known, that no such dialogue, as that, published by Plato, was ever held between Gorgias and Socrates; and there was too much reason for the exclamation of Gorgias, on his first perusal of the work; "how handsomely that same Plato can slander!" The system and the practice of Gorgias were too affected and too presumptuous. The deeper penetration and the more chastened judgment of Socrates led to a higher perfection in the theory of rhetoric. But if it be true, as by the concurrent testimony of all the ancient rhetoricians we are assured, that Gorgias was the inventor of what are called topics, or common places, of oratorical numbers, and of a general plan for extemporaneous declamation upon every subject, he must be considered, as one of the principal improvers of eloquence. These things are peculiarly liable to be abused; but they have been of important use to all the celebrated ancient orators; and to none more, than to Plato himself.

You will find it useful to remember, that the opposition of sentiment between Gorgias and Socrates laid the foundation for two rival systems of rhetoric, the respective pretensions of which have never been definitively settled. They gave rise to two very distinct classes of orators, and two different modes of speaking, distinguished at first by the denominations of the Attic and the Asiatic manners; and which in modern times have been as generally understood by the appellations of the close and the florid style.

Isocrates was a disciple of Gorgias; formed upon the principles of his school. In early life he had been of opinion, that eloquence ought not to be taught, as an art. Deterred by a natural and insuperable timidity, which, in common with many other men of genius, he either had, or fancied, from ever speaking in public himself, he composed orations for others, to be delivered upon the trial of judicial causes. This practice however having exposed him to a prosecution, under a certain Athenian law, which it was supposed to infringe, he abandoned the employment, and opened a school of rhetoric, which soon became highly celebrated, and from which, to use an expression of Cicero, as from the Trojan horse, issued a host of heroes. Isocrates was not only an able rhetorician, but an excellent citizen, and a true patriot. When Socrates fell a victim to the passions of a partial tribunal and a deluded people, and all his disciples were terrified into flight, Isocrates had the honorable intrepidity to appear in the streets of Athens with the mourning garb. When Theramenes was proscribed by the thirty tyrants, Isocrates exposed his own life, by undertaking to defend him at the altar of refuge; and after a life of little less than a whole century, he finally died broken hearted, of mere inanition, upon the fatal issue of the battle of Chaeronea, that final stroke to the agonizing liberties of Greece. Isocrates composed upwards of sixty orations, twenty one of which are still extant. His style is remarkable for its elegance, its polished periods, and harmonious numbers. Like his master, Gorgias, he delights in antithesis and pointed expression, but he is more copious and diffuse. He labored his compositions with such indefatigable assiduity, that he is said to have been ten years employed upon a single oration, entitled the panegyric.

As the school of Gorgias and the other sophists gave rise to the two dialogues of Plato, upon the subject of rhetoric, so that of Isocrates occasioned the rival school of Aristotle, and led to the composition of that work, which is the most ancient treatise, professedly systematic, upon the science, now extant. Plato, as you all know, was one of the disciples of Socrates; and with this fellow scholar Xenophon has published the moral and political doctrines of that philosopher, who left nothing written himself. Socrates was a teacher of philosophy, and as well as his follower, Plato, might have his personal reasons for opposing the theories of the other sophists, who inculcated other principles, but followed the same profession. If the real character of Socrates appears in the writings of his illustrious pupils, his mind must have been of a sterling stamp, and his heart of uncommon excellence. His method of reasoning was so striking, and so peculiar to himself, that to this day it is designated by his name; and though not perhaps the fairest process for a candid logician, it has always been considered, as a mode of close and irresistible argument. It consists in the art of entangling an adversary into absurdity and self-contradiction, by a chain of questions, the first of which seems by its simplicity to admit but of one answer; the last of which with equal simplicity comes to the direct denial of the proposition to be refuted, and the connexion between which is imperceptible to the opponent, until he finds it too late to retreat. The son of Sophroniscus, by the turn of his mmd, was devoted to the rigorous demonstrations of logic, and perhaps too fastidiously disdained the fascinating ornaments of rhetoric. Very different was the character of Plato. With a genius more sublime, though far less correct, he was addicted to the pomp and magnificence of speech, as much as the most ostentatious of the sophists. His imagination is so incessantly upon the wing, and soars to such empyrean heights, that it requires no inconsiderable effort of the understanding to keep him company. His writings are not only poetical to the extremest boundaries of poetry; they often encroach upon the borders of mysticism, and approach the undistinguishable regions of intellectual chaos. It is singular, that two men, of characters so extremely opposite, should have stood in precisely such a relation to each other. That Socrates should have written nothing; and Plato, nothing of his own. That Plato should have held himself out to the world, as the mere amanuensis of Socrates; and that Socrates should have intrusted the registry of his opinions to so wild and eccentric a recorder, as Plato. Hence there is no small difficulty in ascertaining what part of the sentiments, imputed by Plato to Socrates, were really his; but it is known, that the disciple has often ascribed hit, own doctrines to the master. Hence also may be drawn the most natural solution of that inconsistency on the subject of rhetoric, which appears in the two dialogues of Plato; an inconsistency so glaring, that in the Phaedrus, Pericles is mentioned, as a highly accomplished orator, while in the Gorgias he is as positively pronounced to be no orator at all. It is also remarkable, that the Phaedrus closes with a declaration of Socrates, that he intends to repeat the substance of his precepts to his young friend, Isocrates, of whose abilities and virtues he speaks in terms of panegyric, and whom he pronounces superior, as an orator, to Lysias. Yet Isocrates preferred the system of his first master, Gorgias. It is much to be regretted, that the rhetorical work of Isocrates is no longer extant, because, as the admirable work of Aristotle was written in professed opposition to it, we might doubtless derive much useful instruction from a full and fair comparison of the two systems together.

34

Besides the principal work of Aristotle on rhetoric, which is in three books, there is another treatise, seemingly containing a compendium of the whole, published with the common editions of his works, and usually, though I believe not correctly, attributed to him. It is addressed to Alexander the Great, of whom Aristotle was indeed the preceptor; but there are many circumstances, which lead to the inference, that it was the work of another writer, supposed to be Anaximenes of Lampsacus. This was a writer of the same age, and, together with Aristotle, was selected by Philip of Macedon, as one of his son's instructors. His principal writings were historical, and his style has been characterized, as polished and correct, but florid, diffuse, and feeble. This description applies exactly to the rhetoric, addressed to Alexander, though nothing can be a stronger contrast, than the style of all the voluminous works, known to have been written by Aristotle. Demetrius Phalereus lived in the age, succeeding that of Aristotle. He is celebrated, as the last of the Grecian orators; and in that character I shall speak of him more at large on some future occasion. I mention him here, because there is a valuable treatise upon elocution extant, which has been attributed to him; though some learned critics have supposed it the work of another Demetrius, of Alexandria, who lived several centuries later; while others have ascribed it to Dionysius of Halicarnassus. The principal evidence, upon which it has been concluded not to be the production of Phalereus, is, that, being professedly a treatise upon elocution, or style, it not only differs most essentially from that, which was peculiar to this Athenian orator, but passes censure upon all its characteristic features. It is a valuable treatise, discussing at large that important branch of the oratorical art, and serving as a proper supplement to the general system of Aristotle, in which elocution is not so minutely considered.

There are several other rhetorical treatises, full of solid and ingenious criticism, written by Dionysius of Halicarnassus. He is more generally known indeed, as one of the principal historians of Rome; a considerable, though proportionably small part of his work on the Roman antiquities being yet extant. He lived in the age of Augustus Caesar, and spent a great part of his life at Rome, where he is supposed to have been a teacher of rhetoric.

The next of the Grecian rhetoricians in point of time is Lucian of Samosata, who lived[and died in the second century of the Christian era. After having been successively a sculptor and a practitioner at the bar, and becoming disgusted with both these professions, he finally became a teacher of rhetoric. His acquirements in literature and moral philosophy were far above the level of his age; and the turn of his mind inclining to ridicule and satire, he is perhaps the wittiest writer of antiquity. He satirized with so much freedom the gods of paganism, that some learned men in modern times have supposed he was a Christian: though no other evidence of the fact has been adduced.

The treatise, which has led me to speak of him in this place, is entitled Ῥήτοζων Διδάσηαλος, the teacher of orators. It is ironical and allegorical; holding out two systems of instruction for forming a public speaker, as delivered by two fictitious persons. The one indolent, dissipated, and fashionable; the other laborious, severe, and forbidding. Like Swift's directions to servants, which were probably suggested by them, Lucian's instructions mingle the satire of his own age with the lesson to the next; and his moral is only that of the old Greek adage, that the gods sell every thing to labor.

Nearly about the same time lived Hermogenes, one of the most extraordinary examples of early intellectual maturity and decay. At the age of fifteen his celebrity, as a teacher of rhetoric, attracted the personal attendance of the emperor, Marcus Antoninus, at his lectures; and the imperial satisfaction was manifested with princely munificence. The rhetorical works of Hermogenes, parts of which are yet extant, were composed at eighteen. At twenty four he lost his faculties, and continued during the remainder of his life in a state, not far removed from idiotism. With several small fragments, there are two treatises of this author almost entire. One upon the character of an oration in five books, and one upon ideas in two. They are yet in high estimation, and have sometimes been preferred even to the work of Aristotle.

I pass over the writings of Aristides, Apsines, Sopater, Alexander, Menander, Minucian, Cyrus, Apthonius, Theon, Ulpian, Tiberius, and Severus, who all lived near the time of Lucian and Hermogenes. There are short treatises on various rhetorical subjects by all these writers; which contain little else but repetitions of the precepts, taught by Aristotle and Hermogenes. But Longinus must not be thus slightly noticed. His work upon the sublime should be studied by every orator, and even by every writer in any department of literature. Though confined to a single subject, that subject is sublimity; though gnawed and mutilated by the tooth of time into a mere fragment, it is a fragment from the table of the gods.

With Longinus the rhetorical genius of Greece expired; and preserved to its last gasp the proud preeminence of its youth. The luminary, which had so long enlightened the world, after languishing long in decline, at the moment of extinction, kindled into a blaze of transient glory. Longinus lived in the third century of the Christian era. He was at once the rhetorical instructor and minister of state to Zenobia, the celebrated queen of Palmyra. With the prerogative of genuine eloquence he inspired her heroic sentiments into the mind of the princess. But he could not convert a people, degraded by servitude, into a nation of heroes. Zenobia sunk before the victorious legions of Aurelian; and Longinus, like the great orators of better days, paid the usual tribute of transcendent genius, the forfeit of his life, to the principles of an unconquerable soul.

Here I shall conclude the review of the Grecian rhetoricians. It was my first intention, upon mentioning their works, to have given you u brief analytical survey of their contents. This however I soon found would require a course of lectures by itself. Perhaps at some future time, when the principles of the science shall be more familiar to your minds, I shall undertake to make you better acquainted with these venerable relics of antiquity, many of which are so contemptuously undervalued by modern writers. You will also remark, that I have yet spoken only of the rhetoricians, and have left the orators and their works for future consideration. In pursuance of this plan I shall in my next lecture call your attention to the history of the science at Rome.

Lecture Four - Origin and Progress of Oratory at Rome

THE origin of the Grecian, and Roman republics, though equally involved in the obscurities and uncertainties of fabulous events, present one remarkable distinction, which continues perceptible in the progress of their history, through a succession of several centuries. The first principle of human association in Greece, as far as it can be traced, was common consent. At Rome it was force. This striking difference of character is perceptible even in the fables, which form the basis of the respective histories. Thus, while in Greece it was the harp of Orpheus and the lyre of Amphion, which attracted mankind by the fascinations of pleasure into the ties of civil society, the founder of the Roman state is exhibited, as begotten by the god of battles; suckled in his infancy by a wolf; cementing the walls of his rising city with the blood of fraternal murder; and finding no expedient for its population but rape; no means for its subsistence but rapine. It is among the natural consequences of this contrast in the foundations of their municipal associations, that the powers of eloquence were so early discovered among the Greeks, and remained so long concealed among the Romans. Violence and persuasion, being in their nature as opposite to each other, as light and darkness, can never exist together; and by their reciprocal antipathies, wheresoever either predominates, the other must be excluded. Thus we have seen, that in Greece the art of persuasion by speech was held in honor and in exercise of power from the first moment, that any real fact can be discerned. In the Grecian annals history and oratory make their first appearance, entering hand in hand upon the scene. But so far are these personages from presenting themselves on the Roman theatre together, that the first notice we have of rhetoric, in the imperial city, is a decree of the senate, passed in the five hundred and ninety second year from its foundation, and commanding the expulsion of all philosophers and rhetoricians from Rome. The lordly nation seems to have been as averse to thinking, as to speaking. "Tu regere imperio populos" was their only maxim, and they disdained to rule with any thing but a rod of iron. In proportion however as the Romans acquired a more intimate acquaintance with the Greeks, they became accessible to that all-subduing charm, which accompanies the elegant arts. These gradually obtained the same ascendency, which they had so long enjoyed in Greece, and eloquence was successively tolerated and encouraged, until the study became an indispensable part of education to every young man of fortune or distinction in the city. In the first instance, and for several ages, it was taught only in the Greek language and by Greek professors; insomuch, that when Plotius opened the first school of rhetoric in Latin, which had ever been known, Cicero, then a youth, burning with the ambition of acquiring the oratorical art, was dissuaded by his friends from attending the lessons of this Latin teacher, and adhered to the language and instructors of Greece. The progress of the art, in the public opinion, may be discerned in the rank and station of the persons, who at different times engaged in the occupation of teaching it. During a certain period it was confined to the class of freedmen, the lowest order of Roman citizens. In process of time it was deemed worthy of employing the time and the faculties of a Roman knight; and thence continued to rise in reputation and influence, until Cato, the censor, Antonius, the orator, so highly celebrated by Cicero, and Cicero himself, deemed it no disparagement to devote their faculties to the improvement of their fellow citizens in the art of speech. The writings of Cato and of Antonius on this subject have not reached us. And those of several other Roman writers, mentioned by Cicero and Quinctilian, are also lost. They are perhaps not much to be regretted, while we are in possession of Cicero and Quinctilian.

Of Cicero, considered as a practical orator, we shall have occasion to speak much at large in the course of these lectures. In that character he is more or less known to you all. In that character you all admire him already; and I trust, as you advance in years, and in knowledge, will admire him yet more. As a teacher of rhetoric and oratory, he is not so generally read; but his rhetorical works have a recommendation to the student. beyond all others; because they are the lessons of a consummate master upon his own art. His theory holds a flambeau to his practice, and his practice is a comment upon his theory. It is a remark of Rochefoucault, that no man ever exerted his faculties to the full extent, of which they were capable. If there ever was an exception to the universality of this remark, it was Cicero. He presents the most perfect example of that rare and splendid combination, universal genius and indefatigable application, which the annals of the world can produce. There have been other men as liberally gifted by nature. There may possibly have been men, whose exercise of their faculties has been as incessant. But of that mutual league between nature and study, that compact of ethereal spirit and terrestrial toil, that alliance of heaven and earth, to produce a wonder of the world in human shape, which he has described with such inimitable beauty, in one of his orations, there never was so illustrious, so sublime an instance, as himself.

His rhetorical treatises are seven in number, besides a system in four books, addressed to Herinnius, printed in all the general editions of his works, but probably not written by him. As a poet, a historian, a philosopher, a moralist, and an epistolary writer, the rank of Cicero is in the very first line. But by a singular fatality his reputation has been offuscated by its own splendor, and his writings in half a dozen departments of science, which would have carried as many silent writers to the pinnacle of fame, have been shorn of their beams, in the flood of glory, the one unclouded blaze of his eloquence.

The uncontrollable propensity of his mind was undoubtedly to oratory. From the twenty sixth year of his age, when he pronounced his oration for Quinctius, to the last year of his life, when he delivered the philippics against Mark Antony; that is, for the space of nearly forty years, his studies in the closet, and his practice in all the stages of oratory, were without intermission. Hence arose the numerous treatises upon the art, which at different times he composed. Some while yet a student, and before he plunged into the bustle of active life; others in the midst of those great political events, in which he bore so distinguished and so admirable a part. But the principal of these works, the work, over which the future orator must consume the last drop of his midnight oil, and hail the first beam of returning dawn, is the treatise in three books, written in the form of dialogues, and entitled de oratore. They were composed at the request of his brother, when the author's judgment was matured by experience, and his genius in the meridian of its vigor. The substance of his system is collected from those of Aristotle and Isocrates, the two rival systems of Greece. The form of dialogue, into which he has thrown the work, he adopted from Plato. He supposes a conversation, on the subject of oratory, to have arisen between Antonius, Crassus, and Caesar; three persons of high rank and distinction, the most celebrated orators of their age, and who lived about half a century before him. Each of these interlocutors had been noted for a peculiar characteristic manner, and Cicero, by observing to make each of them speak conformably to his known character, avails himself of the occasion to discuss the important questions, involved in the theories of the art.

The first of these dialogues begins by discussing the various opinions concerning the talents, essential to the composition of an orator. This is in substance only settling: the true definition of the art. Yet this gives rise to a useful and instructive examination of fundamental principles. Crassus affirms, that the only able statesman must be an orator, always prepared to speak:, and to excite admiration upon every subject. Scevola, who is introduced as occasionally taking part in the dialogue, insists, that the philosopher is the only suitable ruler of a nation, and that the art of government is to be learnt only in the schools of philosophy. For example, says he, how can a man be qualified for the management of a state, without the knowledge of physical nature, the structure of the earth, and the phenomena of the universe; to be acquired only by the study of natural philosophy? And how can a man obtain the confidence of a whole people in his moral character, or that knowledge of the human heart, which alone can establish his control over the will, without a profound investigation of the science of moral philosophy or ethics?

From this diversity of opinion Crassus proceeds to affirm, that for the genuine orator nothing less can suffice, than universal knowledge. And he successively shows how an acquaintance with the science of government, with the forms of administration, with the doctrines of religion, with laws, usages, history, and the knowledge of mankind, may be applied to the purposes of the orator. Physics and mathematics, he contends, are in their own nature inert sciences, of little use even to their professors, without the talent of the speaker to give them life; while in the whole circle of science there is not a particle of knowledge, which can be condemned to sleep, in the mind of an orator.

Besides this broad basis of universal knowledge, the orator of Crassus must be endowed with a fine natural genius, and a pleasing personal appearance. He must have a soul of fire; an iron application; indefatigable, unremitting assiduity of exercise in writing and composition; unwearied patience to correct and revise; constant reading of the poets, orators, and historians; the practice of declamation; the exercise and improvement of the memory; the attentive cultivation of the graces; and a habit of raillery and humor, sharpened by wit, but tempered with the soberest judgment, to point their application.

This is rather an ideal description of what an orator ought to be, than what among the common materials, of which human nature is composed, will readily be found. But Crassus has a substantial reason to allege for every one of the accomplishments, which he requires, that his speaker should possess. the orator must excel in his profession, or he cannot deserve the name. The orator must please; he must captivate; he must charm; he must transfix affected wisdom and hypocrisy with the blasting bolt of ridicule; he must dart the thrills of terror into the souls of his enemies; he must overwhelm guilt with confusion; he must lead innocence to the throne of triumph. The orator must wield a nation with a breath; he must kindle or compose their passions at his pleasure. Now he must cool them to justice, and now inflame them to glory. To discharge functions like these, it is obvious, that no penurious or scanty stock of knowledge will suffice, and no provision, however abundant, can be superfluous.

After this magnificent enumeration of the qualifications, necessary for a perfect orator, Antonius is requested to point out the means of acquiring them. Antonius however was of opinion, that the reputation of universal knowledge was by no means necessary, and might be very prejudicial to a public speaker. Antonius begins then by controverting the opinion of Crassus. The talent of Antonius was principally defensive. His greatest power consisted in refuting the opinions of others, and, instead of admitting universal knowledge to be necessary for an orator, he contends, that an orator scarcely needs any knowledge at all. This doctrine he supports with so much ingenious plausibility, that the hearers are left in some suspense, and scarcely know which of the two opinions to adopt. In this method of treating the subject, Cicero purposely followed the example of Plato; who in most of his dialogues, after fully discussing the two sides of a question, leaves the judgment of the issue to the sagacity of the reader. Plato indeed generally makes this a compliment rather of form, than of substance; for one side of his argument is so strong, and the other so weak, that the decision is apparently drawn up by himself, and left for the reader only to pronounce. Nor has Cicero chosen to leave his reader in the dark with regard to his own opinion, and in the second dialogue he brings Antonius to the confession, that his opposition to the sentiments of Crassus on the preceding day was a mere trial of skill for his amusement, and that his affectation of ignorance was an artifice to elude the suspicion and distrust, which a high reputation of learning is apt to excite in the minds of judges against an advocate; a prejudice, not without example in later ages, than that of Antonius or Cicero. In this dialogue however Antonius enters into a minute investigation of the art; assigns its limits; marks its divisions; and in the familiar, easy style of elegant conversation, introduces the most important precepts of Aristotle. He passes in successive review the subjects of proof, observance of manners, and management of the passions; and particularly urges the advantages of ready wit, and a talent at ridicule, in judicial oratory. Crassus is the principal speaker of the third dialogue, and his subject is elocution. Crassus was distinguished for the elegance of his oratorical compositions; but, like those of Demosthenes, they were charged by the speaker's enemies with smelling too much of the lamp. He alleges two distinct sources of ornament in discourse, one of which must arise from the dignity of the subject, and will naturally communicate some part of its elevation to the expressions, used for its development; and the other from the diction, the choice and collocation of words, and the figures of speech. This distinction is at once rational and useful; and a natural inference from it is, that the graces of the subject ought to pervade every part of the discourse, while those of diction should only occasionally be introduced, and scattered with a sparing hand. Another observation of Crassus will be found of eminent utility to be held in remembrance by the student. In maintaining, that an orator ought to have some tincture of every science, he cautions against the application of too much time to studies of minutiae, and especially of science merely speculative. The knowledge, necessary to discourse with propriety upon any art, is very different from that, which is indispensable to practise the art. The orator is to obtain such knowledge, as may be useful to him in the exercise of his own profession; and that, without being equally profound, will enable him to discourse upon the art more copiously, and more accurately too, than, can the very artists, who make it the exclusive occupation of their lives.

The principles of the oratorical art, like all other knowledge, may be taught by the analytical, or by the synthetical process. These terms and the ideas, annexed to them, may not be perfectly clear to the minds of some of you. But you will perceive by the derivation of the words themselves, which is from the Greek language, that analysis is the process, which takes to pieces; and synthesis is that, which puts together. Thus in the dialogues de oratore, Cicero has analyzed, and exhibited separately the various qualifications, which contribute to the formation of an eloquent speaker. In the orator he has combined and embodied the same precepts, to show how they are to be brought into action. The dialogues give a dissection of the art into its constituent parts; the orator gathers the parts, and connects them into an organized body. The dialogues are a delineation of the talent; the orator is a portrait of the speaker.

The Grecian philosophers first conceived, and Plato has largely expatiated upon, what they call the beautiful, and the good, in the abstract. Beauty and goodness are properties, and, as to any object perceptible to the senses, neither of them can exist without some substance, in which they may exist. A good man, or a beautiful woman, is perceptible to the eye and to the reason of us all; but the qualities themselves we cannot readily discern, without the aid of imagination. But as imperfection is stamped upon every work of nature, the imagination is able to conceive of goodness and beauty more perfect, than they can be found in any of the works of nature, or of man. This creature of the imagination Plato designates by the name of the good and fair. That is, goodness and beauty, purified from all the dross of natural imperfection. And then, by one step more of the imagination, we are required to personify these sublime abstractions, and call up to the eye of fancy images, in which goodness and beauty would appear, if they could assume a human shape. this principle was applied to the fine arts, as well as to morals; and the painters and sculptors, in imitating the productions of nature, improved upon them by these ideal images, and created those wonders of art, which still excite the astonishment of every beholder. The antique statues of the Apollo and Venus have thus been considered, for nearly three thousand years, the perfect models of human beauty. Such exquisite proportions, such an assemblage of features was never found in any human form. But the idea was in the mind of the artist, and his chisel has given it a local habitation in the minds of others. It was the conception and the pursuit of this ideal beauty, which produced all the wonders of Grecian art. Cicero applied it to eloquence. It appears to have been the study of his whole life to form an idea of a perfect orator, and of exhibiting his image to the world. In this treatise he has concentrated the result of all his observation, experience, and reflection. It is the idealized image of a speaker, in the mind of Cicero; what a speaker should be; what no speaker ever will be; but what every speaker should devote the labors of his life to approximate.

Let it be remembered, that this inflexible, unremitting pursuit of ideal and unattainable excellence is the source of all the real excellence, which the world has ever seen. It is the foundation of every tiling great and good, of which man can boast. It is one of the proofs, that the soul of man is immortal; and it is at the foundation of the whole doctrine of Christianity. It is the root of all real excellence in religion, in morals, and in taste. It was so congenial to the mind of Cicero, that in the treatise, of which I am now speaking, he took the most elaborate pains, and the most exquisite pleasure, in setting it forth. He addressed it to his friend Brutus, at whose desire it was written; and in one of the familiar epistles Cicero declares, that he wishes this work to be considered, as the test of his capacity; that it contains the quintessence of all his faculties.

The principal difficulty of the subject was to settle a standard of eloquence; for the original controversy between the rival Asiatic and Attic schools, which I have mentioned, was so far from being decided, that it had given rise to a third system, partaking of both the others, and usually known by the name of the Rhodian manner. Cicero therefore determines, that there are subjects, peculiarly fitted to each of these three modes of speaking, and that the perfection of the orator consists in the proper use and variation of them all, according to the occasion. The most remarkable example of which, he thinks, is to be found in the famous oration of Demosthenes for Ctesiphon; commonly called the oration for the crown. In the distinction, which he draws between the schools of Isocrates and of Aristotle, we find the true criterion for judging their respective pretensions. The first he pronounces to have been the cradle of eloquence. Its florid colors, its dazzling splendors, its studied and laborious decorations, he thinks peculiarly adapted to representation, and not to action; to the first essays of youth, and not to the serious labors of manhood. But it is in judicial controversies, where the conflict of rights must be decided by the conflict of talents, that the manhood, the highest energies of the art,, must be exerted. Here all the resources of invention, of selection, of arrangement, of style, and of action, must successively be applied, and here alone can the highest perfection of the art be found.

To professional speakers, the orator of Cicero is a work, which they should familiarize and master, at the very threshold of their studies. It contains a lively image of what they ought to be, and a specific indication of what they ought to do. It is in many passages a comment upon the writer's own orations. It points out the variations of his style and manner, in many of those eloquent discourses, and gives you the reasons, which inspired his sublime, indignant vehemence in the accusation of Verres, and of Catiline; his temperate, insinuating elegance upon the Manilian law, and the solicitations for Ligarius; and his close and irresistible cogency of argument in disclosing and elucidating the intricate case of Caecina. I would particularly recommend it to those of you, who may hereafter engage in the profession of the law, to read over these orations, and compare the management of the cause with this account, given by the author, of his motives for proceeding, as he did in each of them.

But to whatever occupation your future inclinations or destinies may direct you, that pursuit of ideal excellence, which constituted the plan of Cicero's orator, and the principle of Cicero's life, if profoundly meditated, and sincerely adopted, will prove a never failing source of virtue and of happiness. I say profoundly meditated, because no superficial consideration can give you a conception of the real depth and extent of this principle. I say sincerely adopted, because its efficacy consists not in resolutions, much less in pretensions; but in action. Its affectation can only disclose the ridiculous coxcomb, or conceal the detestable hypocrite; nor is it in occasional, momentary gleams of virtue and energy, preceded and followed by long periods of indulgence or inaction, that this sublime principle can be recognized. It must be the steady purpose of a life, maturely considered, deliberately undertaken, and inflexibly pursued, through all the struggles of human opposition, and all the vicissitudes of fortune. It must mark the measure of your duties in the relations of domestic, of social, and of public life. Must guard from presumption your rapid moments of prosperity, and nerve with fortitude your lingering hours of misfortune. It must mingle with you in the busy murmurs of the city, and retire in silence with you to the shades of solitude. Like hope it must "travel through, nor quit you when you die." Your guide amid the dissipations of youth; your counsellor in the toils of manhood; your companion in the leisure of declining age. It must, it will, irradiate the darkness of dissolution; will identify the consciousness of the past with the hope of futurity; will smooth the passage from this to a better world; and link the last pangs of expiring nature with the first rapture of never ending joy.

You are ready to tell me, that I am insensibly wandering from my subject into the mazes of general morality. In surveying the character and writings of Cicero, we cannot choose but be arrested, at almost every step of our progress, by some profound and luminous principle, which suspends our attention from the immediate cause of our research, and leads us into a train of reflections upon itself. Yet these, though indirect, are perhaps the fairest illustrations of our primary object. In Cicero, more than in any other writer, will you find a perpetual comment upon the saying of Solomon, that "the sweetness of the lips increaseth learning." Cicero is the friend of the soul, whom we can never meet without a gleam of pleasure; from whom we can never part, but with reluctance. We have yet noticed only two of his rhetorical works; and must reserve for another occasion our considerations upon the rest.

Lecture Five - Cicero and His Rhetorical Writings

WITHIN a century after the death of Cicero, while his language was yet flourishing, and the events of his age, and institutions of his country were in recent remembrance, it was observed by Quinctilian, that a young man, desirous of ascertaining his own proficiency in literary taste, needed only to ask himself how he relished the writings of Cicero, and if he found the answer to be, that they highly delighted him, he might safely conclude himself far advanced in refinement. If this remark was then correct, it must apply much more forcibly to the self-examination of any young man in our times. The difficulties to be vanquished, before you can obtain access to those inestimable treasures, are incomparably greater, than they Mere in the age of Quinctilian. The youth of that day, to understand Cicero, needed little other preparatory knowledge, than merely how to read. Some little acquaintance with the history of the time, the sources to which flowed copious and frequent; some little recollection of republican habits and manners, which had indeed vanished from practice, but were fresh in the memory of all, and yet lurked in the wishes of many; was all the information, necessary for a Roman of that epocha to master every page of Cicero. Your labors to obtain the same possession must be far more severe, and their success at best must fall far shorter of being complete. You have a language, long since deceased, to revive; you have a circumstantial history of the age to familiarize; you have a course of painful studies into the civil, political, and military constitution of the Roman republic to go through, before you can open an unobstructed avenue between the beauties of Cicero and your own understandings. How much more reason then must you have to be pleased with your own acquirements, if you can honestly answer it to your hearts, that you are charmed with the works of Cicero, than a pupil of Quinctilian could have from the same cause? Yet I am not sure, that originally the remark was very judicious. To a Roman in the age of Quinctilian, methinks the fondness for Cicero could not be so clear a demonstration of an excellent taste, as the dislike or contempt of him would have been to prove the contrary. Not to admire him must have shown a want of the reason and feeling, which belong to man. To delight in him could indicate only common sense and common sensibility. Even now, my friends, I doubt not but many of you are sincere admirers of Cicero; and yet I cannot advise you to draw from that sentiment any very pointed inference of self-complacency. Taste was never made to cater for vanity. I would rather recommend it to you to turn the pleasure you take in those exquisite compositions to better account. Make your profit of your pleasure; scrutinize the causes of your enjoyments; pass the spirit of the Roman orator through the alembic of your reason, until every drop of its essence shall be distinctly perceptible to your taste. As a general hint to guide you in this examination, I mentioned to you in my last lecture the distinguishing characteristics of his two principal rhetorical treatises. I told you, that the dialogues de oratore contained an analytical decomposition of the art of public speaking, while the orator put together the same precepts, to exhibit them in the person of a perfect speaker. But instruction is to be derived as much, perhaps more, from example, than from precept; and Cicero has also availed himself of this process for the illustration of his favorite art. The treatise, which bears the double title of Brutus and de claris oratoribus, contains, as this latter title imports, a summary review of all the famous orators, Greek and Roman, until his own time. In form it partakes both of the didactic manner, in which the author speaks in his own person, and of the dialogue, where interlocutors are formally introduced. The Brutus is a narrative of a dialogue, or conversation between the orator and his friends, Atticus and Brutus; for it is not immaterial to observe how Cicero, in writing so many works upon the same general subject, has given to his discussions the charm of variety. The Brutus is a practical commentary upon, the dialogues and the orator. In examining the several excellencies and defects of the most renowned Greek and Roman speakers, the true principles of eloquence are naturally unfolded. But it is further valuable, as it teaches the principles of rhetorical criticism; the art of appreciating the real merits of a public speaker. The natural graces of simplicity, the splendor of ornamented diction, the elegance and purity of a correct style, the charms of urbanity, the stings of ingenious sarcasm and raillery, are exhibited in the shape of historical proof. Specific instances are produced of temperate insinuations, of strength, of vehemence, of dignity, of copious facility, of fertile invention, discerning selection of argument, novelty of expression, art in the choice and arrangement of words, readiness of action, quickness of repartee, skilful digression, and the rare talent of the pathetic, are held up to admiration with the force of example. And as the detection of faults is no less instructive to the student, than the display of beauties, in rendering all justice to the perfections of the illustrious orators, Cicero has not been blind to their blemishes. Boldness of invention, barrenness of fancy, affectation, singularity, treacheries of memory, heaviness, carelessness, exaggerations, awkwardness, penury of thought, meanness of expression, and many other imperfections, occasionally pass through the ordeal, and never escape the discriminating and accurate judgment of Cicero. The acuteness and variety of his remarks are adorned by the liveliness of his manner, and embellished with that richness of fancy, and glow of coloring, which mark every production of his pen.

There is in this work a very perceptible partiality, favorable to his own countrymen. He bestows upon them a much larger share of attention; extends greater indulgence to their faults, and warms with more fervent admiration at their excellencies, than he is willing to bestow upon the Greeks. He acknowledges elsewhere this predilection, and ascribes it partly to his national feelings, and partly to the wish of stimulating them by commendation to superior excellence. But all these sentiments are subordinate to his enthusiasm for the transcendent merit of Demosthenes.

The Brutus concludes with two parallels. The first between the eloquence of Antonius and that of Crassus; the two principal interlocutors of the dialogues de oratore; and the other between Cicero himself and his rival, Hortensius. We have none of the writings of Antonius or of Crassus left, upon which we can form an opinion of Cicero's accuracy in the comparison between them; we must take it upon the credit of his general correctness and ability. He speaks of them in terms probably more favorable, than the judgment of posterity would have confirmed; and as for Hortensius, it is praise enough for him to have been remembered for twenty centuries, as the antagonist of Cicero. But the view, in which this last parallel may be turned to advantage by us, is the signal example, which it furnishes, of industry triumphant over indolence. In point of natural genius, Hortensius was perhaps not inferior to his great competitor. But it is from the example of Cicero's life, that the only means of obtaining unrivalled excellence is to be learnt. The diirst for distinction, as an orator, was felt by Cicero from his very childhood. He frequented assiduously all the scenes of public speaking, and listened with eager avidity to the eminent orators of the age. He was continually reading, writing, meditating upon this favorite pursuit. He sought instruction in jurisprudence from Scevola, in philosophy from Philo, the Athenian, in oratory from Molon of Rhodes, in logic from Diodotus, the Stoic; associating with the study of rhetoric a close application to every branch of learning, connected with it, and composing by turns, both in the Greek and Latin languages, according as the attendance upon his several instructors required.

After a long and unremitting course of preparation like this, he made his first appearance at the bar; and in his oration for Rosciiis of Ameria, delivered in his twenty seventh year, unfolded those wonderful powers, which were to make him the glory of his own age, and the admiration of all succeeding times. His constitution was naturally feeble, and had probably suffered by the intenseness of his application. His friends and physicians advised him to abandon the profession, and sacrifice his hope of glory to his health. But these were not counsels for the soul of Cicero. With the genuine, inflexible enthusiasm of genius, he resolved to persevere in his high career, though it should cost him his life. With the united view however of recovering his health and enlarging the sphere of his improvement, he visited Greece and Asia Minor. He spent six months at Athens, during which he went through a renewed course of moral philosophy, and of mechanical oratorical exercises, under Demetrius Syrus. Thence he travelled over Asia, never losing an opportunity to hear the public speakers, celebrated throughout those regions. On his return he made some stay in the island of Rhodes, where he took further lessons of practice from his old instructor, Melon, whom he eulogizes for friendly severity, in remarking his faults. At the expiration of two years he returned to Rome; his health confirmed, and every faculty improved by the labors of his absence. He was very soon sent, as quaestor, into Sicily, and there with unwearied industry continued his rhetorical studies; so that he was qualified to display the full blaze of his talents in his accusation of Verres.

Hortensius was then without a rival at the bar. He had attained the highest official honors of the republic. Among the characters of his own age and standing, he knew there was none able to contest the first rank in oratory with him; and he had no suspicion, that a younger man was arising to wrest the prize from his hands. The relaxation so naturally consequent upon success, the desire quiet)}' to enjoy the fruits of his former labors, rendered him indolent and careless. Cicero continued persevering and indefatigable. In less than three years the reputation of Hortensius began, among competent judges, to decline; and it was not much longer, before the waning of his fame was perceptible to the multitude. By the time, when Cicero obtained the consular dignity, Hortensius was almost forgotten; and although roused to transient exertions by the swelling celebrity of his new competitor, he was never able to recover that leading and commanding station, which he had so long enjoyed undisputed; but which, once outstripped by his more active successor, he had lost forever.

Cicero had never indulged himself with an hour of relaxation. His only intermissions were from one study to another; or from study to practice, and from practice to study. Nothing, that could promote his great purpose, was by him neglected, or overlooked. He labored all his compositions with anxious vigilance. He followed up his practice at the bar with exemplary assiduity. He introduced a new style and character into his discourses. His hearers fancied themselves in a new world. Until then they had heard talk of eloquence. He made them feel the powers, of which they had only heard. His orations commanded undivided admiration, because they soared far above the possibility of imitation by any of his cotemporaries. Not one of the public speakers in repute had any extent of attainment in literature, the inexhaustible fountain of eloquence; nor in philosophy, the parent of moral refinement; nor in the laws municipal or national, so indispensable to all solid eloquence at the bar; nor in history, which makes all the experience of ancient days tributary to the wisdom of our own. They had neither the strength of logic, that key-stone to the arch of persuasion; nor its subtlety to perplex, and disconcert an opponent. They knew neither how to enliven a discussion by strokes of wit and humor, nor how to interweave the merits of the question with the facts of the cause; nor how to relieve tediousness by a seasonable and pertinent digression; nor finally to enlist the passions and feelings of their auditors on their side.

Cicero does not tell us, that he himself possessed all these qualities, in which the other barristers of his time were so deficient. He leaves the inference to those, who had heard, and those, who should read him. The critical examination of his judicial discourses is his unanswerable evidence of the fact, and that evidence is happily still in our possession. This is that basis of adamant, upon which his reputation arose, while that of Hortensius was crumbling into dust. Unfortunately for him another circumstance concurred to its decay. He had addicted himself to the Asiatic style of oratory; a style more suitable to the airy vivacity of youth, than to the grave and dignified energy of years and station. Hortensius wanted either the ability or the attention to vary his style in conformity to the changes in his situation; and the same glitter, which had given him fame in youth, served but to expose his age to censure and derision.

Such is the parallel, which, long after the death of Hortensius, Cicero drew to exhibit the relation between himself and the most powerful oratorical competitor, with whom he ever had to contend. It is interesting, as it introduces so much of his own biography; and useful, as it furnishes so striking a commentary upon the maxim, that indefatigable industry is as essential to the preservation, as to the attainment of eminence.

The little dissertation de optimo genere oratorum, of the best kind of orators, was only the preface to a translation, which Cicero made and published, of the two orations for the crown; of Demosthenes and Eschines. The rigorous critics , at Rome had censured Cicero himself, as inclining too much to the Asiatic style; and the tribe of small writers, and talkers, and thinkers, whose glory consisted in finding something to blame in Cicero, armed with their watchword the Attic Style, delighted in cavilling at every excursion of fancy, and every splendid ornament, which the active and elegant mind of

Cicero so profusely lavished in most of his orations. To give this censure greater weight, they drove the principles of their Atticism into its remotest boundaries, and affected to consider the plain, unseasoned simplicity of Lysias, as holding forth its most perfect model. By way of self-defence, Cicero published the master pieces of the two great rival Athenians, and in this preface directed the attention of his countrymen to them, as to the genuine models of Atticism. And this he contends is marked, not by the unvarying use of the plain style, which becomes tiresome by its monotony and its barrenness, but by the alternate mixture and judicious application of the sublime and intermediate with the simple style, of which the orations for the crown display the brightest example. The translation is lost. But this preface was included by himself in a general collection of his rhetorical works, and the two orations are happily yet extant in their original language.

The topics are a short essay upon a part of the oratorical art, much esteemed among the ancients, but which in modern times have fallen into great discredit. I shall upon some future occasion give you at large my own opinion concerning them, and endeavour to explain them to you in such a manner, as shall enable you to judge of them for yourselves. The work of Cicero is remarkable, as having been written in the hurry and bustle of a sea voyage, when the author had no access to the book of Aristotle, from which it is abstracted. It is addressed to Trebatius, a lawyer and familiar friend of Cicero, and to whom many of his most amusing letters in the collection of his epistles were written.

The oratorical partitions are a short elementary compendium, written in the form of a dialogue between Cicero and his son; in which, by way of question and answer, all the divisions and subdivisions of the rhetorical science are clearly and succinctly pointed out. It is altogether preceptive, barely containing the rules, without any illustration from example. It is a system of rhetoric in the abstract.

All the writings of Cicero, which I have hitherto enumerated, were composed in the latter part of his life, when the vigor of his genius was matured by long and successful experience. There are two others, less valuable, but of which it is proper some notice should be taken. The one has come to us in an imperfect state. It was originally in four books, only two of which still remain. Their title would indicate, that they treated only of invention; but their intent was to comprise a complete system of rhetoric. they were however a mere juvenile exercise, compiled from the Greek rhetoricians for his own use; and surreptitiously published at a later period of his life, when his name was sufficient to confer celebrity upon any thing. In his dialogues de oratore he mentions them himself, as a mere boyish study; and complains of their publication without his consent.

The other is a system of rhetoric in four books, addressed to Herinnius, published in all the general editions of Cicero's works, but in all probability not written by him. The internal evidence is at least very strong against its legitimate descent. It was ingeniously said among the Greeks, that it would be as easy to wrest the club from the hand of Hercules, as to pilfer a line from, Homer, without detection. By a like reason, you might as well put a distaff into the hand of Hercules, and call it his club, as call this a work of Cicero, because it is bound up with his works. Not that it is a despicable performance. The language is pure; the style not unpleasant. As a compilation from Aristotle and Hermogenes, set forth in classical Latin, and with a very good method, it may be perused with profit. But the manner is dry and barren; totally stripped of Cicero's copious exuberance. Cornificius, to whom it has generally been ascribed, or whoever was the author, appears rather in the form of a grammarian or logician, than of a rhetorician. Never in a single instance does he rise to that of an orator. Cornificius is always a precise, correct, cold schoolmaster; Cicero never ceases to be the eloquent speaker. Cornificius chills you, as he instructs; Cicero warms you, as he teaches. From Cornificius you may learn the theory of rhetoric; from Cicero you must learn by feeling the practice of the art.

I cannot conclude this account of the rhetorical writings of Cicero, without once more urging upon your attention all the works, as well as the life and character of this extraordinary man. When you have dilated your understanding to the full conception of his merit, you will learn from his history the process, by which it was acquired. He lived in the most eventful period, recorded in the annals of the world, and contributed more, than any other man, to its splendor. In a republic, where it had been observed, that the distinction of ranks was more strongly marked, than in any other nation under the sun, he rose, on the sole foundation of personal merit, against all the influence and opposition of the proudest of all aristocracies, not only to the highest official honors and dignities, but to a distinction, never attained by any other mortal man. To be proclaimed by the voice of Rome, "free Rome," the father of his country.

> Roma parentem,
> Roma pattern patriae Ciceronem, libera dixit.

> Juv. VIII.

Compared to this how mean and despicable were all the triumphs of Caesar, "the world's great master and his own." How small, how diminutive is the ambition of that soul, which can be satisfied with a conquest of the world by force, or with a mastery over itself so partial, as to be only a composition with crime, a half-way forbearance from the extreme of guilt, compared with the sublime purposes of that mind, which, not by the brutal and foul contest of arras, but by the soul-subduing power of eloquence and of virtue, conquers time, as well as space; not the world of one short lived generation, but the world of a hundred centuries; which masters, not only one nation of cotemporaries, but endless ages of civilized man, and undiscovered regions of the globe. These are the triumphs, which Caesar, and men like Caesar, never can obtain. They are reserved for more exalted conquerors. These are the palms of heroic peace. These are the everlasting laurels, destined for better uses, than to conceal the baldness of a Caesar, destined to be twined, as a never fading wreath, around the temples of Cicero.

As an orator, the concurring suffrage of two thousand years has given him a name above all other names, save only that of Demosthenes. As a rhetorician, we have seen, that he is unrivalled by the union of profound science with elegant taste; by the extent, the compass, the variety of the views, in which he has exhibited the theory of his favorite art; by that enchanting fascination, with which he allures the student into the deserted benches of the Grecian schools. His correspondence with Atticus and his other familiar friends contains the most authentic and interesting materials for the history of his age. His letters introduce you at once into his domestic intimacy, and to a familiar acquaintance with all the distinguished characters of an era, which seems to have spurned the usual boundaries of human existence, and destined in the memory of mankind to live forever. But those same letters are the most perfect models of epistolary style, that the world has ever seen; and such is the variety of the subjects, they embrace, that the student may find in them finished examples of the most perfect manner, in which a letter can be written, from the complimentary card of introduction to the dispatch, which details the destinies of empires.

His philosophical writings make us acquainted with the most celebrated speculations of antiquity upon those metaphysical topics, which, unless fixed by the everlasting pillars of divine revelation, will forever torture human reason, and elude human ingenuity. On the nature of the gods, on the boundaries of good and evil, on those moral paradoxes, which Milton has represented, as constituting at once the punishment and the solace of the fallen angels in Pandemonium, Cicero entertains us in lively language, dignified by judicious reflections with all the eccentric vagaries of the ancient philosophers, who, like those rebellious spirits,

"Found no end in wandering mazes lost."

But the most amiable and warmest coloring, in which the character of Cicero presents itself to the eye of contemplation, is as a moralist. With what a tender and delicate sensibility has he delineated the pleasures and prescribed the duties of friendship! With what a soothing and beneficent hand has he extended the consolations of virtue to the declining enjoyments and waxing infirmities of old age! With what all vivifying energy has he showered the sunshine of virtue upon the frosty winter of life! His book of offices should be the manual of every republican; nay it should be the pocket and the pillow companion of every man, desiring to discipline his heart to the love and the practice of every virtue. There you will find the most perfect system of morals, ever promulgated before the glad tidings of Christianity. There you will find a valuable and congenial supplement, even to the sublime precepts of the gospel.

It is not then to the students of eloquence alone, that the character and the writings of Cicero ought to be dear. He is the instructor of every profession; the friend of every age. Make him the intimate of your youth, and you will find him the faithful and incorruptible companion of your whole life. In every variety of this mutable scene, you will find him a pleasing and instructive associate. His numerous and inveterate enemies, while he lived, solaced the consciousness of their own inferiority, by sneering at his vanity, and deriding his excessive love of glory. Yes, he had that last infirmity of noble minds! Yes, glory was the idol of his worship. His estimation of mankind over-rated the value of their applause. His estimation of himself is not liable to the same censure. His most exulting moments of self-complacency never transcended, never equalled his real worth. He had none of that affected humility, none of that disqualifying hypocrisy, which makes virtue consist in concealment, and indulges unbounded vanity at the heart, on the single condition of imposing silence upon the lips. As he thought of himself, so he spake, and without hesitation claimed the approbation of the world for talents and virtues, which he would have celebrated with ten-fold magnificence of panegyric in others. To his contemporaries let us admit, that the sense of his immeasurable superiority was of itself sufficiently burdensome, without the aggravation of hearing his encomium from himself. But to the modern detractors of his fame it may be justly replied, that his failings leaned to virtue's side; that his heaviest vices might put to the blush their choicest virtues. Of his own age and nation he was unquestionably the brightest ornament. But he is the philosopher, the orator, the moralist of all time, and of every region. A modern poet has beautifully said, that it is

> "Praise enough
> "To fill the ambition of a common man,
> "That Chatham's language was his mother tongue,
> "And Wolfe's great name compatriot with his own."

But in contemplating a character, like this, we may joy in a more enlarged and juster application of the same sentiment. Let us make this the standard of moral and intellectual worth, for all human kind; and in the reply to all the severities of satire, and all the bitterness of misanthropy, repeat with conscious exultation, "we are of the same species of beings, as Cicero."

Lecture Six - Institutes and Character of Quinctilian

IN a former lecture, you may remember, that I noticed a remarkable difference between the history of rhetoric in Greece and at Rome; and observed, that in the former eloquence appeared to have been the twin-sister to history, while in the latter she appears to have been the child of the republic's old age, at first discarded, long banished, but finally adopted, and rising to the most unbounded influence in the person of Cicero. But the duration of the period, in which rhetoric was cultivated, is equally remarkable in Greece by its length, and in Rome by its shortness. From Pittheus to Longinus, the two extremes in the chronology of the Greek rhetoricians, you perceive a line of more than thirteen hundred years, filled with a catalogue of writers, distinguished by their numbers, as well as by their ingenuity. At Rome we have seen the science began with Cicero. It ended with Quinctilian. These two writers lived within one hundred years of each other; and in them alone are we to seek for all, that Roman literature can furnish to elucidate the science of rhetoric. Their Writings may indeed, in point of real value, contend for the prize with the more copious stores of Greece; and if a complete system were to be collected exclusively from the one or the other language, it would perhaps be difficult to say which would be most reluctantly given up, the Grecian numbers, or the Roman weight. Of the Greek rhetoricians I have given you an account, a very lame and imperfect one indeed, in a single lecture; while the writings of Cicero alone, on this theme, have already occupied two; and I now purpose to devote another to the institutes and the character of Quinctilian.

It will however be proper previously to notice a collection of declamations, under the title of controversies and deliberations, different from those, which bear the name of Quinctilian, and published as the compilation of Seneca. Not of Seneca, the philosopher, the preceptor, the accomplice, and the victim of Nero; but another Seneca, generally supposed to be his father, and a native of Cordova in Spain. This collection was not of his own composition; but collected from upwards of one hundred writers, and accompanied by the critical remarks of the editor.

The practice of declamation among the ancients was deemed of so much importance, it was so different from that exercise, bearing the same name, to which you are accustomed, it was at one period so useful in promoting the improvement, and at another so pernicious in hastening the corruption of eloquence, that it will be "proper to give you a short historical account of its rise, progress, and perversion.

There has been some controversy, by whom it was first introduced; nor is it of much importance to ascertain whether its inventor were Gorgias, the celebrated sophist, or Eschines, who, after his banishment from Athens, opened a school of oratory in the island of Rhodes, or Demetrius Phalereus, the last of the Attic orators. It is more generally agreed to have been introduced at Rome by Plotius, the first teacher of rhetoric in the Latin language; and was practised constantly, by most of the Roman orators, from the age of Cicero to that of Quinctilian. These declamations were composed and delivered by the same person; which rendered them a much more laborious, but at the same time a much more improving exercise, than that of repeating the compositions of others. They were suited, by their gradations of difficulty, to the degrees of proficiency, which the student had attained. They began with short themes upon any topic, selected at pleasure, similar to those, upon which you sometimes exercise your ingenuity. From this the progress was to controverted questions, resembling what we now call forensic disputes; and finally a fictitious narrative or fable was invented, to raise upon its events a moral, political, or legal question, either simple or complicated, for discussion. Thus you perceive, that what they called declamation rather resembled our performances at commencements and at the public exhibitions, than that repetition of the writings of others, to which our practice limits the original name. Its advantages were much greater, inasmuch as it was an exercise of invention, as well as of delivery, and sharpened the faculties of the mind, while it gave ease and confidence to that mechanical operation, which Cicero has called the eloquence of the body.

Of the importance given to this exercise, during the splendid era of Roman oratory, you may form an opinion from the unquestionable fact, that it was practised by Cicero, not only while a student, before his appearance at the bar, but throughout his whole life. In the midst of that splendid and active career, when the fate of the Roman empire and of the world was at his control, he continued the custom of declaiming himself, and of assisting at the declamations of men, as far advanced in years, and as highly exalted in dignity; such as Pompey and Piso; Hirtius and Pansa; Crassus and Dolabella. Nay, so essential was this discipline to every public speaker of that age, that even Mark Anthony, the luxurious, the dissolute Mark Anthony, prepared himself, by constant declamation, to contend against the divine philippics of his adversary; and Augustus Caesar, during the war of Modena, in that final struggle for the dominion of the world, learned, by assiduous declamation, to achieve nobler victories, than he could obtain by all the veteran legions of his father. When the revolution in government had destroyed the freedom of speech, the practice of declamation was still pursued, but underwent a corresponding change of character. Dignified thought, independent spirit, bold and commanding sentiment, then became only avenues to the scaffold. Declamation was still valued, but soon changed its character. Instead of leading the student to the art of persuasion, it taught him the more useful lesson of concealment, the safer doctrine of disguise. The themes of declamation were studiously stripped of every thing, that could bear a resemblance to reality. The most extravagant fictions were made the basis, and a dazzling affectation of wit the superstructure of their oratory. Hence it soon passed into a maxim, that pleasure, and not persuasion, was the ultimate purpose of eloquence. "The author of a declaration," says Seneca, the person, of whom I am now speaking, "writes not to prove, but to please. He hunts up every thing, that can give pleasure. Arguments he discards, because they are toilsome, and disdain decoration. He is content to charm his audience with pointed sentences, and flights of fancy. He asks your favor, not for his cause, but for himself." Here you see the root of corruption, plucked up and exposed. Instead of assimilating declamation to the realities, for which it was first taught, it was purposely and systematically made to deviate from them as widely, as possible. But this unnatural affectation could not fail to spread infection over the reality, and the fribbling declaimer of the school became, in regular progression, the nerveless and tawdry talker in the senate, or at the bar.

From this history you may infer a general opinion of the rate, at which the declamations of the rhetorician, Seneca, are to be estimated. They might perhaps have been more valuable, had they come down to us in a perfect state; but mutilated, as they are, and formed on such a defective foundation, they can be of little use in the study of modern eloquence, and their intrinsic merit cannot entitle them to much attention. Those, which pass under the name of Quinctilian, are not much better, and are well known not to have been composed or even compiled by him.

There exists also a dialogue of that age, on the causes of the corruption of eloquence, which has occasionally been ascribed both to Tacitus and Quinctilian, and is usually published among the works of both those writers. It contains an ingenious parallel between eloquence and poetry, with a warm eulogium upon these sister arts; a comparison between the celebrated orator's of that day, and their predecessors in the age of Hortensius and Cicero. It concludes with an inquiry into the causes, whence the corruption of eloquence, then so universally perceived, had proceeded. The causes assigned deserve our particular attention. The first is the general dissipation, to which the youth of the age had abandoned themselves. For indolence and pleasure are more fatal to the understanding, than to the constitution; they clog the circulations of the soul still more, than they deaden the energies of the body; and, by one simultaneous operation, emasculate the physical, while they stupefy the intellectual man. The next cause, and inseparably connected with it, is the neglect and carelessness of the parents, who were grossly heedless of the education of their children. In that universal degradation of taste and of morals, the very ties of nature were unstrung, and, as the sons had no sense of what was due to themselves, the fathers had lost all memory of their duties to their offspring. The ignorance of the rhetorical teachers, their preposterous methods of instruction, alternately both cause and effect of the degeneracy in the public taste, that degraded taste itself, the impatience of the judges, who, under that arbitrary government, abridged the freedom of speech, so essential to an orator, but above all the form of government since the extinction of the republic; all these are justly enumerated, as the causes of that corruption, which a Quinctilian or a Tacitus could not but lament, but which it was not even in their genius and talents to heal. It is much to be regretted, that a considerable part of this valuable treatise is lost.

To rescue the art from this state of degradation, Quinctilian did all, that human ability could accomplish. His institutes embrace the most comprehensive plan, formed by any of the ancient rhetoricians; and the execution of the work is in all respects worthy of the design. Like Seneca, he is said to have been a native of Spain; and some have asserted, that he was the grandson of the Quinctilian, who collected the declamations. Twenty years of his life were passed at Rome, in the two-fold profession of a teacher of rhetoric and a practitioner at the bar; in both of, which characters he is mentioned honorably by the epigrammatist, Martial, in the following lines.

Quinctiliane, vagae moderator summe juventae,
Gloria Romanac, Quinctiliane, togae;

which, for the benefit of a less classical auditory than mine, might be thus translated.

Sure, to the public speaker's fair renown,
Henceforth, the wildest Roman youth may reach;
Since thy instructions, glory of the gown,
At once by precept and example teach.

During part of the time, that he exercised the rhetorical profession, he received a salary from the public treasury; and he obtained from one of the Roman emperors the honors, if not the official dignity of the consulship. He was appointed to superintend the education of two grandchildren to the sister of the emperor Domitian; and had two sons and a daughter, connected by marriage and adoption with some of the most illustrious families in Rome. He is often noticed with distinction by the satirist, Juvenal, who ascribes his wealth however rather to his good fortune, than to his talents, and who scourges, with a merciless hand, the proud and tasteless grandees of the age for their neglect of the rhetorician. After twenty years of this laborious occupation, Quinctilian was permitted to relinquish the employment, and enjoy the fruits of his toils. But many of his friends, who had witnessed the happy effects of his system of instruction, intreated him to publish, and leave it for the benefit of posterity. Two considerations finally prevailed upon him to comply with these requests. The excellency of his lectures had occasioned partial and incorrect copies of many of them to be surreptitiously taken by some of his scholars, and in that state of imperfection they had been published to the world. He also thought, that in all the rhetorical works, then extant, there was a defect to be supplied. They were not sufficiently elementary. They presupposed the knowledge of many things, essential to the formation of an orator; and took up their pupils, as already initiated in all the preparatory learning. For the purpose therefore of vindicating his own reputation, and of giving a complete system of rhetoric for the benefit of succeeding ages, he undertook the work, which he divided into twelve books. It is addressed to Marcellus Victorius, one of his most intimate friends; a man of elegant taste and literary accomplishments, who felt a more than common interest in the undertaking, as having a son of great promise, then in the course of his education. Quinctilian therefore supposes, that he has a child to educate in the manner, best adapted to make him an accomplished orator; for which he takes him in the first years of infancy, yet lisping from the arms of the nurse, and conducts him by fair degrees through every preliminary study, and every appropriate branch of discipline, until he has attained the perfection of the art. He carries him through life; suggests to him the various studies, occupations, and amusements, best suited to the purpose of his destination. Accompanies him through a long career of active eloquence; follows him in the decline of life into honorable retirement, and teaches him how to render even that season of his existence useful to others, and agreeable to himself. I had prepared an analysis of this work, as well as of some treatises of the Grecian rhetoricians, with the intention of presenting them, in one comprehensive summary, to your view. But I have thought on reflection, that it would waste too much of your present time, and involve the consideration of some parts of the science, which require a previous elucidation, to be clearly understood. I shall therefore at present only notice a few passages, which even now may furnish useful hints for your meditation and improvement.

The first book is altogether preparatory; containing advice, relative to the selection of the child's earliest instructors; a discussion of the comparative advantages and disadvantages of public schools, and of domestic tuition; hints for ascertaining the natural dispositions and intellectual faculties of children; grammatical disquisitions, and miscellaneous observations upon reading, composition, music, geometry, gesture, and pronunciation; all of which he considers, as preliminary acquisitions; and which he thinks may be most advantageously learnt at the same time. In reply to the objection, that this system is too laborious, he says, with a warmth of eloquence, and a soundness of sense, which cannot too strongly be impressed upon our minds:

The whole day neither can nor ought to be engrossed with learning grammar; for the mind of the scholar should not be wearied into disgust. And how can we do better, than assign the intervals of leisure to these subsidiary studies of music and geometry; taking care not to overburden him with any of them? I do not undertake to form a musician by trade, nor a very minute proficient in geometry. In teaching pronunciation, I am not training: an actor for the stage; nor, in giving rules for gesture, do I propose to make a dancing master. Not that there is any lack of time. The years of youthful discipline are many; and I do not suppose my pupil a dunce. What made Plato so eminent for possessing all the knowledge, which I suppose essential to an orator? It was because, not content with all the learning of Athens, he travelled into Italy for that of the Pythagoreans; and even into Egypt to obtain access to the secret mysteries of her priests. Let us be honest. It is our own idleness, that we endeavour to shelter under the mantle of difficulty. We have no real affection for the art. We court eloquence, not for her native, exquisite, and unrivalled beauties; but as the instrument of sordid purposes, and of base and groveling gains. Let the vulgar orator of the forum hold forth his ignorance for his fee. After all, the pedler with his pack, and the town-crier by his voice will earn more money. For my part, I would not willingly have a reader, who should estimate his learning by his wages; no, give me the man, who, in the sublime conceptions of an exalted mind, has figured to himself an image of real eloquence, of that eloquence, called by Euripides the queen of the world. He will never measure her rewards by his fee-table. He will find them in his own soul; in his own science; in his own meditations. Rewards beyond the reach of fortune, and perpetual in their nature. That man will easily prevail upon himself to bestow upon geometry and music the time, which others waste upon theatres; upon public sports; upoffi gaming; upon idle companions; if not upon sleep, or upon debauchery. And how much more delightfully will he pass his time, than in those coarse and ignorant indulgences! For it is one of the blessings of providence to mankind, that "the most honorable should also be the most exquisite enjoyments." These are the sentiments of Quinctilian. They are the only sentiments, which lead to greatness and to glory; to social usefulness, and individual felicity.

The introductory chapters to the fourth and sixth books are peculiarly interesting, as they relate to important events in the life of the author. After completing the third, and before he had begun upon the fourth book, he had been appointed to superintend the education of the two grandsons of the emperor Domitian's sister. He appears to have been too much elated by the honor of this appointment; and, in the effusions of his gratitude or of his servility, prostitutes his eloquence in strains of adulation to the emperor, which cannot wipe off a stain from the infamy of Domitian, but which shed some portion of it upon his panegyrist. For the manners of the age, and the nature of the government, some allowance must be made; and, if any thing could be wanting to complete our abhorrence of arbitrary power, it would be sufficient to behold a man of Quinctilian's genius and industry prostrate in the dust before a being, like Domitian. In the midst of this degradation, it is however some consolation to observe gleams of unquenchable virtue, still piercing through the gloom. We rejoice to find him sensible, that the advancement of his dignity was a call upon him for redoubled industry and energy in the prosecution of his work.

If the introduction to the fourth book compels us reluctantly to pass a censure upon our excellent instructor, that of the sixth exhibits him under the pressure of such cruel calamities, that the natural and pathetic eloquence, with which he laments his fate, will yet claim a generous tear from the eye of sensibility. When he began upon his great work, his condition was blessed with the possession of a young and amiable wife; and of two promising sons. The ardor of his spirit had been inflamed by the hope and the prospect, that his own children would participate in the benefit of his toils; and the fire of his genius blazed with brighter fervency for being kindled at the torch of parental affection. But during the progress of his labors, and before he had commenced upon the sixth book, all his actual enjoyments and all his flattering prospects were blasted by the hand of death.

"The shaft flew thrice; and thrice his peace was slain."

The feelings of a husband and a father alone can conceive the anguish, which inspires his complaints. They are the agonies of nature, when unsupported by the everlasting pillars of Christian consolation. He breaks out into maledictions upon his own writings, and curses upon his attachment to literature; charges heaven with injustice; denies an eternal superintending providence, and scorns his own weakness for supporting the burden of his existence, while his own hand could release him from its thralldom. When we compare these sentiments with that genuine doctrine of fortitude under the miseries of life, which the precepts of the Christian's faith inculcate, we cannot but compassionate the unhappy sufferer; while we feel with redoubled conviction the superiority of that philosophy, which teaches us to consider this world, as no more than a course of discipline to prepare for another; and resignation as the only genuine heroism in misfortune. The soft overflowings of the father's heart succeed the bitterness of his execrations, and the copious enumeration of trivial incidents, to display the opening virtues and fond attachments of his child, awakens a congenial sense in the reader, and touches the finest fibres of sympathy. But finally, after paying the full tribute to sensibility, the energy of Stoic virtue recovers her ascendency; and we admire the resolution, with which he struggles against the rigor of his fate, and seeks consolation in the bosom of literature.

In the twelfth and concluding book Quinctilian discusses a variety of miscellaneous topics, all having relation to the oratorical profession. Here it is, that he maintains, in a long and elaborate chapter, a maxim, much dwelt upon by most of the ancient rhetoricians, and -which, if properly understood and qualified, is undoubtedly true; but which a good intention has led him to assert in terms, and to defend by arguments, irreconcilable to truth and virtue.

To form the perfect ideal orator, that model of a fair imagination, to the imitation of which every public speaker should constantly aspire, honesty, or virtuous principle, is the first and most essential ingredient. None but a good man therefore can ever be such an orator; and incorruptible integrity is the most powerful of all the engines of persuasion.

But if by an orator is meant only a man, possessed of the talent of public speaking to such an extent, as has ever been witnessed in the experience of mankind; if it be meant, that no man can be eloquent without being virtuous, the assertion is alike contradicted by the general constitution of human nature, and by the whole tenor of human experience. Bad men may be, many a bad man has been eminently gifted with oratory; and the dignity of virtue disdains a recommendation of herself at the expense of truth.

The arguments of Quinctilian, in support of his favorite position, are not all worthy of his cause. They do not glow with that open, honest eloquence, which they seem to recommend; but sometimes resemble the quibbling of a pettifogger, and sometimes the fraudulent morality of a Jesuit. "A bad man," says he, "not only by the judgment of philosophers, but oftentimes even by the vulgar, is thought a fool. Now a fool can never be an orator." If this reasoning: is only ridiculous, that, which follows, is something worse. An orator, says he, must be an honest man to enable him, whenever it may be necessary for the success of his cause, to impose upon the minds of his auditors falsehood for truth. And then follows a philosophical disquisition of the occasions, when an honest man may lie, for the good of his client. Perhaps in this last argument we may discover the real nature, as well as the origin of Quinctilian's principle. He insists, that his orator must be an honest man." But he allows his honest man to equivocate, and lie, and abuse the confidence, acquired by honesty, to promote the success of fraud. Where the standard of virtue is so low, it can need little labor to keep on its level. His principle is that of sir Hudibras.

> For if the devil, to serve his turn,
> Can tell truth; why the saints should scorn.
> When it serves theirs, to swear, and lie,
> I think there's little reason why.

No; providence has not thought fit so to constitute the race of man, as to bind in irrefragable chains the virtues of the heart with the faculties of the mind. Nor, could we realize this dream of fancy, would it improve the moral government of the world. Virtue is an injunction of positive duty, of which heaven has at once made the command and the power of fulfilment universal; leaving the execution to individual will. But the distribution of intellectual powers is partial, and graduated with infinite variety. To be honest is the duty and in the power of us all. To be eloquent can only be the privilege of a few. Hard indeed would be the condition of men, if honesty were to wander in all the eccentricities of genius, or to be a sport to the caprices of fortune. Let us then all be honest; for honesty is wisdom; is pleasantness; is peace. If the indulgence of nature and the vigils of your own industry have endowed you with the favors of eloquence, remember, that all your moral duties are multiplied in proportion to your powers; that to whom much is given, of him shall much be required. But in the course of your pilgrimage through this world of trial and of temptation, if you should occasionally meet with a man, blessed with all the power of words, do not too hastily conclude, that his moral worth must be of equal preeminence with his mental faculties. Reserve the treasure of your confidence for the silent oratory of virtuous deeds.

We have now completed our survey of the character and writings of the principal rhetoricians of antiquity. It has been extremely superficial; yet has it consumed no inconsiderable portion of our time. I shall next ask your attention, in passing from the history of the science to the consideration of the science itself.

Lecture Seven - Constituent Branches of Rhetoric

IN the systematic pursuit of science, one of the most important points is a steady attention to order and arrangement. No just survey of any complicated whole can be taken, without keeping a watchful eye both upon the division and upon the combination of its parts. It is the essential advantage of scientific over desultory knowledge, that it discovers to us the various channels and communications between things, which are separated without being severed, and disjoined, but not disconnected. In the construction of the human body, the unlearned observer can scarcely conceive the possibility, that a puncture in the heel should stiffen the jaw, or that a blister between the shoulders should remove an oppression upon the lungs. The anatomist examines the internal fabric, and discovers at once the texture and the coherence of the parts; but, to perceive their mutual influence and operation upon one another, every fibre must be noticed, not only in its positive existence, but in its relative situation; as the cooperating parcel of an organized body, no less than as one distinct, entire, and individual member.

The lectures, which I have hitherto given,, from the beginning of the course have been rather preliminary, than didactic. They consisted, first of a definition and division of the subjects, upon which, by the rules of the institution, I am required to address you. Next of a vindication of rhetoric and oratory from the objections, which are often urged against them; and lastly of a short historical review of the principal rhetoricians of ancient Greece and Rome. These were naturally preparatory to a consideration of the science of rhetoric, upon which we are now about to enter; and which, in conformity to the authority of Cicero and Quinctilian, I shall divide into five constituent parts; invention, disposition, elocution, memory, and pronunciation, or action.

A concise and general definition of these terms is contained in the following passage from Cicero. "The parts of rhetoric, as most writers have agreed, are invention, disposition, elocution, memory, pronunciation.

"Invention is the discovery by thought of those things, the truth, or verisimilitude of which renders the cause probable.

"Disposition is the orderly arrangement of the things invented.

"Elocution is the application of proper words and sentences to invention.

"Memory is the firm perception by the mind of the things and words, applied to invention. And

"Pronunciation is the management of the voice and body, conformably to the dignity of the words and things.

This explanation however is hardly sufficient to convey clear and precise ideas either of the terms themselves, or of the motives for distributing the whole science among them.

There is one important observation, which it will be necessary for you to bear in mind through every part of these lectures, and which is essential for the clear understanding of those terms, which designate the great compartments of the rhetorical science. It is, that in every systematic art there are certain words, which bear a specific technical meaning, very different from that, which is annexed to them in ordinary discourse. A continual attention to this remark becomes the more necessary, when, as in the instances now before us, there are other sciences, in which the same terms are used to indicate a very different modification of ideas, or when the colloquial or vulgar meaning of the word has become prevalent, by a misconception of its technical sense, or a considerable deviation from it.

To illustrate this, trace the word invention to its original source, and compare its primary meaning with the various senses, which it bears in the art of poetry, in mechanics, in ordinary conversation, and in rhetoric.

It was originally compounded from the two Latin words, in venire, to come in, to enter. By the natural progress of all languages from the literal to the metaphorical meaning, it came in process of time to signify discovery; *invenire,* to find; *inventio,* finding. Such is the ordinary meaning of the words in the Latin language. But, in undergoing this transformation of the sense, the verb was at the same time transferred from the neutral to the active class. In its primary meaning the coming in was the action of the external object; and, as applied to thought, supposed the idea active and the mind passive; the thought came into the mind. But, in its transmuted sense, the. action was changed from the idea to the person; and *invenire,* to find, implied not the coming of the thought into the mind, but the going of the mind in search of the thought. This is the sense, in which rhetorical invention is understood. But invention, when applied, as by its most frequent usage it is in ordinary discourse, to the mechanic arts, supposes still greater activity of the mind. It means a higher degree of ingenuity; a more powerful exertion of intellect. In the language of Solomon it is in this sense declared to be the immediate operation of wisdom herself. "I, wisdom, dwell with prudence, and find out knowledge of witty inventions." [1]

But in the language of poetry invention aspires still higher, and lays claim not merely to the praise of finding, but to the glory of creating. Poetical invention disdains the boundaries of space and time. She ranges over worlds of her own making, and takes little heed of being found out by wisdom, or of dwelling with prudence. Her powers are delineated in that exquisite pas» sage of Shakespeare, which you have all heard a thousand times, but which no repetition can make uninteresting.

> The poet's eye, in a fine frenzy rolling,
> Doth glance from heaven to earth, from earth to heaven;
> And, as imagination bodies forth
> The forms of things unknown, the poet's pen
> Turns them to shape, and gives to airy nothing
> A local habitation and a name.

This is poetical invention, described with more than poetical truth. For observe, gentlemen, that in bodying forth the forms of things unknown, in giving to airy nothing what it cannot have, the poet's eye must be rolling in a fine frenzy; his mind must be released from all the restraints of truth and reason, and his imagination emancipated from all the laws of real and even of probable nature. But from this rhetorical invention differs in her most essential characteristics. Truth, or at least the resemblance of truth, as you will perceive by the definition I have quoted from. Cicero, is her most indispensable feature. Not that in the practice of orators she has always been thus rigorously confined; for, among the choicest darlings of eloquence, both ancient and modern, it would not be difficult to quote examples, in which they appear to have mistaken poetical for rhetorical invention, and to have measured the extent of their faculties by the wideness of their departure from truth. But this is no part of the science of rhetoric. Her end is persuasion; and her most irresistible instrument is truth. Poetical invention is the queen of love; arrayed in the magic cestus, and escorted by the graces; mingling in every gesture dissolute wantonness with enchanting attraction, and blending in every glance fascination and falsehood. Rhetorical invention is Minerva, issuing in celestial panoply from the head of Jupiter; beneficent as the morning beam, but chaste as the flake of falling snow; with the glow of beauty enkindling ardor; but with the majesty of deportment commanding veneration. Rhetorical invention however has this in common with the invention of poetry that it is the most powerful test, both of the speaker's genius and of his learning. Though confined within the regions of truth or of verisimilitude, the range of invention is yet coextensive with the orator's powers. It consists in the faculty of finding whatsoever is proper to be said, and adapted to the purpose of his discourse; of selecting from the whole mass of ideas, conceived or stored in his mind, those, which can most effectually promote the object of his speech; of gathering from the whole domain of real or apparent truth their inexhaustible subsidies, to secure the triumph of persuasion.

Disposition is the order, or method, in which the thoughts of the speaker should be arranged. As invention is the standard, by which to measure his genius and learning, disposition is more especially the trial of his skill. The thoughts in the mind of an orator upon any subject, requiring copious elucidation, arise at first in a state, resembling that of chaos; a mingled mass of elemental matter without form and void. Disposition is the art of selecting, disposing, and combining them in such order and succession, as shall make them most subservient to his design. This faculty, though not of so high an order as invention, is equally important, and much more uncommon. You shall find hundreds of persons able to produce a crowd of good ideas upon any subject, for one, that can marshall them to the best advantage. Disposition is to the orator what tactics, or the discipline of armies is to the military art. And as the balance of victory has almost always been turned by the 'superiority of tactics and of discipline, so the great effects of eloquence are always produced by the excellency of disposition. There is no part of the science, in which the consummate orator will be so decidedly marked out, as by the perfection of his disposition. It will deserve your particular meditation;

for its principles are applicable to almost every species of literary composition; and are by no means confined exclusively to oratory. It is that department in the art of writing, in which a young writer most sensibly feels his, weakness; and I venture a conjecture, that it is a difficulty, to which many of you, my young friends, are no strangers. When called to write upon any topic, assigned you, I presume you have often been much more at a loss how to combine and arrange your thoughts, than for the thoughts themselves; and often wanted more the disposing hand of art, than the genial fertility of nature. Elocution, says the definition of Cicero, "is the application of proper words and sentences to invention." And here also you will perceive the necessity of distinguishing the meaning of the term from its ordinary acceptation, as now generally understood. Elocution, in the customary modern sense, means the act of speaking; the delivery. The very thing, which, in the division I have here made of rhetoric, is called pronunciation, or action. In this sense it is used by Sheridan and Walker, the best modern English writers and teachers upon the subject. In this sense it so generally prevails, that I presume many of you are not aware, that among all the ancient rhetoricians it means a thing entirely different. It means what we now call style, or diction j the wording of the discourse. I intreat you to mark and remember this distinction, without which every thing, which I shall hereafter say to you upon elocution, will appear absurd or unintelligible. The elocution, of which I shall speak to you, belongs not to the delivery, but to the composition of the discourse. It is the act, not of the voice, but of the pen. It is the clothing of the thoughts with language; and applies to all written compositions. So that the elocution may be good or bad, of a discourse, which never was spoken, as much as of one, that was. Now the other sense of the word, which makes elocution to consist in speaking, is so much more familiar to you, that I have hesitated, whether I ought in these lectures to use the word in the ancient sense. But, as those of you, to whom the science has a peculiar interest, will naturally recur to the ancient fountains; as you never can understand Cicero and Quinctilian without first knowing, that they always annex to the word this signification; and as the rules of this institution prescribe the consideration of this subject under that meaning; I have thought best not to discard it, but to explain to you so explicitly the sense, in which I am to employ the expression, that you may be in no hazard of mistaking it for any other. Elocution then is the act of committing your discourse to writing.

Memory is the firm possession and ready command in the mind of the thoughts, arrangement, and words, into which the discourse has been reduced.

Pronunciation is the delivery of the discourse by speech. It is also called action; and, as I have already observed, is the same thing, which, in ordinary acceptation, and by the modern English oratorical writers, is called elocution. But both these words, pronunciation and action, furnish fresh instances of the utility you will derive from fixing in your minds, with philosophical precision, the meaning of these important terms, which limit the great divisions of the science. Pronunciation for instance you would probably suppose to indicate only the utterance of a single word. Action you would imagine could only be expressive of the speaker's gestures. Yet this is not the sense, in which either of these words is to be understood in their application here. Here, and among all the ancient rhetoricians and orators, pronunciation and action are used indiscriminately to signify that, which consists of their combination; that is, delivery.

You will now be able to understand the real force of an anecdote, which has often been related of Demosthenes, and which a misconception of the meaning of one of those words has often occasioned to be erroneously apprehended. It is said, that, upon being once asked what was the first qualification of an orator; he answered action. What was the second; action. What was the third; still action. How many blundering comments, and how many sagacious misapplications have been made upon this story, on the supposition, that Demosthenes, by action, merely meant gesture; bodily motion! How many a semi-pedant, knowing just enough to be self-sufficient, has, in the plenitude of his wisdom, discovered by this anecdote, that Demosthenes and the Athenians knew little or nothing of real eloquence! How many a petty babbler, engrafting upon a kinder veneration of the Grecian orator the same misconstruction of his words, has made it an article of his creed, that eloquence consists in gesticulation; and, adapting his conduct to his belief, practised the antic postures of an harlequin, and fancied himself a Demosthenes! I have known even eloquent scholars and accomplished speakers perplexed to account for this opinion of the greatest of orators, and questioning the truth of the story, merely from the same inaccurate idea of his meaning. His meaning was, that the first, the second, and the third thing, to which a public speaker should attend, is his delivery; and although from a variety of circumstances the relative importance of this article was greater in that age, than in ours; yet even now those, who have witnessed in its full extent the difference of effect upon an auditory between a good and a bad delivery, will be at no loss to account for the opinion of Demosthenes, and see no cause to question his judgment.

Such then are the primary divisions, under which I am to treat of the science of rhetoric; and the order, in which I have mentioned them, is that, pointed out by the natural succession of things, in their application to the art of oratory. For suppose yourself called upon to speak in public upon some formal occasion, be it what it may; your first concern will be, what you are to say; what the reflections of your mind can suggest to you, suitable to your subject. This first conception of the thoughts will exercise your invention. Invention therefore is the first chapter in the book of rhetoric. Your next step will be to arrange the thoughts, which your invention has supplied; and this will be disposition. Then you will successively put into language, commit to memory, and pronounce, your discourse, which, it were superfluous to say, must be done in some order, by the means of elocution, memory, and pronunciation; and thus this division comprehends every thing, that can be included in the composition and delivery of an oratorical speech. But divisions like these are always in some sort arbitrary. Rigorously speaking, memory and pronunciation might with more propriety be considered, as subdivisions of elocution, than as constituting separate heads.

An oratorical discourse may be written without being spoken; in which case pronunciation would not be included in the work. It may be spoken without being written; for it may be extemporaneous, or it may be read; the first of which is very common in legislative debates, and on judicial trials; and the last for the delivery of sermons and of lectures. Invention, disposition, and elocution, therefore are essential and indispensable to every oratorical performance. Memory and pronunciation are applicable only to some. The divisions of Aristotle then, who admits only invention, elocution, and disposition, are more conformable to the true principles of analysis, than those of Cicero and Quinctilian; nor is it probable, that any deviation from it would have been made, but for that petty ambition of the minor rhetoricians to distinguish themselves, each by some novelty of his own; an ambition, which sacrifices science to selfishness, and multiplies the difficulties of the student, to gratify the vanity of the author.

To show you how exact the arrangement of Aristotle is, you will find on opening the bible, that it corresponds precisely with the process of the Creator in making the world. "In the beginning God created the heaven and the earth; and the earth was without form and void." Invention.

"And God said, let there be light." Elocution.

"And God divided the light from the darkness; and God called the light day, and the darkness he called night." Disposition.

Thus in the creation of the universe the same identical process is indicated, which Aristotle prescribes for the composition of a discourse. The power of positive creation belongs indeed exclusively to the supreme Creator; where he creates, man can only find. But he is the fountain of all intelligence; and the highest excellence of understanding consists in the imitation, as far as the imperfection of human powers will permit, of his general, unvarying laws. The analytical divisions of Aristotle in this, as in all other instances, were formed on a profound investigation of the laws of nature; but as the later rhetoricians have converted memory and pronunciation into primary branches of the science, and as at all events they must be discussed with all the attention, which their importance requires, I have included them among the principal divisions of the subject, and shall treat of them separately from the others, and combined with them to complete the system.

Invention then is the discovery, by thought, of the things best adapted to obtain the purpose of the speaker; and one of the objects of the rhetorician is to indicate to the practical orator the means of sharpening this faculty, and of facilitating its exercise. To this end Aristotle appears to have been the first inventor of the principal subdivision under this article; and the test of his distinction was drawn from the nature of the purposes, to which the oratorical discourses of that age were applied. He considered, that all public speaking had an object of reference either to past, present, or future time; and with a view to something to be done or omitted. That all such questions must necessarily be subjects of deliberation; and he accordingly called them deliberative discourses. That those, which referred to time past, consisted of controversies in the courts of law, respecting rights previously existing, or wrongs previously committed. This kind of public speaking he therefore denominated judicial eloquence. That the third division consisted of all such speeches, as, having no reference either to deliberation for the future, or to adjudication upon the past, were engrossed by the present moment; and were usually adapted more to exhibition, than to business; rather to show, than to action. These therefore he called by a term indicative of show, and which, as translated by the Latin rhetorical writers and their successors, are called demonstrative orations. This division has been universally adopted until very modern times; and is even prescribed in the rules and statutes of the Boylston professorship, as still to be recognized in this course of public lectures. Nor was this regulation injudicious. For, although the ancient classification in this case does not include all the modes of speaking, usual in modern times; yet it is of material importance, that you should know what that ancient classification was. It is essential to the understanding not only of all the ancient systems of rhetoric, but of many of the most celebrated orations. The rules, derived from these distributions, direct the special character, which marks all the diversities of Cicero's eloquence; and one of the first questions, which the profound student of his orations should ascertain, is, to which of the three kinds, the deliberative, the demonstrative, or the judicial oratory, each of the orations belongs.

The modern arrangement, adopted by the French rhetoricians, and after them by Blair, is into the eloquence of the pulpit, of popular assemblies, and of the bar. And this I suppose to be the division, with which you are most familiarly acquainted. There is one great advantage in it, arising from the circumstance, that two of the three departments are identically the same with those, established by the ancients; the eloquence of popular assemblies being but another word for deliberative, and the eloquence of the bar, for judicial oratory. The third modern division substitutes the eloquence of the pulpit, which to the ancients was altogether unknown, instead of their demonstrative oratory; but, in excluding this latter denomination altogether, they have left a numerous and in our country an important class of public discourses entirely destitute of a name. In the British dominions perhaps there may have been a propriety in omitting this kind of discourses, because they are not much in use among them. But we have resumed in these United States that particular style of speaking, which was so customary among the Greeks and Romans, but which in the island of Great Britain seems to be almost entirely unpractised. On the anniversary of our independence every city and almost every village of this Union resounds with formal discourses, strictly belonging to the demonstrative class of the ancients. There are many other occasions public and private, upon which we are accustomed to assemble in churches, and hear orations of the demonstrative kind. Many of the performances at all our public commencements are of the same description. Funeral orations, as distinct from funeral sermons, are very common among us; and in general the public taste for this species of public oratory is a distinguishing feature in our character. Yet the students, who collect their rules of rhetoric only from Blair, have no knowledge of the critical principles, upon which demonstrative orations ought to be composed. The proper style of eloquence, adapted to them, is therefore little understood, and, as far as my experience has observed, less practised. The great purposes of public benefit, to which these orations might and ought to be applied, that of stimulating genius, patriotism, and beneficence, by honorable eulogy; and that of teaching useful lessons of national virtue, by the honest artifices of eloquence, seldom discover themselves in those discourses, however deeply they may be impressed upon the speaker's mind. We must therefore reinstate demonstrative oratory in the place, from which Doctor Blair has degraded it; and for the eloquence of the pulpit must assign a separate and very distinguished place by itself.

There is also another mode of public speaking, which has arisen from modern usages and manners, of which nothing could be said in the ancient rhetoricians, and which has been generally overlooked by the moderns. It may be termed the eloquence of the bench; and consists in the charges of magistrates to grand-juries, their addresses to petit-jurors, on summing up causes, and the assignment of reasons, which they often give for their decisions. It may be deemed perhaps only one modification of judicial eloquence, but its proper principles are altogether different from those, on which the oratory of the bar is founded; and, like that of the sacred desk, partake of all the ancient kinds, the deliberative, the judicial, and the demonstrative.

In adhering therefore to these ancient distinctions, we are in no danger of wasting our hours upon the acquisition of any useless knowledge. Every one of the three ancient kinds of public speaking is in frequent and common use among us; and every precept, which ever could be useful in the exercise of oratory, remains useful in its utmost extent here. The eloquence of the divine and of the magistrate partakes of them all; and occasionally requires the arguments, appropriated to each of them separately. It has also suggested some additional principles, which we shall consider at the proper time. I shall now conclude with reminding you, that in this lecture you have the outline of all, that the whole course will comprise. That under the successive articles of invention, disposition, elocution, memory, and pronunciation, whatever I have to say upon the science of rhetoric will be included; and that the primary division of oratory, drawn from the different ultimate purposes of the speaker, is into discourses demonstrative, deliberative, judicial, and religious.

[1] Prov, VIII. 12.

Lecture Eight - State of the Controversy

IN my last lecture I informed you, that the whole science of rhetoric was divided into five constituent parts; invention, disposition, elocution, memory, and pronunciation or action. All which terms I endeavoured to explain in such a manner, that your ideas of their import might be clear and precise. Proceeding then to the consideration of the facilities, which it is the object of the science to furnish the orator's invention, I indicated the three great classes, into which all oratorical performances were divided by the ancient rhetoricians, and by them denominated the demonstrative, the deliberative, and the judicial. It will now be proper to say something more, with a view to exhibit tilt; reasons for this division. la undertaking to reduce the most important principles of eloquence to a system of rules, it was obvious that there were certain points, the observance of which applied equally to every occasion, upon which a man should speak in public; and certain others, which could operate only when the object of the speaker was directed to some specific purpose. The scenes, upon which orators were accustomed to exercise their talents, were different. In the popular assemblies, general or particular, the subjects discussed were concerning laws to be enacted, taxes to be levied, distributions of the public force and revenue to be made, accounts to be settled, and all other things of a similar nature. Deliberation upon something to be done was the common character of all such meetings; and the whole drift of the orator in such debates must be to persuade his hearers, that the measure in question is useful, or the contrary. Before the public tribunals, where the litigation of conflicting rights was conducted, the question must necessarily concern some action past; and the common standard, to which the orator must exert himself to bring the cause, which he supported, was justice. But orations, written before-hand, for delivery on some public solemnity, whether in honor of individuals, of communities, or of events, neither having nor intended to have any direct bearing upon the will of other men; neither destined to influence deliberation of the future, nor decision upon the past; the luxury, not the necessity of social intercourse; the pride, pomp, and circumstance, not the broils and battle of oratorical warfare; these, from their showy character, were called demonstrative discourses; and honor was the subject of their story. It will be obvious to you that, in regard to the character of the composition, arrangement, and delivery, there must be a great difference in the style and manner, suited to these several theatres of eloquence. That the same mode of proceeding, which would be proper for an anniversary oration, would be ridiculous upon an argument at the bar; and that neither would befit a debate upon the passage of u law in the legislature. There are some of you, who, in the course of a very few years, may be called to exhibit your talents on each of these different stages; and you will then be fully sensible of the advantage there is in forming, during the process of early education, a distinct idea of the style of eloquence, adapted to each.

A legislature then deliberates whether a law shall be past; a court of justice decides whether a wrong, public or private, has been committed; and a holiday audience is delighted or wearied, instructed or disgusted. I shall in future treat of the arguments, peculiarly proper for each of these occasions, separately; but I am first to notice essential particulars, belonging to them all.

The first and most important of these is what the ancient rhetoricians term the state of the controversy. The passages in the treatises of Cicero and Quinctilian, relating to this subject, are some of the most tedious and unprofitable parts of their works, because they have continual reference to the institutions and forms of proceeding, prevalent in their times; which were very different from those, to which we are accustomed. Some of the translators, and even some editors of Quinctilian, with a freedom highly to be censured, have struck out almost the whole of his chapter on this article. Yet a full and clear understanding of it, properly applied to the usages and manners of our own times, is one of the most important points in the whole science.

The state of a controversy, or, as it is oftentimes denominated, the state of the cause, and yet more frequently by the single word, the state, has probably suggested to your minds either a confused and indistinct idea, or an idea very different from that, which it imports. When I speak of the state of a controversy, you would naturally conclude, that there must be a controversy or disputed point to be settled, and that its state meant its situation in point of time; indicating the progress, made by the parties, and discovering the ground still to be gone over. Such, in the ordinary signification of the words, would be the idea, which the state of the controversy would convey. The state of the controversy among rhetoricians means quite another thing. It is the quod erat demonstrandum of the mathematicians. It is the mark, at which all the speaker's discourse aims; the focus, towards which all the rays of his eloquence should converge; and of course varies according to the nature and subject of the speech. In every public oration the speaker ought to have some specific point, to which, as to the goal of his career, all his discourse should be directed. In legislative or deliberative assemblies this is now usually called the question. In the courts of common law it is known by the name of the issue. In polemical writings it is sometimes called the point. In demonstrative discourses it is dilated into the general name of the subject; and in the pulpit the proper state is always contained in the preacher's text. It belongs therefore to every class of public speaking, and is not confined to judicial or deliberative oratory, where alone you would at first blush suppose the term controversy could properly be applied. It is indeed probable, that it first originated in judicial contests, where it always remained of most frequent use. To the other classes it was transferred by analogy. Whoever speaks in public must have something to prove or to illustrate. Whatever the occasion or the subject may be, the purpose of the orator must be to convince, or to move. Every speech is thus supposed to be founded upon some controversy, actual or implied. Conviction is the great purpose of eloquence, and this necessarily presupposes some resistance of feeling or of intellect, upon which conviction is to operate.

I told you that the state of the controversy was one of the most important points of consideration in the whole science of rhetoric. As I have explained it to you in its broadest acceptation, it is to the orator what the polar star is to the mariner. It is the end, to which every word he utters ought directly or indirectly to be aimed; and the whole art of speech consists in the perfect understanding of this end, and the just adaptation of means to effect its accomplishment. This may perhaps appear to you to be so obvious and so trivial a truth, as to require no illustration. And yet you will find throughout your lives, in the courts of law, in the legislature, in the pulpit, nothing is so common, as to see it forgotten. Our laws have found it necessary to provide, that in town-meetings nothing shall be acted upon by the inhabitants, unless the subject, or state of the controversy, has been inserted in the warrant, which calls them together. In all our legislative bodies rules of order are established for the purpose of confining the speakers to the subject before them; and certain forms even of phraseology are adopted, into which every question must be reduced. Yet even this is not sufficient to restrain the wandering propensities of debate. There is a formal rule in the British House of Commons, that "no member shall speak impertinently, or beside the question." A rule, which I believe none of the legislative assemblies in our country has thought proper to adopt; and whoever has been present at a debate in the parliament of Great Britain has perceived at least with as strong demonstration the inefficacy, as the necessity of such a regulation. In the courts of law so essential and so difficult is it to bring parties or their counsel to a point in litigation, that no cause can be given to a jury, or come to the judges for decision, by the practice of the common law, until the written pleadings have brought the case to an issue, and until that issue has been joined. Now this issue, in judicial trials, as I have already observed to you, is what the ancient lawyers and rhetoricians denominated the state of the controversy. But so loose and so various are the acceptations, in which terms of science are often received in their popular usage, that I find it necessary to explain to you the real meaning even of these two words, issue and pleadings; one of which is liable to be misunderstood by a very vulgar, though not uncommon misapplication; and the other, because in common discourse it is used to signify a different idea. I have heard a divine in the pulpit say, that we might join issue in such or such a remark of some celebrated writer; meaning that we might assent to the remark, and agree with the writer. But to join issue does not mean to agree; it means precisely the contrary. To join issue with a writer is directly to deny what he affirms, or affirm what he denies, and to put the question upon trial. A divine therefore should be cautious not only how, but upon what he joins issue; lest he should find himself unawares denying exactly what he intends to affirm, or affirming what he means to deny.

The case is different with pleas and pleadings. By these words almost every person, excepting professional lawyers, understands the speeches of the counsel to a judge or a jury; and you familiarly say, I heard such a lawyer plead such a cause, and he spoke well or ill; he made a good or a bad plea. The expressions in this sense are not incorrect, because the universality of their usage has forced them into lawful currency. But to a member of the bar pleas and pleadings mean the part of a lawsuit, which is written; not that, which is spoken. They mean the allegations and counter allegations of the parties to a suit; the charge and the answer; the reply and rejoinder; the conflict of opposing assertions, which must all be in writing, and by the means of which the parties must come to some specific point of fact, or of law, affirmed on one side, and denied on the other, before the cause can be tried, or the lawyers argue the issue. The pleadings must all be finished, before the speeches of the lawyer's commence. So you see pleading in the popular sense never begins, until pleading in the professional sense is over. A very material distinction! For although there may be instances in the courts, where even the lawyers' speeches do little more than end where they began; yet the generality of suitors, as well as witnesses, would not be very willing to hear them begin where they end.

The pleadings are the provision, made by the common law to bring litigating parties to an issue, or a state of the controversy. And so anxious has the law been to obtain this desirable object, that a perfect knowledge of the doctrine of pleas and pleadings is equivalent to a knowledge of the whole science. Pleas and pleadings are the logic of the law, as the speeches of lawyers are its rhetoric; and yet, notwithstanding all these pains, those, who have been habituated to attend the trial of causes, know full well how much time is wasted, of judges and jurors, of suitors and witnesses; how much weariness is inflicted upon them, and to how much delay the public justice of a nation is subjected from the forgetfulness of lawyers to observe the state of the controversy.

In demonstrative orations and discourses from the pulpit the orator is controlled only by his own judgment. Here is no formal controversy, as in the other scenes of public speaking. The state, in this department of oratory, is but another word for the subject. Take up then any collection of orations, delivered on public occasions, and examine them barely upon these two questions, what is the subject; and what is the bearing of the discourse upon it; and you will soon discover, that the state of the controversy is a part of rhetoric, of which demonstrative orators are as ignorant, or as heedless, as those of the senate or the bar. The same observation does not apply with so much force to the sermons, which we are accustomed to hear from the desk, and occasionally to read in print. In this, as in every other respect, the modern eloquence of the pulpit approaches nearer to the excellence of antiquity, than that, which is heard in either of the fields of oratory, which are common both to ancient and modern times. The practice of delivering written discourses, and the frequency, with which every clergyman is required to perform this service, have naturally produced in that profession a clearer perception, and a stronger impression of the Utility of methodical arrangement, and of adherence to the subject, than can ever be acquired by the practice of occasional and extemporaneous speaking. The connexion between the sermon and its text is generally better preserved, than that of any other class of discourses, with their state of controversy; yet even in the compositions of the divine, his method is often more formal than substantial, and as often marked by the breach, as by the observance.

Upon this subject however, as well as upon the topics, which are very intimately connected with it, the subtlety of the ancient rhetoricians was ever on the rack to analyze and classify all the kinds of states, which could possibly be devised. Quinctilian devotes a very long chapter to the discussion of this article. According to his usual custom he recapitulates the opinions of preceding rhetoricians, and concludes with giving his own. He apologizes for having changed this opinion since the time, when he had taught rhetoric professionally, and his ideas on the subject still appear to be indistinct or confused. He does not very clearly distinguish between the state of the controversy, as applied generally to every kind of public discourse, and the state of the controversy, as confined to the practice of the bar. Nor does he seem to have settled to his own satisfaction, or to that of his reader very precisely, in what particular stage of judicial controversy the state is to be found. The difficulties of ascertaining the true state are indeed in all practical oratory much greater, than a slight consideration could imagine. They arise principally from three sources, which in the language of the science are called co-ordinate, subordinate, and contingent states.

1. Co-ordinate states occur, when there are more questions than one, which, separately taken, and independent of all the rest, invoke all the merits of the case. Such as the several charges of Cicero against Verres. Such are the impeachments of modern times, both in England and in our own country. Every article contains a coordinate state with all the rest; and they may be met with distinct and separate answers to each charge, or by one general answer to all.

Co-ordinate states are most frequent in the practice of the bar. They seldom occur in deliberative assemblies; though sometimes they may arise upon different sections of one law. In the pulpit also they are rare; the subject being at the preacher's election, and unity being generally a point, which he is ambitious to observe. Yet a sermon may occasionally consist of co-ordinate states. Suppose, for example, you were to take for illustration the following text; "he that justifieth the wicked, and he that condemneth the just, even they both are abomination to the Lord." You would have two co-ordinate states, under one of which you would enlarge upon the guilt of condemning the just, and under the other upon that of justifying the wicked.

2. Subordinate states are questions distinct from the principal point; controvertible in themselves, and more or less important to its decision. They are common to every mode of public speaking. Take, for instance, that very common theme of a sermon; "and now abideth faith, hope, charity, these three; but the greatest of these is charity." The comparative excellence of

faith, hope, and charity, are the subordinate states. The transcendent excellence of charity is the main state; and the preacher's drift is to display, not only the positive beauties of this admirable virtue, but its relative merits, by comparison with the two next highest graces of Christianity,

In deliberative eloquence you will find a remarkable instance of subordinate states, skilfully adapted to the main state, in Burke's speech on his proposal for conciliation between Great Britain and her then American colonies. His main state was the necessity of conciliation. Why? Because America could not be subdued by force. This is a subordinate state. But the proof of his main position depended entirely upon its demonstration; and it was a truth so unwelcome to his audience, that it was incumbent upon him to place every part of his argument beyond the power of a cavil. The depth and extent of research, the adamantine logic, and the splendor of oratory, with which he performs this task, has in my own opinion no parallel in the records of modern deliberative eloquence. It was for wise and beneficent purposes, that providence suffered this admirable speech to fail of conviction upon the sordid and venal souls, to whom it was delivered. As a piece of eloquence, it has never been appreciated at half its value.

3. Incidental states are questions, arising occasionally, and more or less connected with the main question, without being essential to it. They are common to every species of oratory though of rarer use in the desk, where they generally partake of the nature of digressions. But in legislative assemblies every proposition for an amendment, offered to a bill upon its passage; and at the bar every occasional motion for the postponement of a trial, the admission of a witness, the disqualification of a juror, or the like, introduces an incidental question, having some relation to the main state of the controversy.

These are some of the causes, whence it so often happens, that public speakers deviate from their proper subject; and from these you will at once perceive the difficulty and the necessity of eager attention to the state of the controversy. I shall not trouble you with the metaphysical refinements of the ancient rhetoricians, and their inexhaustible multiplication of states. It will suffice to say, that Cicero and Quinctilian reduce them to three; which they call the states of conjecture, of definition, and of quality; equivalent, as they are explained by Cicero, to the questions, whether a thing is; what it is; and how it is; to which Aristotle and some modern writers have added a state of quantity, or whether the thing be more or less. For example, the state of conjecture is what, in our modern courts of justice, is termed an issue of fact. All trials by jury therefore are upon questions with the state of conjecture. The reason given for thus calling it is, that, being a question of fact, asserted by one party and denied by the other, the decision depends upon the conjecture of the judge. If this conjectural etymology be correct, it implies no very flattering compliment to the ancient practice of the law; since it insinuates, that, after all the labors of the learned counsel, the judge is left to decide the question by mere conjecture or guess. One would suspect, that the rhetorician, who first gave the name, meant more than meets the ear, and sheathed a sarcasm in a definition. Quinctilian tells us indeed, that "conjecture is a certain direction of reason towards truth; whence interpreters of dreams and omens were called conjectors." Bui conjecture, if a certain, is by no means a sure direction of reason towards truth. Its essence on the contrary is uncertainty. The illustration, which assimilates the decision of a question of fact to the interpretation of dreams and omens, was doubtless very seriously adduced by Quinctilian; but how far it helps the matter I leave for your judgments to determine; only adding my most earnest recommendation to every one of you. Who may hereafter have occasion to address a jury of your country, that you would entertain a nobler idea of your profession and of its duties, than to leave the cause to be determined upon a state of conjecture, or by the interpretation of a dream.

The states of definition, of quality, and quantity, are all included under the denomination of issues in law in our modern courts of justice. Indeed it is difficult to say what great point of discrimination between them could induce the ancients to place them under separate heads. The state of definition, for instance, is said to be a case, where the fact is admitted; but the question relates to its nature, or how the act should be defined. The instance alleged by Cicero is of a consecrated vessel, pilfered from a private house. The question is, whether this act were theft, or sacrilege; and the determination depends upon the definition of these two crimes. This state is yet very common in trials at the bar upon criminal prosecutions; as there are many offences, which, according to the circumstances, with which they are committed, assume a lighter or a deeper dye, are known by different names, and punishable with different penalties. Thus theft, according to the value of the article stolen, is called grand or petty larceny. Attended with violence to the person, becomes robbery; and, if with breaking open a dwelling house in the night-time, blackens into burglary. These, according to the ancient rhetoricians, might all have been states of definition; that is, when the facts upon a trial concerning them were admitted, their criminality would depend upon the definitions of the crimes. But they might also have been states of quantity; that is, whether the specific act committed was more or less aggravated; whether it was burglary, or robber}', or simple theft. The state of quality is upon agreed facts; but the question is whether they were right or wrong. Not what were the gradations of guilt, but whether there was any guilt at all. But all these distinctions will be of little use to you. In modern practice they are all solved in the clear and substantial distinction of issues of fact, and issues of law. Thus, in the case of Roscius Amerinus, Cicero's oration is upon a state of conjecture; whether Roscius committed the deed; and under our usages would have been an issue in fact. But in the case of Milo it was a state of quality. The fact, that Clodius was killed by Milo or his servants, was undisputed; but Cicero argues, that the act was justifiable self-defence. By our customs it would have been an issue in law.

Thus much for the doctrine of rhetorical states; and to sum up all, that I have said concerning them, you will observe, that the term is used in two different senses; under one of which it is only another word for the subject of the speaker's discourse, and is applied to every species of public oration; while under the other it is limited to judicial practice, and is equivalent to what the common lawyers call the issue. Having thus a clear idea of what the word means, to make the knowledge of use to yourselves and others, the only purpose, for which any knowledge is worth acquiring, let your reflections turn upon the importance, and upon the difficulty to every orator of fixing, and adhering in all public discourses to the state of the controversy, or cause. But it is also of high importance to the hearer of every public speaker. In that point of view it is material to you all. For although some of you may never intend to follow the practice of public speaking, yet you will all occasionally be hearers; and, with your advantages of education, all will be expected to be judges of the public orators. You have been justly told, that there is an art in silent reading. The art of collecting the kernel from the shell; of selecting the wheat from the tares. Let me add, for it is only another modification of the same truth, that there is an art in hearing. And one of its most elaborate exercises is to ascertain the state of a public speaker's discourse. An art perhaps as rare, as that of oratory Pope has very justly represented this contagion of judgments without reflection.

> 'Tis hard to say, if greater want of skill
> Appear in writing, or in judging ill;
> But of the two less heinous is the offence
> To tire our patience, than mislead our sense.
> Some few in that, but numbers err in this;
> Ten censure wrong, for one, who writes amiss.

And these observations apply to speaking, no less than to writing. A great source of erroneous judgment upon public speaking arises from the hearer's neglect or incapacity to ascertain the state of the speaker's cause; yet in this are involved all the essential parts of a correct judgment. From this alone can a just estimate of the merits both of the subject and of the speaker be formed. Listen to the criticisms you will hear on a divine in the pulpit, on a legislator in in the general court, on a lawyer at the bar, and nineteen times in twenty to what will they amount? To a comment upon some unusual word; to a cavil upon some grammatical anomaly; to self-admiring derision at the detection of some unlucky blunder; and to profound admiration at the glitter of some flashy metaphor. These are the trappings and the suits of oratory. They can no more qualify the auditor to pronounce upon the character of a discourse, than a pearl necklace can enable you to judge of a woman's beauty, or a diamond ring can indicate to a surgeon the soundness and vigor of a man's constitution. The state of the cause in rhetoric is the inward man; the internus homo of the anatomists. Here is the seat of life; here all the functions of vitality are performed; and here alone the nature of the being is to be found. But this is not to be discerned by a vacant eye, roaming without direction over the surface. As speakers then or as hearers, let your first attention always be directed to the state of the controversy. Acquire the habit of this attention here, by its employment in all your exercises of composition; and it will soon need no other recommendation, than its own success. Were I required to point out any one thing, which most forcibly discovers the inventive powers of a speaker, the infallible test of oratorical ability, the stamp, which distinguishes the orator from the man of words; I should say, it is the adaptation of the speech to the state of the controversy.

Lecture Nine - Topics

THE division of all oratorical discourses into demonstrative, deliberative, and judicial classes, as explained in one of my last lectures, was made, as I then informed you, for the purpose of facilitating the process of invention, and of marking the discrimination between those topics, which furnish arguments to every kind of discourse, and those, peculiarly incident to each of the separate classes. The topics, which belong alike to every species of public discourse, are those, which first claim our attention; and, in the works of the ancient rhetoricians, assume exclusively to themselves the name of topics. They were originally so called from the Greek word τοπος, a place, as being the common seats or places, to which every speaker must resort for his arguments. They were alike open to both parties in every controversy; which indiscriminate adaptation, together with the abuses, which a misapplication of them has often occasioned, has contributed in process of time to bring them into contempt; and almost all the modern writers upon rhetoric have concurred to explode them from the science. It was not without some hesitation, that I determined to make them the subject of a lecture. But being myself of opinion, that they are not so entirely useless, as in' modern times they have generally been considered; and reflecting, that the purpose of these lectures is to make you acquainted not only with the prevailing systems, but with the history of rhetoric; I concluded to give you such an abstract of them, as may at least open more thoroughly to your view the ancient systems of the science, although they may never answer any purpose of practical oratory for your own use.

The rhetorical topics, or common places then were the general incidents, or circumstances, belonging alike to every subject, and distributed under a certain number of heads, to facilitate the invention of public speakers. The topics were divided into two general classes; internal and external. The internal topics arose from the bosom of the subject itself. External topics arose from any other source without the subject, but made applicable to it. They are in our courts of law included under the general designation of evidence.

The internal topics are said to be sixteen; three of which, definition, enumeration, and notation or etymology, embrace the whole subject. The others, without being equally comprehensive, are derived from its various properties, incidents, and relations. From their names you will perceive the necessity of some further explanation to render them intelligible. They are as follow. Genus, species, antecedents, consequents, adjuncts, conjugates, cause, effect, contraries, repugnances, similitude, dissimilitude, and comparison.

Definition I presume it will not be necessary for me to define. But it will not be improper to tell you, that definitions are of two kinds, that is, of things and of ideas; objects perceptible to the sense, and objects only conceived by the understanding. The forms of definition are various; but the essential character of them all must be to separate the properties, which the defined object has in common with all others, from those, which are peculiar to itself. Definition is of great use in argument, and is at least as serviceable in logic, as in rhetoric. It is much used by the French orators, as an instrument of amplification. Thus, in the funeral oration of Turenne by Flechier, the orator, to display with greater force the combination of talents, required for commanding an army, resorts to an oratorical definition. "What," says he, "what is an army? An army is a body, agitated by an infinite variety of passions, directed by an able man to the defence of his country. It is a multitude of armed men blindly obedient to the orders of a commander, and totally ignorant of his designs. An assembly of base and mercenary souls for the most part, toiling for the fame of kings and conquerors, regardless of their own; a motley mass of libertines to keep in order; of cowards to lead in to battle; of profligates to restrain; of mutineers to control." This definition, you see, is no panegyric, and to a superficial view may appear to have been ill-judged at the court of Louis XIV, and ill-timed in the funeral eulogy of a great general. It is precisely what constitutes its highest merit. In this definition there was couched a profound moral lesson to Louis himself, which that prince had magnanimity enough to hear without offence, though not enough to apply with genuine wisdom to his conduct. I question whether any Parisian orator of the present day would pronounce such a definition of an army.

Enumeration consists in the separation of a subject into its constituent parts. The letters of Junius, ranking in the very first line of eloquence, but far lower in moral and political wisdom, make frequent use of enumeration. His first letter for instance contains an enumeration of the high offices of state, which composed the administration; with a commentary to prove, that they were all held by weak or worthless men. In his address to the king, he asks him on what part of his subjects he could rely for support, if the people of England should revolt; and then answers by enumerating all the other classes of people, then composing the British empire, and proving, that he could depend upon none of them. Enumeration is of great use in elaborate argument, but when employed must be made complete; that is, the utmost care must be taken not to omit any one of the component parts.

Notation, or etymology, seeks the meaning of a word by tracing it to its original sources. Its use is for elucidation; and its application is most suited to discussion of judicial questions. Nearly akin to notation are conjugates, which are nothing more than the different words, derived from the same root. Thus, when Milton's Comus says

"It is for homely features to keep home,
They had their name thence;"

he gives an example both of notation and of conjugates.

Genus and species must be well understood by all the students of logic. They are however often employed in argumentative oratory and the speaker's talent is discerned in the art, with which he descends from a general to a special proposition; or ascends from the special to the general. In technical language the general position is called the thesis, and the special position the hypothesis. In using arguments from these topics you have only to remember, that the species proves the genus; but the genus rather excludes, than proves the species. This is rather abstruse; but perhaps the following little epigram of Prior will make it plainer.

Yes, every poet is a fool.
By demonstration Ned can show it;
Happy, could Ned's inverted rule
Prove every fool to be a poet.

Here fool is the genus, and poet the species; and the very point of the epigram rests upon the axiom, I have just laid down, that the species proves the genus; but that the genus is better in argument to exclude, than to prove the species.

Antecedents, consequents, and adjuncts are circumstances attendant upon the principal point, in the several relations of past, future, and present time. The application of these topics is most common in arguments at law, upon questions of fact; and are there practised in form of comment upon what is called circumstantial evidence. Antecedents and consequents are said by Cicero more properly to belong to logic, than to rhetoric; because they are necessary attendants upon the fact. But adjuncts are more peculiarly rhetorical topics; because mere contingencies, which leave large room for imagination and conjecture. The relation of antecedent and consequent is strongly marked in two lines of Shakespeare.

She is a woman; therefore to be woo'd;
She is a woman; therefore to be won.

Implying, as characteristic of the female character, that a woman can neither be won without antecedent wooing; nor wooed without consequent winning.

I do not vouch for the truth of the sentiment, but only adduce the passage, as an example where these topics are brought into the most pointed opposition.

It requires a minute subtlety of discrimination to distinguish between these places and those of cause and effect. They are however distinguished, as well as the two kinds of cause and effect; the one universal and the other occasional. The inference from effect to cause is more conclusive, than that from cause to effect. Thus the material world, both in reason and in scripture, is the foundation of a never-answered argument to prove the existence of the Creator. The visible things arc the effect; and they prove beyond dispute the invisible things, the cause; the eternal power and godhead of the Creator. But this argument cannot be inverted. The existence of the Creator is not in itself a proof of the creation. A necessary caution in the use of this argument from effect to cause is not to trace the connexion too far, by ascending to a cause too remote. The reasoning in such cases becomes ludicrous. Thus Shakespeare's Polonius undertakes with great solemnity to find out the cause of Hamlet's madness. And, after much circumlocution in praise of brevity, and much prologue to introduce nothing, when he comes to assign the cause, it is, "I have a daughter;" and then, through a long and minute deduction, infers from his having a daughter the lord Hamlet's madness; to make all which elaborate reasoning the more ridiculous, you will recollect, that the madness, so shrewdly deduced from its cause by Polonius, was all the time feigned. So, in the Dunciad, Dennis draws the lamentable conclusion, that he is sixty years of age from a cause still more remote.

And am I then three -score!
Ah! why, ye gods, must two and two make four!

Another nice distinction is that between contraries and repugnancies. Thus, in the passage from Sallust, Concordia res parvae crescunt, discordia maximae dilabuntur; the observation is taken from the contraries, concord and discord. But when Pope, speaking of some character, says he was

So obliging, that he ne'er obliged;

the assertion is drawn from repugnancy; from things generally inconsistent, but sometimes reconcileable. The use of contraries gives energy to the thought; that of repugnancies often gives smartness to the expression. The combination of repugnancies is the most fruitful source of the antithesis; a figure, of which I shall say more hereafter.

Similitude, dissimilitude, and comparison, stand last in the list of internal topics, and are among the most copious sources of rhetorical ornament. These peculiarly belong to rhetoric; as those of cause and effect, antecedent and consequent, are more especially suited to logic. The distinction between similitude and comparison is, that the former has reference to the quality, the latter to the quantity. Comparison is between more and less; similitude is between good and bad. Thus when Livy says of Hannibal, who rested upon the Alps some time with his army, that he hung like a tempest upon the declivities of the mountains, it is a likeness by similitude. But when a learned writer says, that the sublimity of the scriptural prophets exceeds that of Homer, as much as thunder is louder than a whisper, it is a likeness by comparison. Similitude draws objects together to show their resemblance; comparison separates them to mark their difference.

From the internal let us now pass to the consideration of the external, or, as they are otherwise called, the inartificial topics. Inartificial, not that their management requires less art, than that of the others; it requires perhaps more; but because they are not inherent in the subject itself, upon which you discourse; but arise from some external source. There is great diversity and no small confusion among the ancient rhetoricians upon this part of the subject, which varies in the Greek and Roman writers, according to the varieties in their political and judicial institutions; and most of which is altogether inapplicable, except under a different modification, to ours.

The external topics, according to Quinctilian, are six. First, prejudications; second, common fame; third, torture; fourth, written documents; fifth, oaths; and sixth, witnesses.

1. Prejudications were principally confined to the bar. They were of three kinds. First, precedents, or adjudged cases, involving the same point of law, as that in litigations. These are as much used among us, as they were among the Romans; and every lawyer's library principally consists of such adjudged cases in elaborate compilations under the name of reports. Second, previous decisions on the same question between other parties. As for instance in the case of Cluentius; two of the accomplices of Oppianicus had already been tried, and convicted; from which circumstance Cicero strongly urges the argument against Oppianicus himself. Third, decisions of the same cause and between the same parties, before tribunals of inferior jurisdiction, from which there was an appeal. The second and third of these kinds of prejudication are as familiar to our laws, as to the Roman code; but they do not furnish the orator the same fund of argument; because it is a settled maxim of the common law, that the decision of the same question between other parties, or the decision of an inferior tribunal is upon the appeal of no authority whatsoever; and the case must be tried, as if it had never before been judicially examined. Thus the verdict of a coroner's inquest, the indictment of a grand jury, or the sentence of an inferior court, appealed from, cannot with propriety be mentioned, as matter of argument on either side of a cause. In this respect our system of rendering justice has improved upon that of the civil law. Another difference between the common and the civil law makes a different application and modification of arguments, drawn from prejudication, necessary. By the Roman system the questions of law and fact, involved in a cause, were always blended together, and decided by the same judges. By the common law every question of law was decided by the judge, and every question of fact by the jury; and, excepting in cases where the questions of

law and fact are so interwoven together, that the decision of one involves that of the other, this doctrine of the common law still prevails in practice. Hence the authority of precedents, prejudications on mere points of law, is much greater, than in the age of Quinctilian; while his second class of prejudications, chiefly relating to facts, which had so much weight in his time, has none or next to none in ours. I say next to none, because by the principles of our law it ought to have none. Not but that, in your attendance upon judicial courts, you will sometimes hear a speaker argue from this, and even from the third class of prejudications. There always will be some weight in such arguments and therefore they often will be introduced for want of better. But our institutions very justly counteract that natural first propensity to adopt the opinions of others; and forbid juries from putting any trust in the presentment of an inquest, and judges from paying any regard, on appeal, to the judgment of the subordinate tribunal.

There is another peculiarity in our institutions, which in like manner forbids, and yet instigates occasionally the use of arguments from prejudication, in our legislative assemblies, and in deliberative discourses. Our legislatures, as you know, generally consist of two separate assemblies; a senate and a house of representatives. Every law, before it is enacted, must be assented to by a majority of each of these assemblies. It is very common, upon a debate in either branch upon a question, which has been acted upon in the other, to allege the determination of the co-ordinate body, as an argument for or against the thing itself. But the same remark is here applicable, which I have just made with regard to the second and third kinds of judicial prejudications. Such arguments are inconsistent with the fundamental principle, upon which the legislative power is divided between two distinct bodies of men. They are contrary to the rules of order in every such assembly. Yet such is the sympathetic power of opinion, that they are introduced into almost every debate, and are seldom entirely without their influence.

When prejudication is adduced by way of argument, the speaker, adducing it, naturally dwells upon every circumstance, which may contribute to its weight; and enlarges on every favorable incident of reputation and character, which adds to its authority; and upon every feature or similarity between the case decided and that in controversy. His adversary, on the other hand, diligently marks the points of dissimilarity, or assails the reputation of those, from whom the decision is adduced. This requires much delicacy of management. It is usual to profess at least a respect of form for the intentions of those, whose authority is opposed; and when occasions arise, as they sometimes must, requiring an exception to this rule, and corrupt motives are to be denounced, moderation of expression becomes at once one of the most difficult and most necessary parts of the orator's address.

2. Common fame is a copious topic for argument in deliberative and demonstrative discourses, but is generally excluded from the judicial practice of modern nations. As evidence, it is by the rules of the common law never admissible, when other evidence can be supposed to exist. The reputa-

tion of a witness, the marriage of persons deceased, who lived together as man and wife, and some other cases of that kind are allowed to be proved by common fame; but in general the extreme inaccuracy of such testimony has shut the doors of our courts of justice against it. Common fame and prejudication can seldom or never extend further, than to warrant a presumption. The speaker, appealing to it, may exercise his ingenuity in deriving from the concurrent assent of multitudes the probability of truth. But common fame herself is no better reputed in the world, than in the courts of common law. Her testimony stands so degraded in universal estimation, that upon a controverted fact there is some danger in referring to her; as a skilful opponent takes advantage of the very reference to her, and urges, that the truth is to be found in the disbelief of what she asserts, and the full faith of what she denies.

3. Torture, which was a topic of continual recurrence among the Greeks and Romans, is still applied in many parts of modern Europe. It has often been considered, as the most powerful of all the tests of truth; but its use is equally abhorrent to the spirit of freedom, of reason, and of humanity. Among the ancients slaves only were subjected to it; but wherever it has been practised it has been thought to produce evidence of the strongest kind; and the person tortured has been said to be put to the question. Fortunately for us, we can never know its effects, but by speculation and the experience of others. It is not among the ways and means of our oratory.

4. Written documents compose a great proportion of the testimonies, admitted as evidence in the courts of law. Papers of this description give rise to oratorical controversy, either upon their authenticity, or upon their meaning or construction, or upon their legal effect. These are subjects however at this day more proper for the investigation of students at law, than of the mere rhetorician. The law prescribes how every document must be executed for admission, as evidence in the courts. It contains rules, founded upon sound logic, for settling the questions from ambiguity of expression, from disagreement between the words and intention, from repugnances, from analogies of reasoning, and from varieties of interpretation. It has dictated also their forms of expression, the legal operation of which has been settled for many ages. To your future studies I must then refer you for a further elucidation of this subject.

5. The importance of oaths, as oratorical topics, is also principally confined to the practice of the law. The oath of the parties was one of the common modes of trial among the Greeks and Romans. It is also admitted in certain cases both by the common and statute laws of this commonwealth; but the general maxim of our law is, that no man can be received as a witness in his own cause; and it usually disqualifies the testimony of every person, interested in the event of the trial. The oath of a party therefore, even when admitted, can never have much weight, and can be of use to an orator only on the failure of all other testimony.

6. Witnesses constitute the last external topic, concerning which I am to speak. And under this name are included authorities from eminent writers, common proverbs, and oracles among the ancients, instead of which we substitute the sacred scriptures. There are also two modes of collecting the testimony of living witnesses; that is, one when they are present, by word of mouth; the other in their absence, when it is reduced to the form of written depositions. The difference between these two modes of evidence, the advantages and inconveniences, attending each of them, and the cases, in which they are admissible, or must be excluded, belong, like almost every part of these external topics, to the same theory of evidence, which occupies so large a portion of the lawyers' studies.

Such are the topics, both internal and external, which occupy so high a station in all the ancient books upon rhetoric. You will readily conceive what infinite variety of matter they present to the use of an orator. But besides the direct employment of them all, they may be applied also indirectly under a fictitious presentment of facts, with the aid of hypothesis. The hypothesis of an orator bears the same proportion to his thesis, that traverse bears to plane sailing in navigation. It is not included among the topics, but includes them all under a different modification. Hypothesis is the potential or subjunctive mood of rhetoric; frequently used in every kind of public discourse. It is peculiarly calculated to excite attention, and rivet the impression of the topics, employed under it. Read for instance Junius' address, which I have already quoted, and commonly called his letter to the king. It is however in form a hypothetical speech to the king, introduced in a letter to the printer, and a considerable part of its force is owing to the hypothesis, upon which it is raised. Hypothesis is a favorite artifice with all orators of a brilliant imagination. It gives a license of excursion to fancy, which cannot be allowed to the speaker, while chained to the diminutive sphere of relatives. In deliberative and judicial orations, it affords an opportunity to say hypothetically what the speaker would not dare to say directly. The artifice is indeed so often practised to evade all restraint upon speech, that there is at least no ingenuity in its employment. The purposes, for which it is resorted to from this motive, are often so disingenuous, that in seeing it used and abused, as you will upon numberless occasions throughout your lives, you will probably go a step beyond the conclusion of the philosophical clown in Shakespeare, and settle in the opinion, that there is much vice, as well as "much virtue in **if.**"

Thus much may suffice for the doctrine of the topics, or loci communes, which were deemed of vast importance to the students both of logic and rhetoric in ancient times, but which the modern teachers of eloquence have almost unanimously pronounced to be utterly useless. If mere authority were to decide the question, the writers of later ages must excuse me for receiving with great caution any principle in the theory of the science, directly opposed to the opinion and the practice of Cicero. But considering the subject, as divested of all sanction from venerable names, on its own merits I do not deem the topics to be altogether without their use. Their proper use may be illustrated by reference to an usage, with which you are all well acquainted.

In entering an apothecary's shop you have often observed its walls lined with a wainscoting of small boxes, on the outside of which you have seen, painted in capital letters, certain cabalistical words, most of which I presume you found yourselves quite unable to decipher. You ask the attendant at the shop for the medicinal article you want; he goes to one of his boxes, and in a moment brings you the drug, for which you applied; but which you never would have discovered from the names upon the boxes. Now the topics are, as I conceive, to the young orator, exactly what the apothecary's painted boxes are to his apprentice. To the total stranger they are impenetrable hieroglyphics. To the thorough bred physician they may be altogether unnecessary. But in that intermediate stage, when arrangement is needed to relieve the mind from the pressure of accumulation, the painted boxes and the rhetorical topics may be of great use to the young practitioner. The topics are the ticketed boxes, or the labelled phials, in which the arguments of the speaker are to be found. And although telling us where to look for an argument does not furnish us the argument itself, yet it may suggest the train of thought, and add facility to the copiousness of the orator. This is all the benefit, that can be derived, or that I presume it was ever pretended could be derived from a thorough knowledge of the topics. They cannot give, but they may assist invention. They exhibit the subject in all its attitudes, and under every diversity of light and shade. They distribute the field of contemplation among a number of distinct proprietors, and mark out its divisions by metes and bounds. A perfect master of the topics may be a very miserable orator; but an accomplished orator will not disdain a thorough knowledge of the topics.

Lecture Ten - Arguments and Demonstrative Oratory

HAVING in my preceding lectures explained to you the nature, and submitted to your reflections my opinion of the real worth of those incidents in the science of rhetoric, usually known by the denomination of the state of the controversy, and general topics, internal as well as external, the course of my subject now leads me to consider, separately and successively, the arguments suitable to each of the three classes of orations, the demonstrative, the deliberative, and the judicial. This arrangement is enjoined by the regulations of the institution; and is perhaps the best, that could have been devised, as it unfolds to your view the principles of the rhetorical science in the same order of time, as they may be expected to present themselves to your use for practical application. Whenever you shall have occasion to speak in public, the first object, to which your attention will be required, can be no other, than to ascertain precisely the state of the controversy, or in other words the subject of your discourse. The next will be to collect from the whole stock of your ideas those, which may be most subservient to the design, for which you are to speak; and the rhetorical topics were devised to facilitate this process. Your third consideration will be to settle specifically upon those ideas or arguments, best adapted to the particular nature of discourse. The arguments, specially adapted to each of the three kinds of public speaking, may be and often are introduced to the greatest advantage in discourses of the other classes; but there are certain arguments, adapted in a peculiar manner to each of the three departments, which still retain their character and denomination, even when used in the service of the others.

The arguments, suited to either of the three kinds of discourses, are such, as apply more especially to the purpose of that class, to which they belong; and to determine what that is we must recur to those original and fundamental distinctions, which I have already noticed. You will remember then, that the central point, to which all the rays of argument should converge, in deliberative oratory is utility; in judicial discourses is justice; and in demonstrative orations is praise or censure.

Every discourse then, of which panegyric or reprobation upon persons or things is the main purpose, must be included in the demonstrative class. It embraces accordingly a very numerous description of oratorical performances, both of ancient and of modern times. Among the Greeks and Romans panegyrics upon the gods, upon princes, generals, and distinguished men dead or living, and even upon cities and countries, were frequently written and delivered. Funeral eulogies upon deceased persons of illustrious rank, male or female, were often composed and pronounced in public by their kinsmen; a custom, to which the first emperors themselves, Julius Caesar, Augustus, and Tiberius, successively conformed. These were orations strictly and altogether demonstrative. But the panegyric of Pompey, interwoven by Cicero into his oration for the Manilian law, that of Caesar in the oration for Marcellus, that of Literature in the oration for Archias; the panegyric of Trajan by the younger Pliny; and Cicero's invectives against Antony in his philippics, against Piso, Catiline, Clodius, and Verres, in many other of his orations, are applications of the demonstrative manner in certain parts of deliberative, or judicial discourses.

In modern ages and Christian countries funeral sermons are everywhere customary. With the Roman Catholics the panegyric of saints is an ordinary exercise of public eloquence. Some of the most illustrious scientific and literary societies in France were accustomed, upon the decease of a member, to hear a short biographical eulogy pronounced upon him by their secretary. During a long series of years every member of the French academy was expected, on the day of his reception, to deliver a panegyric upon Louis XIV, the first patron, and upon Cardinal Richelieu, the founder of that institution. The learned academies of France were accustomed also to propose the panegyric of some distinguished personage in French history, as a subject for ingenious competition, with the offer of a prize or premium for the best performance.

These were also discourses strictly demonstrative, though, instead of being delivered by their authors, the prize composition alone was read at a public meeting of the society.

But as demonstrative eloquence has been thus assiduously cultivated and zealously encouraged in France, it has in a very singular and unaccountable manner been neglected in England. Of the British nation may emphatically be said, what one of their most eloquent writers has confessed of himself; "they are not conversant in the language of panegyric." How has it happened, that a people, illustrious by a long catalogue of worthies, among the brightest in the fields of fame, should have taken so little pains, or rather should so studiously have avoided, to bestow upon them the merited mead of glory? Their substitute for the clarion of fame is a marble monument in St. Paul's church, or Westminster Abbey. This is indeed a fair and honorable distinction; a powerful incentive to generous deeds, and a noble expression of national gratitude. But after all a tomb-stone is in its proper character a record of mortality. The approbation, the applause of their fellow men, are among the most precious rewards, which prompt the most exalted spirits to deathless achievements; and the sepulchres of the dead are not the stages, upon which this applause and approbation can properly ascend. Non quia intercedendum putem imaginibus, quae marmore aut aere finguntur; sed ut vultus hominum, ita simulacra vultus imbecilla ac mortalia sunt; forma mentis aeterna, quam tcnere et exprimere non per alienam materiem et urtem, sed tuis ipse moribus possis. Have the British nation been insensible to the truth of this sublime sentiment? Have they believed, that such perishable and frail materials, as brass and marble, could bear the proper memorial of imperishable minds? Or why have they been so penurious of their praise? The funeral sermon is the only oratorical form, in which they have been accustomed to utter eulogy j and even that discourse lias rather been devoted to soothe private sorrows, or to gratify personal friendship, than to testify public gratitude or admiration. They once held a theatrical celebration in honor of Shakespeare, and they have commemorated Handel in solemnizing the strains of his own harmony. But on these, on all other like occasions, rhetoric has remained in obstinate and immoveable silence. Alfred and Elizabeth, Shakespeare and Milton, Bacon and Locke, Newton and Napier, Marlborough and Nelson, Chatham and Burke, slumber in death, unhonored by the grateful offerings of panegyric. The British poets indeed have often spoken with exquisite pathos and beauty the language of eulogy; but in the whole compass of English literature there is not one effusion of eloquence, which, like those of Isocrates, Cicero, and Pliny in Greece and Rome, or those of Bossuet and Fléchier, Mascaron and Thomas in France, immortalize at once the speaker and his subject, and interweave, in one immortal texture, the glories of achievement with those of celebration.

Descending in general from British ancestry, speaking their language, and educated in their manners, usages, and customs, we have in some degree inherited this unaccountable indifference to the memory of departed merit. I say in some degree, for funeral sermons are much more frequent in our usage, than in that of the nation, whence we originate. But the funeral sermon is perhaps the most objectionable form, in which panegyrical eloquence could be revived. It is too common to be much valued, and too indiscriminate to be very valuable. But we have occasional funeral orations in honor of distinguished personages; and we have numerous anniversary discourses, which might be made the vehicles of honorable and precious commendation. But the acquaintance of our public orators is generally so exclusively limited to English literature, they are accustomed to look for models of composition so invariably to English example, that, where this has failed them, they seem to have been at a loss where to resort for a substitute; or, with more confidence than safety, they have relied upon the fertility of their own genius, and nobly disdained either to seek models from the past, or to furnish them for the future. Certain at least it is, that our success in this department of literature has not been correspondent to our partialities in its favor. The faculties of our countrymen have been more conspicuous in action, than in celebration. The worthies of elder times have often been commemorated, but seldom eulogized; and the spirit of Washington, in the very abodes of blessedness, must have nauseated at some of the reeking honors, which have issued from his tomb.

Yet although the English language is destitute of orations strictly demonstrative in the line of panegyric, there are however passages of the panegyrical description, interspersed in the speeches of their parliamentary orators, which prove, that its proper style has not always been either unknown or neglected. The speeches of Burke, which were published by himself, contain some admirable specimens of this, as well as of every other kind of eloquence. I refer you particularly to his eulogies of Howard, of Lord Bathurst, of Charles Townsend, of Sir George Saville, and of Mr. Dunning; but above all to that of the American people; the fairest and most glorious tribute of panegyric, that ever was uttered in their honor. As a memorial of the merits of your forefathers, it may be recommended to your patriotism; as an effort of the most splendid eloquence, to your taste; and as a lesson of the most elevated morality, to your imitation. Every line of praise upon the fathers should be received, as a line of duty for the children.

But praise is only the illuminated hemisphere of demonstrative eloquence. Her orb on the other side is darkened with invective and reproach. Solemn orations of invective are not indeed usual. Panegyric sometimes ends in itself, and constitutes the only purpose of the speaker. It has not, I believe, been the custom of any age or nation thus to administer censure; but in discourses of business, deliberative or judicial, reprehension is perhaps of more frequent and extensive use, than applause. It is plentifully scattered over all the most celebrated orations both of ancient and modern times. Familiar alike to Demosthenes and Cicero; to Chatham, Junius, and Burke. The French orators indeed have been most sparing in its use; for the sublimest French orators have been ministers of religion, and have been duly impressed with that truly excellent sentiment of the Athenian priestess, who refused her office to anathematize Alcibiades; because it was her duty to implore blessings, and not to pronounce execrations. She was a priestess to bless, and not to curse. Invective is not one of the pleasing functions of oratory; nor is it her amiable aspect. But she is charged with a sting, as well as with honey. Her terrors are as potent, as her charms; as the same omnipotent hand is manifested by the blasting volley of thunder, as by the genial radiance of the sun.

The ultimate object then of demonstrative eloquence is show; the display of qualities good or bad. Her special function is to point the finger of admiration or of scorn; to deal out the mead of honor and of shame. From this fundamental principle are to be derived all the precepts for the composition of demonstrative discourses; which I shall now present to your consideration in successive reference to the subject, the grounds, and the manner. In other words we are to inquire, what may properly be praised or censured; next, for what, and finally how such praise or censure should be dispensed.

The subjects of panegyric or reprobation may be either persons or things. In the language of Aristotle, which has been adopted by Quinctilian, demonstrative oratory generally relates either to gods or men; but sometimes to other animals, and even to things inanimate." Surely one would think these divisions sufficiently clear and comprehensive; but this is one of the parts of the science, where the rhetoricians of the middle age, from the time of Quinctilian down to the beginning of the last century, wasted a world of idle ingenuity upon petty distinctions, and the multiplication of artificial subdivisions. Vossius for example very gravely discusses the question, whether this division of Aristotle includes vegetables; because they are neither gods, men, other animals, nor things inanimate. Nay, after long and painful argument, he admits, that in the praise or censure of persons, actions, and things, that of the brute creation cannot be comprised; and therefore, in compliance with the scruples of the formidable critics, who insisted upon a more perfect enumeration, he proposes a fourth subdivision of quasi-persons; so that every bird, beast, fish, and creeping thing, of this terraqueous globe, might be regularly entitled to its just proportion of panegyric; or be punished with its proper share of reproach. Unquestionably all being moral or physical, actual or possible, from the Supreme Creator to nothing, "night's elder brother," may seriously or in joke be made a subject of eulogy or of invective. But, in order to establish this proposition, it cannot be necessary to dissect all existence material and metaphysical, and count its every vein and artery, nerve and sinew, for the purpose of converting into legitimate oratory a philippic upon a monkey, or a panegyric upon a parrot.

In Christian countries the great and transcendent object of praise, before which all others vanish, is the Creator and Preserver of the universe. His power and goodness are inexhaustible themes, upon which the duties of the pulpit orator particularly require him to expatiate in all his public performances. It is a part of the regular, stated duties of public worship, and in those churches, where this portion of the divine service has not been reduced to prescribed, unvarying forms, is perhaps the most arduous of all the functions of the sanctuary. With the praise of the Creator is naturally associated that of the Saviour of the world; which will be diversified according to the different views, in which that exalted character is considered by the different denominations of Christians; differences, which it is not my province to discuss, and of which mutual forbearance and charity furnish the best, if not the only solution.

Among the ancient heathens the mythological doctrine and history supplied a copious fund for encomiastic eloquence, in their numberless divinities, demi-gods, and heroes. The Roman Catholics, by an easy substitution, have reserved to themselves the same themes in their hierarchy of saints, angels, and archangels;

"Thrones, dominations, princedoms, virtues, powers."

But the protestant communities know too little of those "orders bright," those supernatural intelligences, to honor them with that panegyric, to which, by their rank and dignity in the scale of being, they may perhaps be entitled; but which in our ignorance has an unfortunate tendency to lead us from veneration to worship, from the adoration of the true God to the idolatry of his creatures.

The persons however, who, in the common affairs of the world, most frequently call for the voice of panegyric or of censure, are men; or at least human beings. And the qualities, for which they may deserve the warmest praise, are those, which contribute to social or individual happiness. And here it is proper to notice a very material distinction, drawn by Socrates, and developed by his disciples, between what they call the fair, and the good; the Καλον, ηαι αγαζον. By the good they understood all those blessings, the direct benefit of which was confined to their possessor; such as health, strength, beauty, and the gifts of nature, which contribute to the happiness of the individual. But the fair was the assemblage of those powers and faculties, which are not only desirable in themselves, but as contributing to the happiness of others. Hence it is that Aristotle remarks, that the whole scope of the demonstrative orator is the fair; το ηαλον; the display of the qualities, which administer to the happiness of mankind. Hence the most perfect theme of human panegyric is virtue. Virtue is the Καλον, ηαι αγαζον; both good and fair; at once contributing to the happiness of its possessor and of other men. Virtue alone unites the double praise of enjoyment and of beneficence. But, as beneficence is her most essential characteristic, it necessarily follows, that those of her attributes, which are most beneficial to others, are those, which merit the highest panegyric. To do good and to communicate is thus the only solid foundation for legitimate praise; and the passage of the holy scripture, which says of the blessed Jesus, that he "went about doing good," embraces within itself the whole compass of applause, the whole system of demonstrative eloquence.

With this general principle always in view, and with continual reference to it, a man may be panegyrized for the qualities of his mind, for bodily accomplishments, or for external circumstances. The highest praise must be reserved for the first. They are most beneficent in their nature, and most extensive in their effects. Mere bodily perfections are of small benefit to the world in a state of civilization, and Hercules himself could, by the cleansing of a stable, or the strangling of a lion, deserve but little praise from mankind, once emancipated from the savage weakness of the heroic age. External circumstances, or the blessings of fortune, can supply no materials for encomium from themselves; but they may be rendered praiseworthy by their application. This they can receive only from the energy of virtue. So that after all, directly or indirectly, virtue is the only pure and original fountain of praise.

But virtue is a term so general and so comprehensive, that the idea annexed to it is seldom very precise. Aristotle therefore, after marking its universal characteristic, beneficence, the property of doing good, enters into a minute enumeration of all its parts; such as justice, fortitude, temperance, magnificence, magnanimity, liberality, meekness, prudence, and wisdom. He gives ingenious and accurate definitions of all these moral and intellectual qualities; but it deserves peculiarly to be remarked, that among the virtues he formally includes revenge. For, says he, retaliation is part of justice; and inflexibility part of fortitude. How striking an illustration is this at once of the superior excellence and of the truth of divine revelation. To mere naked, human nature, this reasoning of Aristotle is irresistible. It is not his wonderful sagacity, that deserts him; it is merely the infirmity of the natural man, in which he participates. On principles of mere natural morality revenge is a virtue, retaliation is justice, and inflexibility is fortitude. But look for the practical comment upon this principle into the fictions of the poets; see the hero of Homer, the goddess-born Achilles, wreaking his fury upon the lifeless corpse of his valiant and unfortunate foe. See the hero of Virgil, the pious Aeneas, steeling his bosom against mercy, and plunging his pitiless sword into the bosom of a fallen and imploring enemy, to avenge the slaughter of his friend. Look for it in real history; consult Thucydides; consult the annals of the French revolution, from the instant, when that peculiar doctrine of Christianity, the forgiveness of injuries, was cast off, as a relic of monkish superstition; and you will trace this virtue of revenge through rivers and oceans of blood, shed in cold and deliberate butchery. But this subject is too fruitful and too important for discussion here. It is a theme for more sacred occasions, and more hallowed lips. Returning to our proper sphere, it now remains to inquire how praise or censure best may be dispensed.

In formal panegyric there are two modes of proceeding, either of which may be adopted, as the circumstances of the case may render expedient. The one may be called biographical, the other ethical panegyric. One proceeds from the object, and the other from the qualities. One takes its departure from the person, and the other from the virtue celebrated.

The biographical panegyric is the easiest. Its divisions are uniform, and are precisely the same in every subject, to which they are applied. It traces the hero of the story through his genealogy to the moment of his birth; accompanies him through life; follows him to the grave, and gathers all the flowers ever scattered on his tomb. The moral panegyric is of more difficult composition. It takes the prominent qualities of the person celebrated for the principal divisions of discourse, and treats them in succession "without regard to chronological order. Of these two methods the first has been pursued by Isocrates and Pliny; the last by Cicero. The French funeral eulogists endeavour to combine the advantages of both, and exhibit a development of virtues in succession, corresponding with the order of a biographical narrative. One of the most beautiful examples of panegyric, thus treated, is the funeral oration of the duchess of Montausier by Flechier.

The rules for the composition of panegyric are neither numerous nor complicated. The first is a sacred and undeviating regard for truth. But the duties, which truth prescribes, are variously modified under various relations. A mere biographer is bound to divest himself of all partialities; to notice the errors and failings, as well as the virtues and achievements of his hero. The obligation of the panegyrist is less rigorous. His purpose is not history but encomium. He is bound to tell the truth. Errors, vices, follies, must not be disguised, nor justified; but they may be covered with the veil of silence; and if more than counterbalanced by transcendent merits, they may even be extenuated; a proceeding perfectly consistent with the pure morality of that religion, which teaches, that "charity covereth a multitude of sins."

The ancient rhetoricians even allowed panegyrical orators the very dangerous indulgence of using what they call moral approximation; and, as all the virtues border very closely upon corresponding vices, they authorize the speaker of praise or invective to transpose them, or mingle up their colors with the view to cause the one to be mistaken for the other. Aristotle formally recommends the occasional substitution of prudence for timidity; of sagacity for cunning; of simplicity for dullness; of gentleness for indolence; and he ingeniously reminds his reader, that this transposition will be most advisable, when the vice is only the excess of its correlative virtue. And thus rashness may easily be pruned into valor, and extravagance whitened into generosity. The aspect, in which moral qualities may be considered, is undoubtedly susceptible of great variety; and nothing falls more frequently under our observation in the common occurrences of life, than the different lights, in which the same act is viewed by different eyes. To deny the speaker of panegyric or invective the use of the faculty, which darkens or illumines the canvass of his portraits, would be restriction too severe. He may present the object in the aspect best suited to his purpose, without deviating from the truth. The use of approximation is more questionable, when employed for censure, than for commendation; unmerited reproach being more pernicious and more odious, than undeserved praise. An example of oratorical approximation in the correspondence between Junius and Sir William Draper is introduced on both sides of the controversy; and refers to a feature in the character of the Marquis of Granby, which one of the writers endeavours to exalt, and the other struggles to degrade. [1] An impartial observer will perceive, that plain fact lay between the two representations. As efforts of skill, the execution of Junius is far superior to that of his adversary. But it is tinctured with bitter and corrosive passions. Sir William Draper is less pleasing and more amiable. Junius is the ablest champion; Sir William has the fairest cause.. If ever engaged in controversy, remember that approximation requires at once firmness and pliancy, steady principle and accommodating address. It obtains more indulgence, used defensively, than offensively; more excuse, urged by way of attenuation, than of reproof; more encouragement in amplifying virtues, than in aggravating faults.

The next rule for the distribution of praise or censure is that it be specific. General encomium is the praise of fools. The quality, which a man has in common with many others, is no theme for panegyric or invective. Dwell on all important incidents, exclusively or at least peculiarly applicable to the person, of whom you speak. Strive rather to excite, than to express admiration; to exhibit, rather than to proclaim the excellence of your hero, if your theme be praise. If invective, pursue the same process, though with inverted step. General abuse may discover anger, but not eloquence. The alphabet of demonstrative oratory is the same, spelt forward or backward. But in descending to specialties, be cautious in the selection of circumstances, which admit of panegyric and embellishment. Assume nothing trivial; applaud nothing really censurable; blame nothing really praiseworthy. The value of praise depends much on the character of the panegyrist, and the selection of incidents for remark is the truest test of both the orator and the oration.

Amplification is the favorite figure of demonstrative eloquence. The speaker then should proceed from the less to the greater, and make his discourse a continual climax. The ears of men are fastidious to praise. When listening to it, they are ever prone to slide into the more pleasant sensation of ridicule. The orator must suit his discourse to the disposition of the audience. Praise or dispraise is relative. To conciliate the favor of his auditory is the first task of the orator in every form of public speaking. To the demonstrative orator it is the alpha and omega, the first and the last.

The last, though not the least important precept for the composition of these discourses is to moralize the subject; an art, which requires the most consummate skill. The amusement of the audience, and the celebration of some favorite occasion or character, are the immediate purposes of the oration; but the speaker should propose to himself the further and nobler end of urging them to virtuous sentiment and beneficent action. Not by assuming the tone of a teacher; not by dealing out driblets of morality from the whole duty of man; not by pillaging the primer, or laying the spelling-book under contribution. Your moral sentiment must be pure, to be useful; it must bear some mark of novelty in the expression or in the modification, to be received without disgust, and to leave a deep impression. Hence you will perceive, that a profound knowledge of human nature, an accurate observation of mankind, and a thorough knowledge of ethics, or the science of moral distinctions, are among the essential qualifications of the demonstrative orator. In this art of mingling moral sentiment with oratorical splendor, modern eloquence has perhaps equalled that of the ancients; and the French orators have excelled all other moderns. Bossuet and Fléchier, in their funeral orations and panegyrics, combine admirable sentiments with ardent panegyric, and irradiate every gem of their eloquence with a lucid beam of instruction.

Thus much for the arguments, suited peculiarly to demonstrative oratory. My next object will be to give you a view of those, most adapted to the eloquence of deliberation.

[1] Heron's Junius i. p. 57, 51, 59.

Lecture Eleven - Deliberative Oratory

To ascertain the arguments peculiarly suitable to each of the three kinds of public speaking, where eloquence may be displayed, we must resort to that special principle, which constitutes the distinctive character of the kind. Thus we have seen, that, as show is the essential property of demonstrative orations, the arguments, best adapted to discourses of that class, are such as display sentiment or character. Proceeding in the same track to discover the arguments, which fall within the province of deliberative oratory, we are to recollect, that the characteristic common measure of this class is utility. Deliberation presupposes a freedom of election in the deliberating body. It presupposes alternatives, which may be adopted or rejected. The issue of deliberation is action, and the final determination, what that action shall be, results from a sense of utility or expediency, entertained by the speaker's audience. The object of the orator then is to persuade his hearers, and to influence their conduct in relation to a future measure. His task is to inspire them with the belief, that the adoption of that, which he recommends, or the rejection of that, which he dissuades, would be useful either to the hearers themselves, or to their constituents, whom they represent.

It is in deliberative oratory, and in that alone, that eloquence and the art of persuasion maybe considered, as terms perfectly synonymous. Demonstrative orations terminate in themselves. They lead to no vote; they verge to no verdict. The drift of the discourse is to display the merits of the subject, and the talents of the speaker. He may indeed exercise powers of persuasion, but they are not essential to his task. He has no call to act upon the will of his hearers. Persuasion is not necessarily his aim.

Judicial discourses terminate in action; and in that respect resemble deliberative speeches. But the drift of the argument is to justice; not to utility. The aim of the speaker must be to produce conviction, rather than persuasion; to operate by proof, rather than by influence. The judge or jury, to whom the discourse is addressed, has no choice of alternatives, no freedom of option, like the deliberative body. That which is just, that which is prescribed by law, once discovered and made manifest, he is bound to follow. Persuasion therefore does not properly belong to that class of oratory. The judge is to act not under the impulse of his will, but of the law. He is the mere minister of justice. He must take the facts according to the proof. He is to presume nothing; to suppose nothing; to imagine nothing. The orator ought not to address himself to the inclinations of his auditor, because the auditor has no right to consult them himself. This distinction is much stronger in modern times and in our country, than among the ancients; because our judicial courts are more closely bound to the letter of the law. So then in demonstrative orations the application of the orator's eloquence is only to the opinions of his audience; in judicial arguments to their judgment: but in deliberative discourses directly to their will.

From these observations you will perceive the solid grounds, upon which these divisions were originally made. So different is the nature of public speaking, on these different occasions, that the talents, required to shine in each of them, are different from those, which give excellence in the others. In our own experience we may observe, that the eloquence of the bar, of the legislature, and of public solemnities, are seldom or ever found united to high perfection in the same person. An admirable lawyer is not always a popular speaker in deliberative assemblies; and a speaker of brilliant orations often sinks into silence at the bar. In the relative estimate of the difficulties and importance of the several kinds of public oratory, Cicero has assigned to judicial eloquence the place of the highest difficulty, and to the eloquence of deliberation that of the highest importance. This arrangement is suited to all republican governments, and indeed to all governments, where the powers of legislation are exercised by a deliberative assembly. From the preponderancy of democracy in the political constitutions of our country, deliberative assemblies are more numerous, and the objects of their consideration are more diversified, than they ever have been in any other age or nation, from the formation of a national constitution to the management of a turnpike, every object of concern to more than one individual is transacted by deliberative bodies. National and state conventions for the purpose of forming constitutions, the congress of the United States, the legislatures of the several states, are all deliberative assemblies. Besides which, in our part of the country, every town, every parish or religious society, every association of individuals, incorporated for purposes of interest, of education, of charity, or of science, forms a deliberative assembly, and presents opportunities for the exhibition of deliberative eloquence. These are scenes, in which your duties, as men or as citizens, will frequently call upon you all to engage. There is only a certain proportion among you, who will ever have occasion to speak in the courts of justice, or in the sacred desk. Still fewer will ever have the call, or feel the inclination to deliver the formal oration of a public solemnity. But you are all citizens of a free republic; you are all favored with the most liberal and scientific education, which your country can afford. That country, in her turn, will have a peculiar claim upon you for the benefit of your counsels; and either in the selected bodies of her legislatures, or in the general assemblies of the people, will give you opportunities to employ, for her advantage and your own reputation, every faculty of speech, which you have received, or which you can acquire.

The principles of deliberative oratory are important also in another point of view; inasmuch as they are applicable to the ordinary concerns of life. Whoever in the course of human affairs is called to give advice, or to ask a favor of another, must apply to the same principles of action, as those, which the deliberative orator must address. The arguments, which persuade an assembly, are the same, which are calculated to persuade an individual; and in speaking to a deliberative body the orator can often employ no higher artifice, than to consider himself as discoursing to a single man.

The objects of deliberative eloquence then are almost co-extensive with human affairs. They embrace everything, which can be a subject of advice, of exhortation, of consolation, or of petition. The most important scenes of deliberative oratory however in these states are the congress of the union, and the state legislature. The objects of their deliberation affect the interests of individuals and of the nation, in the highest degree. In seeking the sources of deliberative argument I shall therefore so modify the rules, generally to be observed, as to bear constant reference to them. They include all the subjects of legislation, of taxation, of public debt, public credit, and public revenue; of the management of public property; of commerce; treaties and alliances; peace and war.

Suppose yourself then, as a member of a deliberative assembly, deliberating upon some question, involving these great and important concerns; desirous of communicating your own sentiments, and of influencing the decision of the body you are to address. Your means of persuasion are to be derived from three distinct general sources; having reference respectively, first to the subject of deliberation; secondly to the body deliberating; and thirdly to yourself, the speaker.

1. In considering the subject of deliberation, your arguments may result from the circumstances of legality, of possibility, of probability, of facility, of necessity, or of contingency.

The argument of legality must always be modified by the extent of authority, with which the deliberating body is invested. In its nature it is an argument only applicable to the negative side of the question. It is an objection, raised against the measure under consideration, as being contrary to law. It can therefore have no weight in cases, where the deliberating body itself has the power of changing the law. Thus in a town meeting it would be a decisive objection against any measure proposed, that it would infringe a law of the state. But in the legislature of the commonwealth this would be no argument, because that body is empowered to change the law. Again, in the state legis-

96

lature a measure may be assailed, as contrary to a law of the Union; and the objection, if well founded, must be fatal to the measure proposed; though it could have no influence upon a debate in congress. There however the same argument may be adduced in a different form, if the proposition discussed interferes with any stipulation by treaty, or with the constitution of the United States. The argument of illegality therefore is equivalent to denial of the powers of the deliberating body. It is of great and frequent use in all deliberative discussions; but it is not always that, which is most readily listened to by the audience. Men are seldom inclined to abridge their own authority; and the orator, who questions the competency of his hearers to act upon the subject in discussion, must be supported by proof strong enough to control their inclinations, as well as to convince their reason.

The arguments of possibility and of necessity are those, which first command the consideration of the speaker, whose object is persuasion. Since, if impossibility on the one hand, or necessity on the other, be once ascertained, there is no room left for further deliberation. But, although nothing more can be required for dissuasion, than to show that the intended purpose is impracticable, barely to show its possibility can have very little influence in a debate; and it becomes the province of the speaker to consider its probability and facility; insisting upon every circumstance, which contributes to strengthen these.

It is to be remarked, that the task of dissuasion or opposition is much easier to the orator, than that of persuasion; because for the rejection of a measure it is sufficient to show, either that it is impracticable, or inexpedient. But for its adoption, both its possibility and its expediency must be made to appear. The proposer of the measure must support both the alternatives; the opponent needs only to substantiate one of them.

In discussing the probabilities and facilities of a measure, the speaker often indulges himself in the use of amplification, which here consists in the art of multiplying the incidents, favorable to his purpose, and presenting them in such aspects, as to give each other mutual aid and relief. As in the arguments of impossibility and necessity, he borrows from demonstrative oratory the art of approximation, and represents as impossible that, which is only very difficult, or as absolutely necessary that, which is of extreme importance.

The argument of contingency, or, as it is styled by the ancient rhetoricians, the argument from the event, derives a recommendation of the measure in debate from cither alternative of a successful issue or of failure. An admirable instance of this kind of argument is contained in that advice of Cardinal Wolsey to Cromwell.

"Still in thy right hand carry gentle peace,
To silence envious tongues. Be just and fear not;
Let all the ends, thou aim'st at, be thy country's,
Thy God's, and truth's; then if thou fall'st, O Cromwell,
Thou fall'st a blessed martyr."

2. With regard to the deliberating body, there are two views, in which they must be presented to the speaker's reflections, as accessible to persuasion; the motives, by which they are to be stimulated, and their own manners and character. As motives of persuasion, an orator may address himself to the sense of duty, of honor, of interest, or of passion; motives, which I have here arranged according to the comparative weight, which they ought respectively to carry, but which in the influence, which they really possess over most deliberative assemblies, should be ranked in precisely an inverted order.

Of the sense of duty may be observed, what I have already said of arguments, pointed against the power of the audience. They are indeed only different modifications of the same thing. To call upon the auditory to perform a duty is to speak the language of command; it virtually denies the power of deliberation; and, although the force and efficacy of the appeal may be admitted, it is seldom listened to with pleasure, and always rather controls, than persuades the will.

The most proper and the most powerful arguments, which are usually employed for the purposes of persuasion, are those, addressed to the sense of honor and of interest. But in the choice and management of these you are to consult in a special manner the character of your audience; for one class of men will be most powerfully swayed by motives of honor, while another will most readily yield to the impulse of interest. "The discourse must be accommodated," I am now speaking the words of Cicero, "not only to the truth, but to the taste of the hearers. Observe then first of all, that there are two different descriptions of men; the one rude and ignorant, who always set profit before honor; the other polished and civilized, who prefer honor to every thing. Urge then to the latter of these classes considerations of praise, of honor, of glory, of fidelity, of justice; in short of every virtue. To the former present images of gain, of emolument of thrift; nay, in addressing this kind of men, you must even allure them with the bait of pleasure. Pleasure, always hostile to virtue, always corrupting by fraudulent imitation the very nature of goodness herself, is yet most eagerly pursued by the worst of men; and by them often preferred not only to every instigation of honor, but even to the dictates of necessity. Remember too, that mankind are more anxious to escape evil, than to obtain good; less eager to acquire honor, than to avoid shame. Who ever sought honor, glory, praise, or fame of any kind, with the same ardor, that we fly from those most cruel of afflictions, ignominy, contumely, and scorn? Again, there is a class of men, naturally inclined to honorable sentiments, but corrupted by evil education and vitiated opinions. Is it your purpose then to exhort or persuade, remember that the task before you is that of teaching how to obtain good, and eschew evil. Are you speaking to men of liberal education, enlarge upon topics of praise and honor; insist with the keenest earnestness upon those virtues, which contribute to the common safety and advantage of mankind. But if you are discoursing to gross, ignorant, untutored minds, to them hold up profit, lucre, money-making, pleasure, and escape from pain. Deter them also by the prospect of shame and ignominy; for no man, however insensible to positive glory, is made of such impenetrable stuff, as not to be vehemently moved by the dread of infamy and disgrace." This passage of Cicero, extracted from the dialogue between himself and his son, I recommend to your meditations, as the truly paternal advice of a father to his child. You will find it not only a most useful guide in the practice of deliberative oratory; but, if properly applied, it will furnish you a measure for many an audience, and many a speaker. It is however proper to remind you, that arguments of interest are in some degree purified of their dross by the constitution of our principal deliberative assemblies. They are representative bodies. Their measures operate upon their constituents, more than upon themselves. The interests, to which you appeal in arguing to them, are not their individual interests, but those of the nation. They are therefore often identified with the more elevated topics of honor; since to promote the interest of the people is the highest honor of the legislator. This however is sufficiently understood by most of our deliberative orators. As for you, my young friends, whenever you may be called to deliberate upon the concerns of your country, I trust you will feel, that the honor, as well as the interest of the public, is the object of your pursuit; and without ever forgetting the sacred regard to the general interest, which becomes a virtuous citizen, you will still perceive the immeasurable distance between those regions of the soul, which are open only to the voice of honor, and those, which are trodden by the foot of avarice.

In all numerous assemblies the characters, opinions, and prejudices of the auditors will be various; a certain proportion of them will belong to each of the classes, enumerated by Cicero. In such cases the deliberative orator will find it advisable to introduce a variety of arguments; some addressed to the generous, and some to the selfish feelings; some to the coarsest, and some to the most refined principles of action. But I cannot with Quinctilian discuss the question, how far an orator may exert his talents of persuasion for base and dishonorable purposes; or urge his hearers to actions, which he himself would detest or despise. In judicial controversies, where the discussion relates to time and actions irretrievably past, it may often be the fortune of the orator to defend what he cannot justify; and in the most rigorous court of justice or of honor, he may say, like Shakespeare's Isabella,

"I something do excuse the thing I hate,
For his advantage, whom I dearly love."

But of deliberative eloquence the first principle is sincerity. No honest man would advise what he cannot approve; and a counsellor should disdain to recommend that, which he would not join in executing himself. And this leads me to the third general head, from which the means of persuasion are to be drawn in deliberative oratory, the speaker himself.

3. The eloquence of deliberation will necessarily take much of its color from the orator himself. He must be careful to suit his discourse to his own character and situation. In early life he may endeavour to make strong impression by the airy splendor of his style, contrasted with the unaffected modesty of his address. If advanced in years, and elevated in reputation and dignity, the gravity of his manner and the weight of sentiment should justly correspond with the reverence, due to his station. It is in deliberative assemblies, more than upon any other stage of public speaking, that the good opinion of his auditory is important to the speaker. The demonstrative orator, the lawyer at the bar, derive great advantage from a fair reputation and the good will of their hearers; but the peculiar province of the deliberative speaker is to advise; and what possible effect can be expected from advice, where there is no confidence in the adviser. This subject however is so important and so copious, that I shall reserve it for a separate lecture, in which I propose to consider those qualities of the heart and of the mind, which are or ought to he best adapted to acquire that benevolence of the auditory, which is so powerful an auxiliary to the power of speech. 4t

In treating this part of the subject, Aristotle, according to his usual custom, has pursued his train of analysis to its deepest root, and lo its minutest ramification. Assuming, as a fundamental position, that utility, that is the attainment of good or avoidance of evil, is the ultimate object of all deliberation, he proceeds to enumerate a catalogue of every thing, considered as a blessing by human beings. These blessings he divides into two classes; first of those, universally recognized, and positive; and second of those, which are only relative, and subject to controversy. Among the former he includes virtue, health, beauty, riches, eloquence, arts, and sciences. Among the latter are the least of two evils; the contrary to what your enemy desires; the esteem of the wise; what multitudes desire; and specific objects to individual men. The forms of government also modify the prevailing estimate of good and evil. The end of civil government, under a democracy, is liberty; under an oligarchy, property; under an aristocracy, law; and under a monarchy, security. These are all positive blessings for all mankind. But their relative importance is greatly enhanced, where they constitute the basis of the social compact. The deliberative orator, whose appeal must always be to the sentiments of good and evil, rooted in the minds of his auditory, must always adapt his discourse to that standard measure of the land.

The ancient practice of declamation was an ingenious and useful exercise for improving in the art of deliberative oratory. A character and a situation, generally known in history, were assumed; and the task of the declaimer was to compose and deliver a discourse suitable to them. The Greek and Roman historians introduce speeches of this kind in the midst of their narratives; and among them are so many examples of the most admirable eloquence, that we regret the cold accuracy of modern history, which has discarded this practice, without providing any adequate substitute in its stead.

As amplification has been said to be the favorite resort of demonstrative oratory, the allegation of examples is the most effectual support of deliberative discourses. There is nothing new under the sun. The future is little more than a copy of the past. What hath been shall be again. And to exhibit an image of the past is often to present the clearest prospect of the future. The examples, which are adduced successfully by the deliberative speaker, are of two kinds; first fictitious inventions of his own, second real events, borrowed from historical fact. The first of these are called by Aristotle fables, and the second parables. The fable, which may be invented at the pleasure of the speaker, is more easily applied to his purpose; but the parable, always derived from matter of fact, makes a deeper impression upon the minds of the audience. In the rude ages of society, and among the uncultivated class of mankind, the power of fable, and still more of parable to influence the will, is scarcely conceivable upon mere speculative investigation. But it is demonstrated by the uniform tenor of all human experience. The fable of Menenius Agrippa stands conspicuous in the Roman annals. It pacified one of the most dangerous insurrections, which ever agitated that turbulent but magnanimous people. The scriptures of the old testament bespeak the efficacy of these instruments in a manner no less energetic. But their unrivalled triumph is in the propagation of the Christian gospel; whose exalted founder we are told "needed not that any should testify of man; for he knew what was in man;" and who delivered his incomparable system of morality altogether through the medium of fables and parables; both of which in the writings of the evangelists are included in the latter term. "And with many parables spake he the word unto them, as they were able to hear it; but without a parable spake he not unto them." (Mark, iv. 33.)

The principal feature in the style of deliberative oratory should be simplicity. Not that it disdains, but that it has seldom occasion for decoration. The speaker should be much more solicitous for the thought, than for the expression. This constitutes the great difference between the diction proper for this, and that, which best suits the two other kinds of oratory. Demonstrative eloquence, intended for show, delights in ostentatious ornament. The speaker is expected to have made previous preparation. His discourse is professedly studied, and all the artifices of speech are summoned to the gratification of the audience. The heart is cool for the reception, the mind is at leisure for the contemplation of polished periods, oratorical numbers, coruscations of metaphor, profound reflection, and subtle ingenuity. But deliberative discussions require little more than prudence and integrity. Even judicial oratory supposes a previous painful investigation of his subject by the speaker, and exacts an elaborate, methodical conduct of the discourse. But deliberative subjects often arise on a sudden, and allow of no premeditation. Hearers are disinclined to advice, which they perceive the speaker has been dressing up in his closet. Ambitious ornament should then be excluded, rather than sought. Plain sense, clear logic, and above all ardent sensibility, these are the qualities, needed by those who give, and those who take counsel. A profusion of brilliancy betrays a speaker more full of himself, than of his cause; more anxious to be admired, than believed. The stars and ribbands of princely favor may glitter on the breast of the veteran hero at a birth-day ball; but, exposed to the rage of battle, they only direct the bullet to his heart. A deliberative orator should bury himself in his subject. Like a superintending providence, he should be visible only in his mighty works. Hence that universal prejudice, both of ancient and modern times, against written, deliberative discourses; a prejudice, which bade defiance to all the thunders of Demosthenes. In the midst of their most enthusiastic admiration of his eloquence, his countrymen nevertheless remarked, that his orations "smelt too much of the lamp."

Let it however be observed, that upon great and important occasions the deliberative orator may be allowed a more liberal indulgence of preparation. When the cause of ages and the fate of nations hangs upon the thread of a debate, the orator may fairly consider himself, as addressing not only his immediate hearers, but the world at large; and all future times. Then it is, that, looking beyond the moment, in which he speaks, and the immediate issue of the deliberation, he makes the question of an hour a question for every age and every region; takes the vote of unborn millions upon the debate of a little senate, and incorporates himself and his discourse with the general history of mankind. On such occasions and at such times, the oration naturally and properly assumes a solemnity of manner and a dignity of language, commensurate with the grandeur of the cause. Then it is, that deliberative eloquence lays aside the plain attire of her daily occupation, and assumes the port and purple of the queen of the world. Yet even then she remembers, that majestic grandeur best comports with simplicity. Her crown and sceptre may blaze with the brightness of the diamond, but she must not, like the kings of the gorgeous east, be buried under a shower of barbaric pearls and gold.

Lecture Twelve - Judicial Oratory

IN the two last lectures, which I delivered from this place, I considered the two classes of public orations, usually denominated the demonstrative and the deliberative; pointed out their peculiar characteristics; the ends, to which they are severally directed; and the arguments, especially suited to them. Demonstrative oratory, I informed you, was that species of public speaking, which consists of discourses, formally prepared, and delivered in celebration of some person or public event. I observed that, whether in the form of such public orations, or introduced incidentally into discourses of business deliberative or judicial, it included all panegyric and invective. That praise or censure was its ultimate object; honor and shame the hinges, upon which it revolved. That demonstration in rhetoric bears a meaning very different from demonstration in mathematics. That the demonstration of a pan-egyric is by no means the demonstration of a theorem. The one is incontro-vertible proof; the other is the breath of fame. Thus, originating from the same source, the signification of the word is modified by the science, to which it applies, until in Euclid it conveys the idea of irrefragable proof; in Quinctilian, that of oratorical display. Here a solid substance; there an insub-stantial pageant.

Of deliberative oratory, I remarked, that the final purpose was utility. That its relation was always to future time; its issue a measure to be adopted or rejected; and the subjects within its competency, under our forms of gov-ernment, the most important and extensive of any, in which oratory can be concerned. The difference between deliberative and judicial oratory, of which I am now particularly to speak, is, in relation to the objects of which it treats, the difference between time future and time past. Judicial oratory manages the litigation of causes public or private, civil or criminal, in the courts of justice. In other words it is the eloquence of the bar.

In delivering the precepts of demonstrative and deliberative oratory, little more was necessary than to form a selection, and arrange into a system the rules, prescribed by the great rhetoricians of antiquity. The nature, the char-acter, the purpose of discourses, belonging to these classes, are precisely the same in the present, as in former ages; in our own country, as at Athens and Rome. Not so of judicial oratory. The fundamental principles, upon which a judicial cause must be managed at this time, are as different, as the institu-tions and the forms of proceeding, under which it arises; and, in order safely to apply any part of the doctrines of the ancient rhetoricians to our own us-ages and practices, it will first be necessary to indicate the difference be-tween their judicial institutions and modes of process and ours.

Now the common standard of all judicial arguments, according to Aristotle, Cicero, and Quinctilian, is justice, or equity; which was to be measured some-times by the written laws, and sometimes by natural reason, independent of positive prescription; and sometimes even in contradiction to it. The tribu-nals of the Greeks and Romans consisted of persons, who were judges both of the fact and of the law. They also exercised a sort of dispensing power, and could exempt a party from the operation of the written law in cases, when that was deemed to act too rigorously, and to interfere with the dictates of natural equity. Something of a similar nature is still customary among us in the courts of chancery; institutions originally borrowed from the Roman law, and still governed in a great measure by the principles, established in the code of Justinian. But the powers of our chancery courts are confined within very narrow limits. In this commonwealth they are admitted only within the extent of jurisdiction, allotted to the courts of the union, and are excluded from the cognizance of all criminal cases whatsoever. The courts of common law, before which almost all our judicial controversies are tried, consist not of a single, but of a double tribunal; the judge or judges, who are authorized to decide all questions of law, and the jury, who pronounce upon every question of fact. Hence arises a division of the subject altogether different from that of the ancient rhetors. Instead of inquiring whether his cause rests upon a state of conjecture, of definition, of quantity, or of quality, the American lawyer must ascertain whether he is to try an issue in fact, or an issue in law; a distinction not only much more clear, but much more important, since the issue in fact is to be argued before a jury, and the issue in law before the judges; tribunals differently constituted; consisting of persons different in station, in character, in powers; accessible to arguments of different descriptions; and swayed only by one inviolable common control, the written law. The whole management of the cause and the nature of all the testimonies vary according to the course, which it assumes, of requiring the determination by the verdict of the jury, or by the opinion of the court.

Let it however be remarked, because it is a consideration of material importance to the judicial orator, that this division of powers between the judges and the jury was made by the common law, not so clearly, nor with a definition of boundaries so precise, as to leave these authorities uncontroverted. In England, the country where the common law, together with this system of judicial proceedings, originated, and even in our own country, there have been very sharp disputes how far the authority of the court and jury respectively extend, and where is the line of separation between them. The ancient maxim of the common law was explicit; ad questionem juris respondent judices; ad questionem facti juratores. But in the administration of criminal justice especially it was not so easy to separate the question of law from that of fact, as to say, that they should be tried by different persons. In all trials for crimes the guilt or innocence of the party depends upon the application of the law to the fact; and, when a jury by their verdict pronounce a man guilty, they not only determine the fact, which he has committed, but also the law, by which that fact is made to constitute guilt.

In all general verdicts therefore the jury pronounce both upon the fact and the law. On the other hand, after the cause has been argued by the parties or their counsel to the jury, the judges are in the constant practice of addressing the jury, and stating to them the law, with its application to the facts upon trial. In this part of the judge's duty it is as difficult for him to confine himself exclusively to the consideration of the law, as it is for a jury, without implicating a decision of the law, to pronounce a party guilty. The judge explains to the jury the injunctions of the law upon a given state of facts; and to make his discourse pertinent it must be that identical state of facts, upon which they are to decide. How then can he speak the dictate of the law, without intimating his opinion of the fact? The obstacle is inherent in the nature of the thing; and the division of powers between judge and jury, professed by the common law, is not always practicable. Thus far however the lawyer has an unequivocal rule for the management of his cause. If any question of fact is involved in the controversy, the cause must go to the jury. But if the parties have no dispute upon the facts, and their contest is merely upon the operation of the law, it is within the ex» elusive province of the judge. Hence the parties often have it at their option, whether they will take a trial by the court, or by the jury; and there are certain forms of pleading, suited to produce an issue in law; and others, which are adapted to an issue in fact.

This system of pleas and pleadings, of which in a former lecture I have taken some notice, embraces in substance the whole code of the common law. Of its importance to those of you, who are destined hereafter to the profession of the law, it were needless for me to speak here at large, as it will occupy a great portion of your time and studies, after you shall take your leave of the university, as pupils. But it is strictly within the province of these lectures to mark its operation upon the eloquence of the bar, and to consider it, as one of the causes, which contribute to render all the precepts of ancient rhetoric so inapplicable to the practice of our judicial courts.

The forms of process, both civil and criminal, among the ancients were very simple and very general. In the accusation against Verres Cicero makes an apology to the judges for passing over the licentious debaucheries of that offender's youth; intimating, that their turpitude was so shocking, that he could not describe them without violating his own modesty. Then, addressing himself to the culprit, he says, "fourteen years have elapsed, since you, Verres, held the office of quaestor. From that day to this I put in judgment every thing you have done. Not an hour of your life through that whole period will be found unpolluted by some theft; some baseness; some cruelty; some villany. During those years you successively disgraced the offices of quaestor, of delegate in Asia, of praetor in the city, and of praetor in Sicily. From the functions of these several public stations will arise the fourfold distribution of my whole accusation." From this passage it is apparent, that under a general impeachment the whole life, public and private, of the party charged was open to scrutiny. So that the accuser might prove against him whatever he pleased to consider as an offence, civil, political, or moral. From the oration for Muraena the inference may with equal certainty be drawn, that the forms of pleading in civil causes were substantially not more difficult nor complicated. Cicero speaks of them with contempt; derides them as a compilation of verbose and unmeaning pedantry; and affirms, that amidst the multiplicity of business, with which every hour of his life was loaded, he would undertake to make himself, in three days, a perfect master of the whole science. And from some specimens, which he introduces in his argument, it is apparent, that the same identical forms were susceptible of adaptation to every case, and that the whole compass of legal controversy was reducible to one common rubric.

This looseness in the system of pleadings still continues to characterize the proceedings in the courts, founded upon the principles and governed by the doctrines of the civil law. It was diametrically opposite to the whole spirit and tenor of the common law. By the original genius of the common law a great proportion of every trial, civil or criminal, consisted of the pleadings. Every charge must be precise, specific, single. The violation of law must be alleged in terms as concise and unequivocal, as human wit could devise. Every fact must be narrated with the minutest accuracy of time, place, and circumstance. The answer must be drawn up with the same logical acuteness. Every fact, charged in violation of law, must be met by a direct denial, in terms expressly adapted to the nature of the charge. Every accusation in vague or general terms, unsupported by positive law, must be repelled by an appeal to the judge, whether the party was bound to answer. The issue consisted of a single question, either of fact for the decision of the jury, or of law for the determination of the judge.

In process of time however, as the increase of commercial intercourse multiplied the sources of litigation, this extreme strictness in the forms of the common law became often inconvenient and troublesome. The hedges of special pleading were found sometimes to obstruct the avenues to truth. The excess of caution sometimes opened to chicanery the door, which it closed upon justice. A multitude of suitors were driven to seek redress in the chancery courts; the pliancy of whose forms was more easily accommodated to the complicated transactions of commerce. Hence arose a conflict of jurisdictions between the courts of common law and of chancery; and, although the former eventually maintained their ascendency, they gradually relaxed from the rigor of their system of pleading, and by the invention of various legal fictions assimilated their forms of process in a multitude of cases to those of the civil or Roman law. The late Lord Mansfield, who for a long series of years presided alternately in the chancery and in the highest common law court of England, went so far towards affecting a complete revolution in the doctrine of pleadings, that his successors have found it expedient to retrace many of his steps. In our own country the prejudices against chancery courts have been much stronger, than they ever were in England. They were altogether excluded from the jurisprudence of this state before the revolution, and until the judiciary system of the United States obtained for them a partial admission. But the common law doctrine of pleadings has occasionally been modified by our local statutes, and by the practice of the bar. And the enlargements, which Lord Mansfield opened to the British pleaders, have generally been imitated in our courts. But all the common law maxims of pleading still remain in full force and unimpaired in all cases of criminal prosecutions. Their operation indeed generally affects only the accuser. The defendent, or prisoner at the bar, is never perplexed with any subtleties of pleading. A simple declaration, that he is not guilty, termed the general issue, reserves to him every advantage of defence, which he can derive from the facts or the law. But the prosecutor cannot advance a step without a written accusation, penned with the most scrupulous, technical accuracy. There is no possibility of putting in judgment every thing, that a man has done for fourteen years. No prosecutor would be suffered, upon a charge of malversation in office, to rake up the rankness of a dissolute youth for the purpose of heaping the measure of opprobrium upon the prisoner. Had the judges upon the trial of Verres possessed powers, circumscribed within the limits of our institutions, almost all the eloquence of Cicero would have been not merely superfluous, but inadmissible. The official misdemeanors would have been cognizable by one tribunal; the private wrongs by another; the thefts and acts of cruelty by a third; and in all, every infraction of right must have been charged in language, stripped of every blossom of oratory by an article of impeachment, a writ of trespass, or an indictment. These written accusations would have marked the limits, within which all his evidence and all his argument must have been confined. Like the stakes and floating buoys, which edge the narrow channel of an expansive but shallow river, they would have continually reminded him, that he could not proceed a foot beyond them without stranding. Not a witness could he have called to any offence, not specified in the pleadings. Not a word could he without rebuke have uttered, unconnected with his allegations and his proofs. Had he lifted his torch upon the midnight revels of his adversary's boyish days, some learned judge would have told him, that those scenes might be left to their own darkness. Had he apostrophized the Alban groves, and lakes, and fountains, he would have been stopped by a hint from the bench, that he was traveling out of the record.

While the shackles of pleading thus restrain the excursive powers of oratory on the part of the prosecution, those of the defendant, or party accused, are scarcely less cramped by another limitation of our judicial authorities. The judges of ancient times had not only the powers of deciding both upon the law and the fact; they also exercised a sort of dispensing power; or rather the power of pardoning offences was accumulated upon that of inflicting punishment. This power of pardon has in our country been most carefully separated from the judicial functions, and vested exclusively in the executive government. Among the ancients the judges had before them not only the question, whether the accused was guilty or innocent; but the subsequent question, how far his punishment should be aggravated or mitigated; and whether it should be inflicted or remitted. This discretionary power of determining the degree of punishment was even paramount to the written and positive law; a striking example of which we have in the sentence, passed and executed upon the accomplices of Catiline. The law was clear and express, that no Roman citizen should be punished with death. Yet the associates of Catiline were executed by a decree of the senate. The question, whether they should suffer death, or only perpetual imprisonment with confiscation of their estates, was earnestly debated in senate. The fourth of what are called Cicero's orations against Catiline is upon this question; and in Sallust you have read the speeches of Caesar and of Cato upon the same occasion. From this latitude of discretion in the powers of the court we perceive the foundation of all those appeals to the passions of the judges, so earnestly recommended by the precepts of Cicero, and so often exemplified in his practice. Hence it was, that every man under accusation was expected to throw himself upon the compassion of his judges; to assume the garb of mourning; to apply for the countenance and solicitations of his friends; to exhibit his family in the agonies of distress; and to count upon the tears of his infant children among his most powerful means of defence.

But our courts of justice possess neither the power of aggravating nor of remitting a punishment. Guilty or not guilty is the only question for the determination of the jury upon criminal prosecutions; and this question they are solemnly sworn to decide according to the evidence. When their verdict is delivered, their functions are at an end. The punishment of the offender is not within their province. The sentence is awarded by the judges, to whom in this respect some discretionary power is entrusted, in cases less than capital, to proportion the penalty to the degree of the offence. But even this discretion is very scantily bestowed. In all cases of life and death, and in many others, the judges are merely the living voices of the law; empowered barely to pronounce the decree, which that has prepared before the commission of a crime. The administration of public justice is in substance a strict logical syllogism, of which the written law forms the major proposition, the verdict of the jury the minor, and the sentence of the court the conclusion. Every man, guilty of treason, shall be put to death, says the written law, A. B. is guilty of treason, says the verdict of the jury; therefore, says the sentence of the court, A. B. shall be put to death.

This distribution of the judicial powers between judge and jury, together with this separation of the dispensing or pardoning power from both, affords a copious and a profitable subject of reflection to the legal student, and to the philosophical inquirer into the organization and principles of our government. It is a distribution and division perhaps as important to the liberties of a nation, as the separation of the legislative and executive powers, and the division of the former between two assemblies. But in the light, in which I now consider it, I am barely to point out its necessary effect upon judicial eloquence; and you will immediately perceive, that it cuts up by the roots all the precepts of ancient rhetoric, which place the perfection of the art in the address, with which the orator assails the passions of the judge. It calls for a management of causes upon principles not merely different, but opposite to those of antiquity. The common standard of judicial arguments is no longer natural justice or equity, but positive law. The first fountains of the art are no longer the same.

It is indeed true, that this difference is much greater in criminal, than in civil jurisprudence. An estimate of damages for a breach of contract, a settlement of accounts between merchants, the mere controversies of bargain and sale, are determinable in all ages and nations upon nearly the same principles; and in the very few orations of Greece and Rome, still extant, of this description, there is little, which might not with equal propriety be said in a modern court of justice. And yet, if a modern lawyer were to open an argument to a court, as Cicero begins his oration for Quinctius, by observing, that the personal influence of the suitor and the eloquence of his counsel were the two principal sources of success, he would run a great risk of a severe reprimand from the bench. If an American barrister should undertake by an elaborate argument to prove, that the Abbé Delille was a citizen of the United States, because he was an excellent French poet, if all the muses should combine to compose his oration, not five sentences of it would he be suffered to deliver. Yet examine that inimitable, that immortal oration for Archias, and amidst that unbounded blaze of eloquence, with which it beams, observe the nucleus of argument, upon which it revolves. Archias was a Roman citizen, because he was a Greek poet. Were a counsellor in the courts of these states to start a train of reasoning like this, the judges would instantly arrest the career of his oratory by calling for the certificate of naturalization.

Yet we are not to conclude, that judicial eloquence is to be excluded from the systems of modern rhetoric. Restricted and limited, as the orator at the bar must now be, there is yet an unmeasured difference between speaking well and ill on a judicial trial. If there is less room for powerful addresses to the passions of the judges, there is more necessity for convincing their understandings. The success of a suitor does not depend upon the eloquence of his counsel; but his failure may follow from the want of it. Oratory will not prove so often the victorious auxiliary to a bad cause; but it will be an equally necessary aid to a good one.

I have thought it necessary to lay open to your minds the primary causes, which make it necessary to vary the very principles of judicial oratory from those transmitted by our ancient teachers. Many of their precepts however, in detail, may still be used to great advantage. In a subsequent lecture I shall notice those of their instructions, which are still susceptible of adoption or modification, and suggest some further observations respecting the course, to be pursued in judicial causes tinder our own institutions.

Lecture Thirteen - Judicial Oratory

FROM the tenor of my preceding lectures you must have collected, that, while the principles of demonstrative and deliberative oratory are the same in every age and country, where the art is practised, those of judicial eloquence must be varied and modified by the laws and judicial institutions of the time and place. The importance of this idea must plead my apology for dwelling with earnestness upon its development, for recurring again to it at this time, and for presenting it, with the hope of giving it additional illustration, under another point of view to your reflections.

Observe then, that demonstrative and deliberative oratory are not of necessity connected with any particular social institutions. The subjects of panegyric, of invective, or of deliberation, are indeed diversified under different forms of government, but do not necessarily result from them. An eulogy or a philippic may be pronounced by an individual of one nation upon the subject of another. Deliberation may occur between persons, bound by no social compact together. Civil or political institutions may incidentally be the subjects, but are not of the essence of such discourses. Praise, censure, exhortation, and advice, are dispensed and bestowed by man, as a rational being, to his fellow creature, endowed with the same faculty. The Greeks and Romans, as we have seen, allowed much of the same latitude to their municipal tribunals. But under our improved theories of natural and social rights positive institution is the indispensable ingredient of all judicial discourse. The whole amount of every trial can be neither more nor less, than a conflict between law and transgression. To try a man by the laws of one nation for an offence against the laws of another would be at once the extreme of oppression and the height of absurdity. The common standard then, by which all judicial argument must be measured, is law; the whole drift of an advocate's eloquence, to display the conformity between the cause of his client and the law; the whole purpose of a prosecutor, to vindicate its violation; the whole defence of innocence, to disprove its infringement.

Now the particulars in our judicial institutions of the most material importance to the forensic speaker are three.

1. The division of all offences against the laws into public and private wrongs; Math the consequent distinction between courts of criminal and civil jurisdiction.

2. The division of public wrongs into two classes; personal wrongs, which may be committed by every man, as an individual; and official crimes or misdemeanors, committed by public officers, and triable by impeachment. And

3. The division of powers, mentioned in my last lecture, between the judges and jury, in the course of ordinary jurisdiction; and the separation of the power of pardoning offences from both.

1. Under our state of society every individual is entitled to certain rights, recognised and defined by the original social compact, or by the laws, enacted under it. It is the primary object of civil society and of government to protect every individual in the enjoyment of these rights. Some of them are of such magnitude, that their support and vindication are exclusively retained in the hands of the body politic itself, while others are secured to the individual only by a pledge of assistance from the public authority, whenever its aid may be found necessary. Such is the distinction, so well-known to all lawyers, between private and public wrongs; the private wrong consisting of the violation only of the right of individuals; the public wrong, in an outrage upon the rights of the whole political society. Thus a breach of promise, a non-payment of debt, or a disputed title to land, is barely a private wrong, for the redress of which the injured party is authorized to call upon the powers of government; but which he must first prove by suit in his own name, and at his own risk, before the competent tribunals. But treason, robbery, murder, theft, and all those offences, which are included under the denomination of crimes and misdemeanors, are of so much importance to the whole society, that, although the direct injury, committed by them, often affects only an individual, the cause is adopted, as that of the nation; and the punishment of the offender is prosecuted in the name of the sovereign. Hence the distinc-

tion between the civil and criminal jurisdiction of our courts; a distinction sedulously to be remembered by the judicial orator, because, although these jurisdictions are among us united in our highest courts, yet there are different rules of evidence, different maxims of law, and different modes of practice, established in them. Under the civil jurisdiction the cause is brought forward by the party, and is called an action; under the criminal jurisdiction it is prosecuted by the government. In civil causes the controversy is only between two or more individuals, the plaintiff and the defendant. In criminal causes it is between the public on one side, and the person accused on the other. The right of action must be pursued by the individual himself, or by his agents. The public wrong is not entrusted to the pursuit of any individual. Select bodies of men are from time to time appointed, whose task it is to inquire into all such offences, committed in their vicinity, and to present them to the competent courts for trial. The accusation is drawn up under the name of an indictment, and is managed by a permanent public officer. The person accused is then arraigned, and usually pleads, that he is not guilty of the offence, charged against him; and by this answer he makes it necessary for the attorney general, or person conducting the prosecution, to prove both the law and the facts. If the accusation fail in the proof of either, the accused must be discharged.

The influence of these particulars in our judicial institutions upon the eloquence of the bar will be most readily discerned, by recurring to the instructions of the ancient rhetoricians for the management of judicial argument, and observing what would now be their application.

They make no distinction between causes of civil and of criminal jurisdiction. Their rules and precepts are all calculated for the management of criminal prosecution or defence; and they tell us, that all the necessary variations upon the conduct of civil causes will be so obvious to the practitioner, that they need not to be specially indicated. In our courts so great is the difference between these two descriptions of cases, that the same rules, which would be prescribed for the one, must be proscribed for the other; and the same practice would appear on one side in the form of injunction, on the other in that of prohibition.

Thus for example Quinctilian lays it down, that, in discussing the state of conjecture upon a question, whether the party accused is guilty of the crime, charged against him, the course of inquiry will be directed to three distinct points; the will, the power, and the fact; that is, that the natural division of the prosecutor's argument must be to prove, first, that the accused had the will to commit the offence; secondly, that he had the power; and thirdly, that he actually did commit it. The means of investigating the first of these points, the will, are largely discanted upon by Quinctilian. The object was to scrutinize the motives of the inculpated party; to pry into his general impulses to action, resulting either from personal character or from special inducement. Thus, if a man was accused of murder, his prosecutor was to labor in the first instance to establish the belief, that his personal character was bold, rash,

111

violent, cruel; that he was addicted to turbulent and angry passions; or that his interest was liable to be promoted by the result of the act. The argument, derived from interest, was indeed deemed so forcible, that we learn from Cicero, it was a general salvo for all deficiencies of other evidence in the practice of a celebrated Roman judge, whose only question to ascertain the criminal in all doubtful cases was, cui bono; who was to be the gainer by the deed. A great proportion of argument, in all the judicial orations of Cicero himself, is devoted to this investigation of motives, or research into the will. His address in handling the subject will always command our admiration; and the inquiry naturally leads an ingenious and reflecting mind into a profound and acute perception of the operations of the human heart. But the principles of our criminal jurisprudence by no means admit so great a latitude of inquiry, nor open such a range for eloquence upon presumptions, drawn from the will. The humane maxim of the common law considers every man as innocent, until he is proved guilty. The general reputation, the personal disposition, or even the incitements of passion or interest to the commission of a criminal act, may indeed occasionally have an involuntary weight upon the mind of a juror; but they are scarcely ever topics, upon which a prosecutor can enlarge. The sound and merciful logic of our laws always infers the motive from the action, and not the action from the motive. The mercies of the common law are not entrusted to the discretion, nor to the passions of individual judges; they are converted into fixed and uniform principles. In our criminal jurisprudence justice herself holds an uneven balance. She never lifts her scales without throwing the weight of mercy into that of the accused. She lays no claim to impartiality. She avows freely her preference, that ten guilty should escape, rather than that one innocent should suffer. She not only permits, but commands her judges to be of counsel for the prisoners. She directs juries, even though the balance of testimony should preponderate against the accused, yet if a reasonable doubt can be raised in his favor, to dismiss him unpunished. She catches with eagerness at every gleam of probability, which leads to acquittal. She admits with reluctance even a certainty, which compels conviction.

Hence you will readily perceive, that the principles for the management of a criminal prosecution are toto coelo different from those for conducting its defence. The inquiry into the will, the motives, or the interest of the party can seldom afford any assistance to the prosecutor; but it may be of material service to the defendant. The attorney general is rarely indulged with an opportunity of arguing the guilt of a culprit from his personal character, or common fame. Still less can he urge, as a proof against him, that his interest was promoted by the event. But these topics may be employed with success in favor of the accused. An irreproachable character, a fair reputation, are presumptions in favor of innocence, of which a skilful advocate never fails to avail himself. Still more confidently may he rely upon the efficacy of arguments to show, that there was no temptation of interest, that could operate upo«i his client to stimulate his commission of the act; and if his interest can be shown to have suffered detriment from the issue, it furnishes an argument of the most conclusive nature in his behalf.

The second source of argument, mentioned by Quinctilian, is the power; a track of reasoning more exclusively confined to the defence of causes in our criminal courts, than even that of the will. A public prosecutor, who should at this day attempt to raise the conclusion, that a prisoner at the bar was guilty of the crime charged against him, upon so frail a basis, as that he had the power to commit it, would be suspected of having lost his senses. But nothing is more natural and more visual in a course of defence, than for the party to alledge, that the act imputed to him had not been in his power. The most usual form, in which this defence appears, is in undertaking to prove, that the accused was at the time, when the crime was committed, in another place; a defence perfectly decisive of the cause, when clearly made out; but which has been so often resorted to by desperate offenders, who depend only upon the testimony of their accomplices to accredit the fact, that to set up an alibi is proverbial among those, who are conversant in the practice of our criminal courts, as the last, desperate refuge of an all but convicted felon. In ordinary cases therefore this defence terminates in a question upon the credibility of the witnesses; for however desirous all juries are to find the person upon trial innocent, they understand too well the common refuges of guilt, lightly to credit the pretence of an alibi.

There remains then only the third of the points, recommended by Quinctilian to the consideration of the judicial orator, which in our courts of justice affords materials for argument both upon the prosecution and the defence; that is, the discussion of the fact. Upon our principles the fact, once proved, renders all investigations of the will or the power useless; and without proof of the fact no indication of the will, no demonstration of the power is admissible.

The general result, which the judicial orator must draw from the division of offences into public and private wrongs, and the consequent distinction between the civil and criminal jurisdictions are, that a speaker at the bar must conduct the prosecution and the defence of a criminal cause upon principles altogether different, and in some respects opposite; and that those for the management of a civil action again essentially differ from both. On a civil suit, a mere controversy between party and party, the rule of perfect impartiality returns to govern our courts and juries. No bias in favor of a defendant is allowed; no destruction; no permission even to the judges to be of counsel for him; no direction to the jury to grasp at every rational doubt, as conclusive in his favor. Justice again becomes even-handed; she balances probabilities; she admits on both sides inquiries into the will and the power, as well as into the fact; she receives the testimony of written depositions, which on all criminal trials she rejects. The parties stand in court on equal ground, and their advocates possess precisely the same latitude of discussion. This difference is peculiarly remarkable in those cases, which are included both among the public and private wrongs; such as assault and battery, defamation, and libels. For these acts a man is liable to a double prosecution; one by the party injured, for the damage specially sustained by him; the other by the public, for the violation of the peace. But so different are the maxims, upon which these two trials of the same act are conducted, that on one of them the testimony of the complainant himself is received, while on the other it is rejected; nor is it unusual to see a man acquitted and convicted of the same act by these two forms of process.

2. The division of public wrongs into two classes, personal offences, triable, as I have above described, by jury, and official offences, triable by impeachment, forms the second of those circumstances, upon which every modern American system of rhetoric ought to be constructed.

By the constitution of the United States, and by that of this commonwealth, the senate of the Union and of the state are respectively constituted courts for the trial of offences, committed by public officers in their official capacity. The power of impeaching such offenders is in both cases exclusively given to the house of representatives; and the power of the senate extends no further, than to remove the person impeached from office, and declare him disqualified from holding any other office of honor, trust, or profit. The operation of this trial is only upon a man's official capacity; for he may individually be tried again by indictment for the same act, upon which he has been tried by impeachment.

Impeachments are events of so rare occurrence, and a judicial orator will so rarely be called to take a part in them, that it can scarcely be necessary to spend much time in prescribing a formal system -of rules for his observance. As the power of accusation is entrusted only to a branch of the legislature, its exercise is assimilated as much to deliberative, as to judicial functions. The question in every individual case, whether the house will impeach, is purely deliberative; and is decided like all others of a similar nature. When the impeachment is resolved upon, the house usually appoint a small number of their own members, as managers for its prosecution. The senate sit as judges both of the law and of the fact; but a concurrence of two thirds of the members is essential to the conviction of the person impeached.

The field of argument, opened upon a trial of this description, is obviously very different from that presented by an ordinary jury trial. The subject in controversy is the discharge of official functions; the questions at issue are upon the nature and extent of public duties; and the interests implicated are those of the nation at large. The principles of the ordinary criminal jurisprudence are partially, but not entirely applicable to the proceedings of this extraordinary tribunal. The judges are less rigorously bound to consult alone the prescriptions of positive law. Moral and even political considerations may contribute in some degree to the formation of their judgment. They may therefore be urged both upon the attack and the defence of these charges. But if it should ever hereafter be the lot of any of you, as probably it may, to be called to act in cases of this nature, whether as prosecutors or as judges, the most important precept I can give you, and that, which I most earnestly wish you from this day to remember, is never to make impeachment, nor, as far as may depend on you, never to suffer it to be made an engine of party.

3. The division of the judiciary powers between the judges and the jury, and the separation of the dispensing or pardoning power from both, have already been largely considered in my preceding lecture. You have there seen, that in general questions of law are to be argued to the judges, and questions of fact to the jury. The materials of argument are therefore as different, as the characteristics of the persons, to whom they are addressed. To the bench their common centre of reference is the law; to the jury they hinge almost entirely upon the evidence.

The judges are always few in number; often there is but one. They are usually men of profound legal learning, trained to their office by a long course of study, and a career of full practice in the profession. The tenure, by which they hold their offices, is permanent during good behaviour; which in ordinary cases is equivalent to a tenure for life. The rule of their duty is uniform and invariable; having nothing to consult but the law. With minds so highly cultivated, and with a line of duty so clearly marked out, they are generally inaccessible to any influence of passion. They are not to be swayed by the artifices, which are sometimes successful in deliberative assemblies. It is vain to address any application to their hopes or their fears. They are not allowed even to indulge the most amiable weakness of compassion. As ministers of the law, they are bound indeed to dispense the mercies of the law; but these, as I have shown you, are not left to their discretion. The benefits, provided for the party upon trial, are secured to him as a right. They are not discretionary in the breast of the judge. These are all intended for the protection of innocence. Mercy should sometimes also be extended to the guilty. But this power the laws have chosen to vest elsewhere. A compassionate would therefore be a guilty judge. When the judge ascends the tribunal, he must leave his heart behind him. There he must be all head; all intellect; impassive and impenetrable to the sensibilities, the most endearing to the human character. Whatever conviction can be carried to his mind must be accomplished by the means of cool, solid reasoning and lucid development.

Our juries consist of a very different description of men. They are occasional and not permanent bodies; selected for a single cause, and consisting of the same men, only during one session of a court. They are appointed from among the respectable citizens of various employments; but the members of all the learned professions are either exempted or excluded from service upon them. There are of course no regularly bred lawyers, and few men of refined mental cultivation among them. Their principal, and in most cases their only functions are to ascertain controverted facts. For even when they decide upon the law, as by a general verdict they always may, they usually receive it from the bench, and pronounce conformably to the opinion of the judge.

Thus then it follows as a corollary from our judicial institutions, that an argument to the court is essentially a disquisition of law; an argument to the jury, a comment upon evidence. In both the ultimate object of the orator is not to persuade, but to convince; the triumph of the art to operate not upon the will, but upon the understanding. To accomplish this an able advocate must vary the style and substance of his discourse to suit the diversities of situation and characters of the two auditories. To the bench his most powerful instrument of conviction is profound and accurate deduction. To the jury his most effectual weapon is copious elucidation. His address to the judge should be concise without obscurity; to the jury, copious without confusion. He must incessantly bear in mind, that the court is not an ignorant, nor the jury a learned body of men. The consummation of eloquence is in the adaptation of the ideas in the speech to the ideas already in the minds of the hearers. To the judge it will suffice to present results. To the jury you must often unfold principles.

The customary mode of transacting business in our judicial courts makes it seldom possible, and perhaps never advisable to address either the bench or the jury in speeches, previously written. In criminal causes the testimony must all be oral, delivered by witnesses in open court. The cause always takes its complexion from their relations, and after they have been heard the counsel are scarcely ever allowed any time for preparation. Their discourse must be immediate and extemporaneous; and when a case comes on for trial, the advocates, by whom it is managed, seldom precisely know themselves what its state will be. The examination and cross-examination of the witnesses is itself one of the severest tests of a lawyer's talents. The testimony often assumes its color from the feelings and character of the witnesses. They are sometimes unable and sometimes unwilling to testify what they really know. They are sometimes inclined to put their own gloss upon the facts, to which they are knowing, and sometimes need reminding, that the truth and the whole truth are not always identically the same. They are often discovered to have their partialities, and to sympathize too much with one of the parties. Even with a sacred and inviolate regard for truth, different witnesses often relate the same transaction with great diversities of circumstance. One incident struck the observation or remains upon the memory of one witness; another upon that of his neighbour. To eviscerate the truth from a body of testimony is perhaps the most arduous task of a modern lawyer; but it seldom admits of previous preparation, and never of writing. Upon civil causes, although depositions of absent witnesses are admitted, the course of trial is commonly of the same kind, and alike extemporaneous. Arguments to the court are more susceptible of previous writing. As they are exclusively confined to the establishment of some doubtful point of law, they consist of a continual chain of deductions, resembling mathematical, rather than oratorical demonstration. But sometimes the opinion of the court is settled before the argument commences. The advocate often asserts positions, which the judge, deeming erroneous, immediately controls or denies. Every interruption of this kind would disconcert a written speech. So that of all public speaking judicial oratory is that, which most requires previous meditation, and least admits of previous writing.

Yet although the eloquence of the bar so materially differs from that, of which Cicero and Quinctilian were masters, in one respect it still retains the same character. The bar is beyond all question the scene of the greatest difficulty to the public speaker, and that, where the rarest combination of talents is indispensable for the attainment of eminence. The demonstrative orator stands alone. He has no antagonist before him. He has had his own time for every species of preparation. He runs for an undisputed prize, and bears away the palm, if he can but succeed to amuse his hearer. The deliberative speaker must make his way against opposition, but he stands only as one among many. His sources of argument are more abundant and more general. Deliberation relates to future time. The decision turns upon a balance of contingencies. The question of expediency is decided by a majority of votes, but leaves it still undetermined whose foresight of futurity was most accurate. The out-numbered voters may still appeal to the issue of future events. But at the bar time past, right and wrong, existing law, are the materials in contest. Property, liberty, reputation, life, are the objects at stake. The fame and fortune of the speaker himself are bound up in the issue with the dearest interests of his client. He stands under the eye of a sharp-sighted adversary, eager to snatch at every error, and to turn every unwary concession to his own advantage; of learned and able judges, jealous of their own honor and reputation, quick to detect false reasoning, fastidious to trivial declamations, and ever cautious to shelter their understanding from being taken by surprise. He is ever liable to be misled by his own client, whose self-delusion and partialities often represent his cause more favorable, than it proves upon investigation; and he must be incessantly upon the watch against the arts of a zealous opponent. In the management of an important cause, an advocate seems placed in a state of warfare against all mankind. The antagonist is an open and inveterate foe. The judge must at least be redeemed from neutrality to join his side; and the client himself, by his anxieties, his fears, and his prejudices, hangs continual and irretrievable ruin over his cause. Success is attended with little honor. It passes but for the ordinary course of justice. Failure is accumulated mortification. It consists not alone in the sentence of the court. A triumphant adversary, and a client, as prone after the issue to impute his misfortune to his counsel, as he was to prepare it by his mismanagement, are the ordinary and unavoidable aggravations of defeat. This active and incessant collision however sharpens the faculties, while it tries the temper of the mind. It brings every talent at once to the test, and to the light. Men of other occupations may have feeble capacities without exposure, or great abilities without discovery. As a speaker at the bar, a man must open to public view all the strength and all the weakness of his mind. Dullness has no refuge from detection. Envy has no shroud for the kindling radiance of genius. The first and most distinguished station in the ranks of oratory must still be assigned to the eloquence of the bar.

Lecture Fourteen - Eloquence of the Pulpit

THE purpose of my lectures hitherto has been in the first instance to make you familiarly acquainted with the principles, transmitted in the writings of the ancient rhetorical masters; and in the next to discriminate those parts of their precepts, which were inseparably connected with the social institutions and manners of the ages and nations, for which they wrote, from those, which, being founded upon the broad and permanent basis of human nature, are still applicable, and will ever retain their force, while gratitude and admiration shall swell the voice of praise; while freedom shall prompt to deliberation, and while justice shall hold her balance upon earth. For the doctrines of demonstrative and deliberative oratory we have little else to do, but to receive and register in our memory the instructions of our ancient guides. But we have been compelled to depart widely from them in tracing the proper course of judicial eloquence; and we are now to enter upon an element, where their guidance entirely fails us. The eloquence of the pulpit is to the science of rhetoric what this western hemisphere is to that of geography. Aristotle and Quinctilian are as incompetent to mark its boundaries, as Pausanias or Strabo to tell us the latitude of Davis' Straights or Cape Horn. In exploring this new region, like Columbus on his first voyage to this continent, we find our magnet has deserted us. Our needle points no longer to the pole.

Pulpit oratory may be considered, as coeval with the first introduction of Christianity. And it has undoubtedly been one of the most effectual means, by which that religion with all its blessings has been so extensively propagated throughout the earth. It has been practised at every period and in every region, favored with the Christian dispensation; and during several centuries preserved the only glimmering of literature and eloquence, which remained in the world.

The opinions respecting the substance and the manner, most proper for the addresses of the Christian orator, have fluctuated with the revolutions of doctrines and of taste. At one time the pulpit has been made the vehicle of unintelligible mysticism; at another of unfathomable metaphysics; at a third of fanatical inflammation. It has been the instrument of the worst abuses of the Romish church, and the most effectual weapon of the reformation. Athanasius, Peter the Hermit, Wicliff, Huss, Luther, and Calvin, successively and successfully employed this mighty engine for the propagation of error and of truth. During the space of four hundred years it poured the myriads of Europe upon the shores of Palestine, to recover from infidels the sepulchre of Christ. For three succeeding centuries it armed nation against nation upon questions of speculative doctrine and ecclesiastical discipline. Since the invention of printing its powers have indeed been more circumscribed, both by the participation and by the control of that art. Yet to this day it remains among the most energetic instruments of power, exercised upon mankind.

Many modern writers of learning and genius have written upon the theory of pulpit oratory; but they have treated it in a manner so different from that, which was pursued by the ancient rhetoricians, that it will not be easy to assimilate this to the other parts of these lectures. To give the whole that unity and consistency of plan, which is best adapted to your information, it will be most advisable to apply the principles and the method of Aristotle, so far as they can be applied, to this more recent species of public speaking.

What then is the end of pulpit oratory? What is that common central point, round which the eloquence of the sacred orator should revolve; bearing the same relation to his discourse, which we have seen praise and censure bear to demonstrative, utility to deliberative, and law to judicial orations?

The functions of the Christian divine in the pulpit are of two kinds; in one of which he addresses his hearers, and in the other the supreme Creator. In one he speaks to his fellow mortals, in the other, to their Maker. In one he is the monitor of their duties, in the other, the organ of their wants. The ultimate object in both cases is the same, to improve the condition of the auditory. But the means are different, being in the one case by obtaining the favor of providence, in the other by their own advancement in virtue. Life and immortality, the happiness of this world and of the next, these are the objects, which should inspire every word, uttered by the divine from the sacred desk. But the form and the substance of the discourse must be diversified according to the office, in which he is engaged. Neither the matter nor the style of address can be the same in expostulating to mortals upon their own obligations, and in supplicating the Father of the universe for his favor and forgiveness.

There are several sects of Christians, who have judged it proper not to leave the subject nor the language of social prayer discretionary with individual divines; but hive regulated the intercessions in public worship by the establishment of settled forms of prayer, diversified and adapted to the conditions and situations of men. Among those classes of Christians this part of the minister's duty requires only the talent of reading well; the proper observations upon which will arise in another part of the course. But when the divine is expected to compose, as well as to pronounce these addresses to the Father of spirits, the execution of the task becomes one of the most important parts of his duty.

The purposes of social worship are specifically and accurately enumerated in a passage of the episcopal liturgy. They are there declared to be first, confession of sins; secondly, the return of thanks for benefits received; thirdly, the praise of the Creator's transcendent perfections; and fourthly, petition, founded on the wants of the congregation, whether spiritual or corporeal. Of these four distinct purposes there are two, derived from the attributes of the Creator, and two from the necessities of the creature. Confession and petition are founded upon the consciousness of our own infirmities, manifested in the former case by our transgressions in time past; in the latter, by that incessant recurrence of wants, which from the cradle to the grave beset our animal and corporeal nature; and by those necessities equally urgent, which assail the imbecility of our minds. Confession therefore has always reference to past and supplication to future time. Another distinction to be drawn is, that confession is always general. Supplication is principally special. The minister makes a general acknowledgment for himself and his congregation of those sins, errors, and imperfections, which are incident to all mankind; but he is neither required nor authorized to make confession of any individual or particular sin. But besides the general petitions, alike applicable to all men and at all times, there are special occasions, which give rise to particular supplications in behalf of individual persons or families. Thanksgiving and praise are acts of immediate homage to the Sovereign of the universe. The first resulting from a grateful sense of those innumerable blessings, received at his hands, by which we live, and move, and have our being. The last, from that wonder and veneration, mingled with love, which the displays of infinite benevolence and unbounded power necessarily enkindle in the human heart. In these constituent parts of prayer there is also a difference corresponding with that, noticed in the two preceding. Thanksgiving is offered for benefits, specially conferred upon ourselves; praise, for the general attributes of excellence, belonging exclusively to the Deity. Thanksgiving is the return of grateful hearts for their own enjoyments; praise is the general tribute of benediction for those energies and bounties, which created and preserve the universe. From the analysis of the several principles, upon which associated prayer is composed, will result the proper materials to be used in each of its departments; and the minister will readily perceive the manner, best suited to each part of the service, by reflecting on the special characters, by which it is distinguished.

Some of the ancient rhetoricians divided all eloquence into reasoning and feeling; addressed the one to the understanding, and the other to the passions; under which are included oil the accesses to the will of man. The orators of ancient times employed both of these powers in every kind of public speaking, to which they were accustomed. The judicial eloquence of modern times, as I have explained to you, is almost exclusively confined to the avenue of the understanding. The eloquence of the pulpit in prayer is still more rigorously limited to that of feeling. It neither requires nor admits of argument. The object of the speaker is neither persuasion nor conviction. It is the prostration of the creature before his Maker. It is the effusion of sentiment and of duty. Its essential characters are ardor and simplicity. Coldness and prayer carry an inconsistency in the very terms. All the objects of prayer are calculated to excite the most active and vivid sentiments, which can arise in the heart of man. "Words that burn" are the native language of deep feeling. They can never be translated into the dialect of a temperate, much less of a frozen region. Affectation is yet more irreconcilable to the spirit of prayer, than coldness. All affectation is a species of hypocrisy. Affectation in prayer is hypocrisy of the darkest hue, the hypocrisy of religion.

120

It might be supposed superfluous to deliver any precepts for the composition of prayer, other than those contained in the scriptures. The Founder of Christianity himself taught his disciples how to pray, both by precept and example. He warned them against the ostentatious hypocrisy of the pharisees, who displayed themselves in the synagogues and comers of the streets "to be seen of men," and against the affected elegance of the heathens, who used vain repetitions, and thought to be heard for their much speaking. These instructions, with a proper attention to the comprehensive and perfect simplicity of that form of prayer, which he gave as a model to his disciples, will render every critical injunction unnecessary, and would seem to render it impossible, that a Christian pulpit should ever resound with pompous inanity, to be heard of men, or with vain repetitions, having no claim to be heard, but that of much speaking.

The other department of pulpit oratory, the only one, which the modern writers upon eloquence have considered as reducible to the theories of human discourse, is that, which consists of addresses from the pastor to his flock; discourses on topics of religion and morality, which in all Christian countries are delivered at periodical intervals, and constitute so important a part of the duties of a divine. The end of these discourses or sermons, as I have before intimated, is the improvement of the auditory in knowledge and virtue. It combines the purposes of the ancient deliberative oratory with those of the drama. Its means are persuasion; its object, to operate upon the will of the hearer; its result, to produce action, not joint and corporate, nor immediate, like that of deliberative assemblies by the taking of a vote, but individual, progressive, and sometimes remote action by a change of life and reformation, or amelioration of temper and conduct in the auditors. The speaker may take advantage of every possible argument resting on the basis of utility. The attainment of good and the avoidance of evil is the aim of his discourse. His powers of exhortation are multiplied and enhanced by the magnitude of the interests, which they embrace. The objects of his advice and admonition are not merely temporal and momentary, good and evil, but immortal happiness and misery. He pleads the cause not only of time, but of eternity.

In common deliberative assemblies, however successful the eloquence of the speaker may be to persuade many of his healers, yet, if a majority of the assembly remain unconvinced, his argument has no more efficacy, than if it had been impotent upon every mind. But it is high encouragement to the zeal of the pulpit orator, that not a particle of his persuasion can be lost. It operates separately upon every individual. However numerous his assembly, however hardened the multitude of his hearers may be against his exhortations, if the seed he scatters strike root but in a single heart, his labors are not lost. His audience may consist of thousands, but he speaks to them all as to one. To each individual in the language of Solomon he may say, "if thou be wise, thou shalt be wise for thyself; but if thou scornest, thou alone shalt bear it."

The sources of his arguments may be derived from his subject or his audience; and the divine, duly qualified to treat the great variety of subjects, which fall within the compass of his duties, will often find the exercise of his judgment necessary to adapt the choice of his subject to the character of his audience. It has long been remarked, that there is a striking difference between the eloquence of the pulpit, as it has appeared in the compositions of the French and of the English divines. A French sermon is a popular discourse, addressed almost exclusively to the feelings of the auditory; clothed in the most gorgeous attire of rhetoric, and calculated only to make an impression upon the heart. An English sermon is, or rather was until of late years, a cold, unimpassioned application to the understanding; abounding with solid reason and logical argument, but seldom attempting to warm or interest the passions of the hearers. The practice appears in both instances to have preceded the theory; but the French system first found an able advocate in the celebrated Fenelon, archbishop of Cambray; and the modern English writers upon rhetoric, without duly considering the principal cause of the difference, have adopted his ideas, and yielded perhaps too readily the palm of victory to the French doctrine.

The cause to which I allude, and which I apprehend contributed much more to influence the character and composition of English sermons, and to mark their difference from those of the French, than the mere diversity of national character, to which it has generally been ascribed, is no other than the protestant reformation. In France and in other Roman Catholic countries, where every point of doctrine was an article of faith, the exclusion of reasoning from the desk is just and consistent. The Christian is not allowed to be a reasoner; he is only a believer. His religious opinions are given him not for examination and scrutiny, but for implicit and unhesitating assent. The sacred scriptures themselves are held to be mysteries above his understanding, and his creed is never submitted to the decision of his judgment. The French doctrine of pulpit oratory, is a natural consequence from the doctrine of an infallible church, and inseparably connected with it. Under such a church there can be no occasion for argumentative sermons, and reasoning is very naturally expelled from their pulpits. But the protestant churches profess to make the reason of every individual the umpire of his faith. They admit no infallible rule of faith, other than the scriptures. The assiduous perusal of these they not only permit, but enjoin upon all their followers; and abandon their construction and exposition to his own judgment. The explanation and elucidation of the scriptures thus become one of the most arduous and important duties of the protestant preacher; a duty, which he can discharge only by enlightening the understandings of his people.

In order to test the correctness of this French system of sermonizing, and to show that it is adapted only to the practice of an infallible church, let us attend only to those classes of subjects for the disquisitions of the pulpit, which are among the most suitable for a protestant divine, but which become useless and improper, where they are prescribed, as undeniable articles of faith.

If the end of the preacher's discourse is the happiness of his hearers both in this and the future life, by means of their improvement in knowledge and virtue, that portion of the duty, which consists in the communication of knowledge, must of necessity be addressed to the hearers' reason. The faith of the protestant layman must often depend upon the degree of information, which he may receive from his religious instructor. The existence and attributes of the Deity, the nature and immortality of the soul, the doctrine of future rewards and punishments, the evidences of revealed religion, the peculiar character of its precepts, a comparison of its system of morals with those of the Chinese, Indian, Persian, Egyptian, Greek, and Arabian legislators and philosophers, an internal comparison between the Mosaic and Christian dispensations, or in other words between the principles of the law and those of the gospel, these are all themes, upon which the protestant teacher may and ought freely to expatiate for the improvement of his hearers in knowledge. But they admit of no discussion, where the preacher himself and all his flock are compelled to believe whatever has been prescribed to them on these all important questions, and have no further to look for their creed, than to the decisions of the church. A Roman catholic believes in the existence of a God, in the immortality of his own soul, and in a future state of retribution, because the holy church has told him they are articles of faith. But he is not allowed to ask the reason why. A protestant is told to believe these fundamental points of religion, because upon examination he will find them as satisfactorily proved to his reason, as he will discover them to be important to his happiness. Now the evidences of these primary principles are not obvious to every mind. They are liable to numerous and plausible objections. Not only the thoughtless and the profligate, but shallow reasoners and philosophical dogmatists dispute and deny them. The wolves of infidelity are prowling around every fold. Surely under such a state of things it is the duty of the pastor to guard his flock by every kind of security. It is as much his duty to detect the sophistical semblance of reason, as to repel the impetuous onset of the passions.

These three articles form the basis of what is called natural religion; and the belief in them does not always imply that of Christianity. This is barely a question of evidence, which in this, as in all other objects of controversy, is partly external and partly internal. When the truth of the Christian revelation is contested, it becomes the minister of the gospel not only to be able to give a reason for the faith that is in him, but to furnish those of his hearers, less qualified to search into the depths of such inquiries, with a reason equally satisfactory to themselves.

When both these difficulties at the threshold of religious persuasion have been removed, when the atheist and the deist have both been silenced, and the firm belief in divine revelation is established, then the volume of sacred inspiration is opened before the preacher, and it is his duty to make it profitable to his hearers for doctrine, for reproof, for correction, for instruction in righteousness. The field here opened to the protestant divine is inexhaustible. To the Roman Catholic preacher it is never opened at all. For with what propriety could he reason to his audience from a book, which they are not permitted to read?

In making these observations it is not my design either to pass a censure upon any prevailing system of Christianity, or to question the correctness of the French theory of pulpit eloquence, as adapted to the church, where it originated; but to caution those of you, who may hereafter assume the pastoral office, against the implicit adoption of the critical creed of the French school, which the recent English theorists have too much countenanced. A protestant divine, who looks upon his pulpit merely as a chair for the delivery of moral lectures, or a stage to work upon the passions of his auditory, as at a theatrical representation, has a very inadequate idea of his duties and of his powers. The earnest and ardent inculcation of moral duties is undoubtedly one of the essential obligations of the preacher; and in discharging it he is bound to lay hold of every hope and every fear, that can influence the heart of man. But to enlighten the mind is one of the most effectual means of amending the heart; and the societies of Christians, who place themselves under the ministration of a spiritual monitor, have a right to expect, that he should consider and treat them as rational, no less than as sensitive beings.

Let not the youthful candidate for the ministry entertain an idea too contracted of the functions, to which he aspires. Let him be deeply impressed with the principle, that his task in the pulpit will be to enlighten ignorance and to refute error, as well as to reclaim from vice and exhort to virtue. Let him not consider the celebrated French preachers or their English imitators, as furnishing the only proper models for the composition of a sermon. By enlarging the number and the nature of the topics, upon which he shall discourse, he will find his own duties more easy to discharge, and his people will be more extensively benefitted by his labors. In discussing topics of doctrine or of controversy the more ancient writers of English sermons will be more instructive guides, than those of recent date. From the frequency of the occasions he will have to address his people, he cannot too much diversify both the matter and the manner of his discourses.

In adapting the subjects of his sermons to the occasions and the audience the preacher must be governed by circumstances and by his own situation. The same disquisition, which might be seasonable and judicious before one auditory, would be worse than useless before another. Even the discourses of the moral and practical class ought to be diversified according to the time and place of their delivery. There are certain errors and vices more congenial to one state of society than to another. The inhabitants of populous cities are exposed to temptations and allured by opportunities to transgressions, different from those most incident to rural and sequestered regions. Different situations in life are prone to different offences. The rich and the poor, the ignorant and the learned, the ploughman and the mariner, the aged and the young; each is addicted to the sin, which most easily besets him, from which the others are more usually exempt. The divine is in some degree in vested with the functions of the censor among the ancient Romans. He has indeed no authority to punish the offender; but it is his right and his duty to reprove the offence.

From the imperfect and transient view of pulpit speaking, which I have here taken, you will perceive, that it includes within itself the principles of all the ancient classes of oratory. For the discussion of doctrines, its process must assume all the characters of judicial investigation. In manifesting the praise of the Supreme Creator, or unfolding the loveliness of that moral virtue, in which he delights, the displays of demonstrative eloquence can be limited only by the finite powers of the human imagination; while those addresses to the heart, which exhort to the practice of virtue, and urge the sinner to repentance, are marked with the features of deliberation.

In point of form it is precisely the same, as the demonstrative oration. The speaker stands alone, subject to no contradiction, and in undisputed possession of the whole field. His discourse may be extemporaneous, or previously written, at his option. The practice varies among different denominations of Christians, and among individuals of the same denomination. There are advantages and inconveniences, inherent in each of these modes of address; and the preference of the one to the other ought perhaps to be decided rather by the character of the preacher's talents, than by any rule of uniformity. There is a force, an interest, an energy, in extemporaneous discourse, "warm from the soul and faithful to its fires," which no degree of meditation can attain or supply. But the stream, which flows spontaneous, is almost always shallow, and runs forever in the same channel. The talent of speaking well without preparation is rare, and that of uttering fluent nonsense, so often substituted in its stead, though far from being uncommon, is not so well adapted to the oratory of the pulpit, as to that of the forum or of the bar. Amidst the infinite variety of human capacities there are some, whose floods of eloquence are more rich, more copious, more rapid, rushing from the lofty surface of unpremeditated thought, than drawn from the deepest fountains of study. But the productions of ordinary minds are improved by reflection, and brought to maturity by labor. The preacher should endeavour justly to estimate his own faculties, and according to their dictates prepare his written discourse, or trust to the inspiration of the moment. The talent of extemporal speaking may suffice for the ordinary duties of the preacher, but the sermon, destined to survive its hour of delivery, must always be previously written.

Lecture Fifteen - Intellectual and Moral Qualities of an Orator

AT an early period of this course, in pointing out the several sources of invention it was observed, that they were to be derived, first from the subject of the discourse; secondly from the speaker; and thirdly from the audience. The materials for invention, which can be supplied by the subject, have been now fully considered; as well those, which belong to all the classes of oratory in common, as those more distinctly suitable to the demonstrative, deliberative, judicial, or pulpit eloquence apart. It is now time to fix our attention upon the speaker himself, and to inquire what resources for the success of his cause he may be enabled to derive from his own personal character and address.

There are three particulars in the character of an orator, which may naturally and essentially affect the success of his eloquence. They are manifested by the qualities of the heart, the endowments of the understanding, and the dispositions of the temper; of which I propose to speak successively in the order here assigned them, according to my estimate of their relative importance.

The first and most precious quality then, which contributes to the success of a public speaker, is an honest heart; a sentiment which I wish above all others may be impressed with indelible force upon your minds. On a former occasion I freely acknowledged my own opinion, that the maxim, upon which the ancient rhetoricians, and especially Quinctilian, so emphatically insisted, that none but an honest man could possibly be an orator, was not strictly true. That from a laudable but mistaken intention it strained too far the preeminence of virtue, and supposed a state of moral perfection as extant in the world, which was at best but imaginary. The position in so broad an extent is not only erroneous in itself, but dangerous in its tendency. For if no other than a good man can possibly be a great orator, the converse of the proposition must be also true, and every great orator would of course be proved an honest man. An opinion of this kind might be pernicious to youth and inexperience. It is incompatible with the uniform constitution of human nature, and the unvaried tenor of human history. It leads to conclusions, which must confound the distinctions between fair profession and honorable action; and makes a smooth and fluent tongue the incontrovertible test of moral excellence.

It is however unquestionably true, that in forming that ideal model of an all-accomplished orator, that perfect master of the art, which a fruitful imagination is able to conceive, the first quality, with which he should be endowed, is uprightness of heart. In mere speculation we cannot separate the moral character from the oratorical power. If we assume as a given point, that a man is deficient in the score of integrity, we discard all confidence in

126

his discourse, and all benevolence to his person. We contemn his argument as sophistry. We detest his pathos as hypocrisy. If the powers of creation could be delegated to mortal hands, and we could make an orator, as a sculptor moulds a statue, the first material we should employ for the composition would be integrity of heart. The reason why this quality becomes so essential is, that it forms the basis of the hearer's confidence, without which no eloquence can operate upon his belief. Now if the profession and the practice of virtue were always found in unison with each other, it would inevitably follow, that no other than a good man could possess high powers of oratory; but as the world is constituted, the reputation of integrity will answer all the purpose of inspiring confidence, which could be attained by the virtue itself.

The reputation of integrity is sometimes enjoyed without being deserved, and sometimes deserved without being enjoyed. There is however no safer maxim, upon which a young man can proceed in the career of life, than that the reputation is to be acquired and maintained by the practice of virtue.

To estimate at its proper value the importance to a public speaker of an irreproachable character, consider its general operation upon the auditory at the several scenes of public oratory, with which we are conversant, and the distinctive characters of which have been delineated in my preceding lectures.

Our demonstrative orations are generally delivered upon some public anniversary or before some charitable or humane society, or in the form of funeral eulogy. Whether as the vehicles of persuasion to charity, or of moral or political sentiment, or of fair and honorable fame, how much more forcible and impressive must be the words of a speaker esteemed and respected for his personal character, than of one degraded in reputation. To influence the public opinion for some purpose of public benefit is the great end, to which the demonstrative orator should always endeavour to direct his discourse. This he will seldom find difficult. The occasions, upon which he will be called to speak, seldom fail to furnish him the opportunity. But to ensure his success the esteem and confidence of his hearers will contribute more than the substance of his discourse. The demonstrative orator should imagine to himself what truth and virtue and honor would say, could they appear in person, and speak with a human voice. What they would speak is precisely what he should say; and what can so surely fix the seal upon generous and noble sentiment, as the universal testimonial of the public voice, that it issued from a noble and a generous soul?

Still more important is a pure and spotless reputation for integrity to the general success of a pleader at the bar. The profession of the law requires a life the more scrupulously pure, for being more than perhaps any other occupation exposed to temptations, and stimulated by opportunities of departure from the path of rectitude; and for being far more than any other obnoxious to popular prejudices and suspicions. But although a fair character will certainly promote the general success of an advocate, it can have little or no influence upon the issue of any particular cause. Here again we discover different consequences from the different judicial institutions of ancient and modern times. One of the reasons most earnestly urged by Quinctilian, in recommending to his orator integrity of character, is, that it may enable him to succeed in advocating a bad cause. And it is obvious from the whole scope of his argument, and from that of Cicero to the same purpose, that the personal character of the advocate influenced in no small degree the fate of almost every cause. But in our courts of law it is the duty and the practice both of the judges and the juries to separate entirely the merits of the cause from those of its advocate. In the greater part of our criminal trials neither the prosecution nor the defence is conducted by men, who voluntarily assumed the office. The attorney general is bound by the duties of his station to conduct before the courts all accusations, preferred by the grand-jury; and although there are certain cases, in which he may proceed by way of information, that is, he may himself commence a prosecution without the intervention of a grand-jury, yet those cases are rare, and of little comparative importance. On the other hand our laws and constitutions, in that spirit of humanity, which marks all their regulations of criminal process, have expressly provided that all persons, charged with crimes, shall have the benefit of counsel; and it is generally made the duty of the practitioners at our bar to defend the party, who applies for his assistance. In all capital cases, if the prisoner under indictment is unable to defray the expense of an adequate fee, the judges themselves appoint individual members of the bar to manage his defence, and the task, thus imposed upon the advocate, he is bound to assume and to discharge with as much zeal and fidelity to the client thus allotted him, as if it had been the effect of his choice. The moral character of the lawyer can therefore have not the weight of a feather upon the scales of justice in causes of criminal jurisdiction. With regard to civil suits there is certainly a line of discrimination strongly marked between the general practice of different men in extensive business. There is a reputable and a disreputable practice. But even in these cases the result is different from that of ancient times. The complexion of the cause is often reflected upon the reputation of its supporter, but receives neither light nor shade from it. There are causes, which a man of moral delicacy never would undertake; and there is a management of causes, when undertaken, which a person solicitous for his own reputation never would adopt. Such causes and such a mode of conducting them are consequently found in the hands of men less scrupulous, and generally settle their reputation. But even in their hands every cause stands, as it ought to stand, upon its own merits, and is submitted to no criterion of decision, other than the law.

It is impossible on this subject to prescribe any uniform rule, which can be recommended to your observance. It is neither practicable nor necessary for a lawyer to pretend in the course of his professional practice to be always on the right side. A great proportion of causes, litigated in the courts of civil jurisdiction, consist of questions, the right or wrong of which can be ascertained only by the decision of the court. To insist upon having always the triumphant side of the cause would be to abandon the character of an advocate, and to arrogate that of a judge. The personal integrity of the lawyer is therefore by no means implicated in the failure of the causes, which he may support. On the other hand there are sometimes cases, in which the operation of the law itself is so harsh, so unfeeling, so at war with that natural justice, which can never be obliterated from the heart, that a man of principle would refuse his ministration for carrying it into effect. The only advice I can give you for all such emergencies is before you enter upon that profession, to lay the foundation of your conduct in a well digested system of ethics; to make yourselves thoroughly acquainted with the general duties of the man and the citizen; to form for yourselves principles

> Beyond the fixed and settled rules
> Of vice and virtue in the schools,
> Beyond the letter of the law;

and, when once thus well-grounded in the theory of your moral obligations, you may safely consult the monitor in your own breasts for direction upon every special occasion of difficulty, which may afterwards occur in your intercourse with mankind.

To the deliberative orator the reputation of unsullied virtue is not only useful, as a mean of promoting his general influence, it is also among his most efficient engines of persuasion, upon every individual occasion. The test of deliberation you remember is utility. Its issue is some measure to be pursued or rejected. The purpose of the speaker is to persuade his hearers that the act, to which he exhorts, will be advantageous to themselves; or, if the discourse is held before a representative body, to their constituents. It is obvious then, that the hearers of a deliberative speaker will listen to him with a disposition much more favorable to the adoption of his opinions, when they have an unshaken confidence in his integrity, than when they suspect or disbelieve the purity of his intentions.

In our country the legislative bodies of the state or of the union are the assemblies, in which all the most important deliberative discussions are agitated. Generally speaking, a reputation for integrity must to a certain degree be established, before a citizen can obtain a seat in those assemblies, and enjoy the right of taking a part in their debates. I do not mean to say, that these stations are universally or exclusively filled by men of exemplary virtue, or even of fair fame. There always are and always will be some exceptions. The places are all elective, and all granted for a short space of time. But the instances of polluted characters ushered into the halls of legislation are rare. An election by popular suffrage to a place of trust and honor is conclusive proof, that the person chosen was an object of esteem to those, by whom he was elected. If not always decisive evidence of merit, at least it is an indication of good repute. And as uprightness of character is the most effectual passport to a seat in the legislative councils, so is it the most certain instrument for acquiring influence in them. Without it the most brilliant eloquence loses half its lustre; with it every faculty of speech acquires a ten-fold energy.

To the worldly orator then of whatever denomination, good name is a jewel of inestimable price. But to the preacher of the gospel it is the immediate jewel of his soul. Not that there is any principle of religion or of virtue, binding upon a clergyman, from which men of other occupations are entitled to an exemption. Heaven has not prescribed one system of morality for the priesthood, and another for the people. The divine precepts are the same for us all; and that, which would be criminal in a divine, can never become innocent in a layman. Nevertheless usages of society, and the general opinions of mankind apply a more rigorous standard of piety and virtue to the duties of a clergyman, than to those of other men. High offences partake of aggravated enormity, when committed by them; and indulgencies, deemed innocent in the ordinary characters of mankind, become transgressions in the cloth. By their profession they are teachers of religion and virtue. If then by his example a divine should give the lie to his own instructions, his guilt is complicated. Besides the criminality, which he incurs in common with every other offender, he commits a sort of moral and professional suicide. He destroys all possibility, that his lessons to others should obtain credit. He is an apostate from the cause, to which he has pledged himself. He is not merely a worthless man; he is an impostor to mankind, and a traitor to his God. This character, I add with pleasure, is no less rare, than it is odious. There is no class of men in society so generally distinguished for pure morals and blameless lives, as our clergy. For dignity of mind and decency of manners, for uprightness of conduct and delicacy of sentiment, no other profession can bear a comparison with the ministers of the gospel of every sect and denomination. To men of this vocation the maxim of Quinctilian might be applied in its utmost extent. The orator of heaven must be a saint upon earth.

And truths divine come mended from his tongue.

Thus then, for the purpose of conciliating the benevolence of the auditory, an object so indispensable to the success of all eloquence, the reputation of integrity appears of momentous consequence to the orator of every description. But there is an advantage, which genuine integrity will secure to the speaker, independent of the fallacious estimates of his hearers, which no baseless reputation can usurp, and no delusive prejudice can destroy. The advantage of that natural alliance, which always subsists between honesty and truth, guided by that spirit of truth, which is no other than the perception of things, as they exist in reality, an orator will never use, for he will never need any species of deception. He will never substitute falsehood for fact, nor sophistry for argument. Always believing himself what he says, he will possess the first of instruments for obtaining the belief of others. Nor is the respect for truth in a fair and ingenuous mind a passive or inert quality. It is warm with zeal. It never suffers carelessness to overlook, nor indolence to slumber. It spurs to active exertion; it prompts to industry, to perseverance, to fortitude. Integrity of heart is a permanent and ever active principle, exercising its influence over the heart throughout life. It is friendly to all the energetic virtues; to temperance, to resolution, to labor. It trims the midnight lamp in pursuit of that general knowledge, which alone can qualify the orator of ages. It greets the rising dawn in special application to the cause, for which its exertions may be required. Yet more; integrity of heart must be founded upon an enlarged and enlightened morality. A truly virtuous orator must have an accurate knowledge of the duties, incident to man in a state of civil society. He must have formed a correct estimate of good and evil; a moral sense, which in demonstrative discourse will direct him with the instantaneous impulse of intuition to the true sources of honor and shame; in judicial controversy, to those of justice; in deliberation, to the path of real utility; in the pulpit, to all that the wisdom of man, and all that the revelation of heaven have imparted of light for the pursuit of temporal or eternal felicity.

Finally, an honest heart is the fountain of all irresistible argument, and all overpowering sentiment. Mankind are indeed liable to be occasionally led astray and deluded by their passions; but all the lasting sympathies of the human soul are with virtue. So true is this, that the most abandoned instigators to criminal acts are ever solicitous to varnish over their purposes with some plausible pretext; and the prince of darkness holds forth temptation in the garb and image of an angel of light.

But integrity of heart, although the first, is not the only essential qualification for the eminence of a public speaker; nor is it a distinction more peculiarly adapted to his profession, than to all others. It forms a general duty, obligatory alike upon all, though I have here considered it only, as it operates upon the oratorical character. The endowments of the mind are the next ingredients in the composition of a public speaker; and though subordinate to that all-surrounding orb of moral principle, they are equally indispensable to the harmony of the system.

The faculties of the mind are either natural or acquired. There is no occupation among men, excepting the exercise of the military art, which affords so wide a scope for the operations of genius, as the practice of oratory. So far however as genius is the gift of nature, it cannot be a subject of much useful discussion. It is a property neither to be suppressed where it exists, nor given where it is not. The natural endowments however, which are indispensable for a distinguished orator, are not of that rare and extraordinary kind, which that common mother bestows only upon a darling of twenty centuries. Fluency of speech, strength of lungs, and boldness of heart, these appear to be the only natural gifts, which an orator can require, excepting the powers of invention. But the attribute, which of all others exclusively bears the mark of genius, is the power of overcoming obstacles; and in the history of Demosthenes it seems as if nature had purposely denied him all those physical powers, for the express purpose of exhibiting the triumph of genius over nature. The sublimest of human orators became such in despite of an impediment in his speech, of feeble lungs, and of the timidity, which dreads the sound of its own voice before an assembled multitude. The example of Demosthenes can be safely recommended however only to those, who have not to struggle with the same difficulties. Let the youth more liberally provided with the physical organs of speech, whose ambition points him to the paths of oratorical fame, let him remember, that the same indefatigable assiduity, the same inflexible perseverance, and the same inventive ingenuity, which enabled Demosthenes to disarm the very rigors of nature, are the weapons, with which he must learn to improve her favors.

It will not be necessary for me to dwell with tedious earnestness upon the importance to the orator of those faculties, which his own industry can acquire. The rhetorical dialogues of Cicero and the institutes of Quinctilian are so ample and so comprehensive on this article, that the most elaborate discourse I could frame to the same purpose would in substance consist of nothing but of repetitions from them. It were easy to transcribe, and perhaps impossible to add to the weight of their opinions, or to the energy of their instructions. If it were possible to suppose any of you seriously doubtful, and inclining to the belief, that shallow draughts of learning suffice for the purposes of oratory, there would be reason to apprehend, that on such a mind neither Cicero nor Quinctilian could make much impression. As students at this place, I cannot imagine the use of an argument to recommend to you the pursuit of knowledge. It is the purpose, for which you are here, and a dissertation to convince you of the benefits of learning would be like a medical treatise to prove that food is conducive to health, and that respiration is one of the luxuries of life. There is however one observation, which may perhaps not be so obvious to all. An university by its name imports a seminary, where youth is initiated in all the sciences; and it is an idea too flattering to indolence and vanity not to have many believers, that all the knowledge of the sciences, which can be of use in the common affairs of life, is to be acquired at the university. According to this estimate of things a liberal education means no more, than the acquisition of a degree; and the pursuit of the sciences here taught is regularly laid aside with the square cap and the collegiate gown. But the practice upon this doctrine will never make an accomplished orator. The student, who aspires to the attainment of that proud eminence, must consider himself as able to acquire here nothing more, than the elements of useful knowledge, a mere introduction to the porches of science. These fountains of the muses are destined not to quench but to provoke his thirst. Here he can only learn to be his own teacher hereafter.

But to say that the orator must be a man of universal knowledge is to speak in terms too general for practical utility. The objects of human learning are so multifarious, and its several branches are so complicated, that no human wit or industry can be adequate to a mastery equally minute over the whole. The comparative importance and value of the various classes and kinds of knowledge is worthy of your most deliberate inquiry; that no precious time may be wasted upon unprofitable researches, and that no hasty conclusion may discard studies, adapted to useful purposes.

The professional studies, which succeed the termination of your academical education, will be different, as your choice may lead you to the ministry of the gospel, or to the practice of the bar. To enlarge upon these would lead me into a field too extensive for the present occasion, and would anticipate subjects, which may more properly be presented to your consideration hereafter. The materials, upon which the mind of a deliberative orator is called to fix a special attention, are still more various and extensive; and the period, at which they may become necessary to be investigated by you, still more remote. But as art is long and life short, there is no precept, which I can more earnestly recommend to you, than that of exercising your own understandings upon all the knowledge you acquire. Endeavour to methodise your studies. Habituate yourselves to reflect upon what you read and what you hear. Let the streams of knowledge never stagnate upon your souls. Learning in the head of indolence is like the sword of a hero in the hand of a coward. The credit and the usefulness of a merchant depends at least as much upon the employment, as upon the extent of his capital. The reputation of learning is no better, than that of a pedantic trifler, unless accompanied with the talent of making that learning useful to its possessor and to mankind.

With this talent the orator must also be governed by a corresponding disposition. And the disposition, manifested by the temper of the speaker, was the third and last of the properties, which I have deemed important, as affecting the merits of the oratorical character. The temper of the speaker operates in a twofold manner; like the reputation of integrity, it influences the affections of the auditory; and like integrity itself, it modifies his management of every subject. The qualities, which operate most powerfully upon the hearers, are benevolence, modesty, and confidence. That, which affects the treatment of the subject, may be comprised in the single term self-command. Benevolence is not merely the first of moral and Christian virtues, it is the most captivating of all human qualities; for it recommends itself to the selfish passions of every individual. Benevolence is a disposition of the heart, universal in its nature; and every single hearer imagines that temper to be kindly affected towards himself, which is known to be actuated by good will to all. It is the general impulse of human nature to return kindness with kindness, and the speaker, whose auditory at the instant of his first address believe him inspired with a warm benevolence for them, has already more than half obtained his end. Modesty is a kindred virtue to benevolence, and possesses a similar charm over the hearts of men. Modesty always obtains the more, precisely because it asks nothing. Modesty lulls all the irritable passions to sleep. It often disarms, and scarcely ever provokes opposition. These qualities are so congenial to the best feelings of mankind, that they can never be too assiduously cultivated. In them there is no counteraction. If they do not always succeed, they never totally fail. They neutralize malice; they baffle envy; they relax the very brow of hatred, and soften the features of scorn into a smile. But the purest of virtues border upon pernicious failings. Let your benevolence never degenerate into weakness, nor your modesty into bashfulness. A decent confidence is among the most indispensable qualifications of an accomplished orator. Arrogance stimulates resentment; vanity opens to derision; but a mild and determined intrepidity, unabashed by fear, unintimidated by the noise and turbulence of a popular assembly, unawed by the rank or dignity of an auditory, must be acquired by every public speaker aspiring to high distinction. It is as necessary to command the respect, as to conciliate the kindness of your hearers.

This decent and respectful confidence is but a natural result of that perfect and unalterable self command, which, though last, is far, very far from being the least ingredient in the composition of an accomplished orator. If it be true of mankind in general, that he who ruleth his spirit is greater than he that taketh a city, to no description of human beings can this preeminence of self dominion be so emphatically ascribed, as to the public speaker. Let no man presume to bespeak an ascendency over the passions of others, until he has acquired an unquestioned mastery over his own. Let no man dare to undertake the guidance of reason in others, while he suffers anger or vanity, the overflowings of an inflated or an irritated mind, to intermingle with the tide of his eloquence. When the ebullitions of passion burst in peevish crimination of the audience themselves, when a speaker sallies forth, armed with insult and outrage for his instruments of persuasion, you may be assured, that this Quixotism of rhetoric must eventually terminate like all other modern knight errantry and that the fury must always be succeeded by the impotence of the passions.

Lecture Sixteen - Excitation and Management of the Passions

IN delineating the qualities of the heart, of the understanding, and of the temper, which must combine to constitute an orator worthy of a station in the memory of ages, I reserved, as the closing and highly important consideration, the necessity, that he should possess a steady and unvarying command over his own passions. The course of my subject naturally leads me next to inquire how far and by what means he will find it expedient to exercise an influence over those of his hearers.

The rhetorical theories of this age must differ very materially from those of ancient times on this part of the science. Among them the management of the passions was considered as including almost the whole art of oratory. Each of the three great writers, who have hitherto been our instructors, appears to consider this as by far the most arduous task, and the most effectual power of a public speaker; and each of them has treated it in his peculiar characteristic manner. One entire book of the three, which contain the rhetorical sys-

134

tem of Aristotle, is devoted to the passions. He selects from the whole mass of habits and affections, which hold dominion over the hearts of men, a certain number, which he comprises under the general denomination of oratorical passions, or passions which are peculiarly susceptible of being operated upon by a public speaker. To each of these he allots a distinct chapter, in which he successively analyzes the passion itself, the classes of men, who are most liable to be stimulated by it, and the manner in which it may be excited. This book is one of the profoundest and most ingenious treatises upon human nature, that ever issued from the pen of man. It searches the issues of the heart with a keenness of penetration, which nothing can surpass, unless it be its severity. There is nothing satirical in his manner, and his obvious intention is merely as an artist to expose the mechanism of man; to discover the moral nerves and sinews, which are the peculiar organs of sensation; to dissect the internal structure, and expose the most hidden chambers of the tenement to our view. Cicero insists also much upon the management of the passions. Not by anatomizing the passions themselves, but by showing how they are to be handled. His example is followed by Quinctilian, whose sentiments on this chapter it may be proper to cite, as explained by himself, in order to mark distinctly how far they can be applicable to present times.

"There is," says he, "perhaps nothing so important as this in the whole art of oratory. An inferior genius, with the aid of instruction and experience, may succeed, and appear to great advantage in all the other parts. You can easily find men able to invent arguments and proofs, and even to link them together in a chain of deduction. These men are not to be despised. They are well qualified to inform the judges; to give them a perfect insight into the cause; nay to be the patterns and teachers of all your learned orators. But the talent of delighting, of overpowering the judge himself, of ruling at pleasure his very will, of inflaming him with anger, of melting him to tears, that is the rare endowment indeed. Yet therein consists the true dominion of the orator; therein consists the empire of eloquence over the heart. As for arguments, they generally proceed from the bosom of the cause itself, and are always the strongest on the right side. To obtain the victory by means of them is merely the success of a common lawyer; but to sway the judge in spite of himself, to divert his observation from the truth, when it is unpropitious to our cause, this is the real triumph of an orator. This is what you never can learn from the parties; what none of their documents will ever contain. The proofs and the reasonings serve indeed to convince the judge, that our cause is the best. But by means of his passions he is made to wish it such; and he will soon believe what he once wishes. No sooner does he begin to catch our passions and to share in our hatreds and friendships, indignations and fears, than he makes our cause his own. And as lovers are ill-qualified to judge of beauty, because blinded by their passion, in like manner the judge, amidst his perturbation, loses the discernment of truth. The torrent hurries him along, and he gives himself up to its violence. Nothing but the sentence itself can indicate the effect of the arguments and witnesses upon his mind. But if he warmly feels the passions excited in him, you can easily discover his sentence before he leaves the bench; nay without his rising from it. When he bursts into tears, as sometimes happens at those admirable perorations, which must move the hardest of hearts, is not the decree already pronounced? Let the orator then direct all his exertions to this point; let him fasten most obstinately upon it, without which every thing else is slender, feeble, and ungracious. So true it is, that the strength and the soul of a pleader's discourse centres in the passions."

Let us here remark, that in this passage, which contains the whole substance of the ancient doctrine respecting the excitation and management of the passions, Quinctilian applies his observations exclusively to judicial eloquence. The ends, for which these energetic machines are to be worked, have no relation to demonstrative discourses. There is no judge to be deceived, no sentence to be falsified. The ideas apply only by a weak and imperfect analogy to deliberative eloquence; and indeed it was a received maxim among all the rhetoricians, that the great field for operating upon the passions was at the bar. In my lectures on the subject of judicial oratory, I have already shown, as a consequence of our judicial institutions and principles, that the means of influencing the issue of a cause, by the passions of the hearers, are less at the bar, than in any other form of public speaking. Our judges are sworn to administer justice according to law. Our juries are under oaths equally solemn to give their verdicts according to the evidence; and even the attorneys and counsellors, practising in all the courts, are under like engagement to do no wrong, and to suffer none knowingly to be committed. That, which Quinctilian tells us to be the most splendid triumph of the art, would therefore now be a high misdemeanor; and the judge, who should suffer his sentence to be diverted from the truth, and should join in the hatreds or friendships of one party against another, would soon get himself removed by impeachment.

This is perhaps one of the principal causes of the superiority, enjoyed by ancient over modern eloquence. It manifests a great improvement in the condition of society. When we see Quinctilian speaking contemptuously of arguments, because they are always strongest on the right side, what must we think of their administration of the laws? If the modern courts have lost on the side of eloquence, they have gained on the side of justice; and if our orators have less brilliancy, our judges have more solidity.

The Christian system of morality has likewise produced an important modification of the principles respecting the use of the passions. In the passage, above quoted from Quinctilian, no distinction is made between the kindly and the malevolent passions. Neither does Aristotle intimate such a distinction; envy, hatred, malice, and indignation, are recommended to be roused, as well as love, kindness, and good will. The Christian morality has commanded us to suppress the angry and turbulent passions in ourselves, and forbids us to stimulate them in others. This precept, like many others proceeding from the same source, is elevated so far above the ordinary level of human virtue, that it is not always faithfully obeyed. But although perhaps not completely victorious over any one human heart, the command to abstain from malice and envy, and all the rancorous passions, has effected a general refinement of manners among men. Is there a rhetorician of modern ages, who would dare utter, as a precept to his pupils, instructions how to debauch the understanding of a judge, through the medium of his passions? Ib there a teacher, who would have the courage to search out the most venomous regions of the human heart, to instruct his scholars how to feed them with congenial poison? Doctrines like these could only suit the times, when the rule of morality was "thou shall love thy neighbour and hate thine enemy." They must be, and they are universally exploded from the lessons of those, who have been commanded to love their enemies; to return blessings for curses, prayers for persecution, and good for evil. Would to heaven, that they were as universally abandoned in practice. Of this there is but too much still remaining. It is too easily learned and too frequently employed, for the worst of purposes. Instead of recommending it to your use, I cannot too earnestly warn you against its adoption.

Addresses to the malevolent passions are not necessary for the highest efforts of eloquence. To convince yourselves of this truth, compare the oratorical compositions of Burke with the letters of Junius. They have been sometimes ascribed to the same author, and there are many particulars, in which the resemblance between them is remarkable. They are both writers of ardent passion and high vehemence. But in regard to the motives and feelings, which they strive to excite, they differ as widely as possible. Burke was upon principle and conviction a Christian. He had examined its evidences, and compared its moral system with every other known theory of ethics. The result of his investigation was a conviction of the truth of Christianity, and its laws of general benevolence and charity appear in every page of his writings. The blaze of passion, the bolt of indignation, flash with incessant energy from his controversial speeches and publications; but the tone and character of his sentiment is invariably generous and benevolent. All his maxims of wisdom, all his remarks upon life and manners, beam with humanity, with good will to men. Junius was probably infected with the shallow infidelity of the French encyclopedists. He seldom suffers an opportunity for a sarcasm upon religion to escape him; and he always speaks of piety with a sneer, as if it conveyed to his mind no image, other than that of hypocrisy. Yet he dares not avow his infidelity; and, when directly charged with it, shuffles with the dexterity of a rope dancer, and cavils with the subtlety of a sophist to disclaim an offence, which at the same moment he repeats, h is obvious from the general tenor of his letters, that Christian principles were as foreign from his heart, as Christian doctrines from his understanding. His eloquence is unshackled by any restraint of tenderness for his species. He flatters the foulest prejudices. He panders for the basest passions. Anger, hatred, and envy, are the choicest instruments of his oratory. There is scarcely a sentiment, calculated to warm the hearts of his readers with kindness to their fellow creatures, in the whole collection. The tender, affectionate feelings never inspire him with a thought; and, whenever an idea of patriotism or philanthropy crosses his mind, his principal address consists in pointing it with individual malignity.

The vindictive and envious passions being excluded from the ways and means of our eloquence by the duties of our religion, and all the passions being so much discountenanced in our judicial courts, it is an obvious inference, that this particular department of the art has lost some of its relative importance. There are still however occasions, in every class of public speaking, when the orator may obtain his end by operating upon the passions of his hearers, and success obtained by these instruments is still the most difficult achievement and the most splendid triumph of the art. It is however an instrument, which requires the management of a skilful hand, and which, to retain its efficacy, must be very rarely employed.

Under the general denomination of passions we include two distinct classes of sentiments or impulsions, which by the ancient Greeks were distinguished by the names of παζος and ηζος. The terms in our language most nearly corresponding with these are passions and habits; in the sense which we apply to this latter word, when we say that habit is a second nature. By the passions they understood the keen and forceful affections of the mind. By the habits they meant the mild and orderly emotions. The passions were tumultuous agitations; the habits quiet and peaceable impulses. The first were more adapted to control; the last to attract. Generally speaking the words marked a difference in duration, as well as in degree. The passions were momentary, the habits constant; the former an occasional, the latter a permanent influence. The passions are the tides of the ocean, ebbing and flowing at short intervals; the habits are the current of a mighty river, always setting in the same direction. From the analysis of Aristotle it appears also, that the habits affect men in classes; the passions only as individuals. Thus he describes the habits of the young, the old, and the middle aged; of the rich and the poor; of the powerful and the feeble; of the prosperous and the unfortunate. But in speaking of the passions he considers them individually; anger and its remission; love and hatred; fear and boldness; shame and honor; compassion and revenge; envy and emulation.

Although the distinction between these two powers, which divide between them the control of the human will, is obvious and important, they are sometimes of precisely the same nature, and differ only in degree. Thus for instance love is included among the passions, but friendship among the habits. Still more common is it to find them in opposition to each other, and the most vehement appeals to the passions are counteracted by addresses to the calmer influence of the habits.

The occasions, upon which an attempt to move the passions properly so called is advisable, do not often occur. In ordinary cases the speaker's manner should be calm and moderate; avoiding all affected elevation or energy. Correctness of thought and expression, pleasantness and probability are the natural characters of discourses, urged to the habits of the hearers. But to stir the passions, the tempests of the soul, grandeur of expression, boldness and irregularity of thought, and gravity, seriousness, inflexibility of manner, become indispensable. In the compositions of the drama, the habits or manners belong exclusively to the province of comedy; the passions to that of tragedy.

One of the most universal precepts, recommended alike by all the writers upon the science ancient and modern, is that the orator himself should feel the passion, which he purposes to excite. This rule however must be received with some limitations. It is applicable only to some of the passions, and even with regard to those requires, that the speaker should be affected only in such degree, as to leave him in perfect possession of all his intellectual faculties. Si vis me fiere, dolendum est primum tibi ipsi. This is the direction of Horace to the writer for the stage; and thus far the rule is unquestionably as applicable to the forum, as to the theatre. But suppose the passion to be excited is fear or shame; is the orator, who would rouse these emotions, to partake of them himself? Suppose it to be anger or indignation; a sentiment justifiable and laudable in a virtuous cause; must he not rather struggle to suppress in himself the natural violence of these passions, to communicate them even in their due degree to his audience? In applying generally to all the passions that rule, which was originally given only for that of compassion, or sympathy with distress, the doctrine has been too far extended, and reminds us of Johnson's reply to some shallow wit, who repeated with great emphasis a verse, which he deemed truly sublime;

"Who rules o'er freemen, should himself be free."

That, said Johnson, is as much as to say,

"Who drives fat oxen, should himself be fat."

Indeed the passions, which are liable to be excited by the powers of oratory, are numerous; and some of those, which act with the most irresistible energy upon the hearts of mankind, are altogether omitted in the catalogue of Aristotle. Ambition, avarice, the love of fame, patriotism, are all passions to be numbered among the sharpest stimulants to action, and to the motives, which they present, much of the most celebrated eloquence of all ages has been addressed. There is however a more restricted sense, in which the terai passion is used, and of which the precisest idea will be formed by tracing its etymology. In this sense it is equivalent to sufferance, distress, anguish. In this sense it has emphatically been applied to the last sufferings of the Saviour; and to this sense it must be confined, when we are inquiring into those pathetic powers of oratory, which awaken the sympathies of the audience. These very words themselves, pathetic and sympathy, are both derived immediately from the Greek παθος, of which the Latin passio is merely a translation. And the meaning, universally annexed to them, has kept closer to their original derivation, than the Latin term. We could scarcely take up an oration of celebrated fame, without discovering in all its parts passages, calculated to move the passions. But we should certainly denominate pathetic only those, which have a tendency to excite our sympathies, with some exhibition of distress. This brings us back to the poetical precept of Horace, which the experience of all ages will verify, and which a public speaker can never imprint too deeply upon his mind. If then your purpose be to stir compassion, begin by feeling it yourself. But would you inflame anger? Be cool. Would you bring to a sense of shame? Sound the trump of unblemished honor. Would you strike terror? Be intrepid; and in general remember, that if it is the nature of some passions to spread by contagion, it is equally characteristic of others never to kindle without collision.

But whatsoever be the passions, upon which the orator is desirous of working, this is the occasion, upon which he must summon all the powers of imagination. By imagination I here mean what perhaps is more properly called fantasy; the power of representing to the mind the images of absent things. The operation of the passions is much more uniform among mankind, than that of reason. The "sensible of pain" or of pleasure is nearly the same in all human beings. It differs only in degree. By the power of imagination the orator undergoes a virtual transformation. He identifies himself either with the person, in whose behalf he would excite the sentiment of compassion, or with the antagonist, against whom he is to contend, or with the auditor, whom he is to convince or persuade; or successively with each of them in turn. In the deep silence of meditation he holds an instructive dialogue with every one of these personages. Of his client he learns what he most keenly feels; of the antagonist what he most seriously dreads; of the auditor what he most readily believes. He sounds the depth of every heart; he measures the compass of every mind; he explores the secret recesses of nature herself. To him, as to the immortal bard, she unveils her face; to him she presents her golden keys, and says,

> This can unlock the gates of joy,
> Of horror that, and secret fears,
> Or ope the sacred source of sympathetic tears.

The power of imagination furnishes a substitute for the evidence of all the senses. It creates and multiplies all those incidents, which, being the constant attendants upon all realities, have always so strong a tendency to enforce belief. So indispensable is this power to the success of that oratory, which aims at the dominion of the passions, that a public speaker can institute no more important self-examination, than the inquiry whether it has been bestowed upon him by nature. If it has, let him cherish and cultivate it, as the most precious of heaven's blessings. If it has not, let him graduate the scale of his ambition to the temperate regions of eloquence, and aspire only to the reputation of being the orator of reason.

In each of our three great scenes of public speaking, the legislature, the bar, and the pulpit, there is one master passion, which bears, or is supposed to bear an ascendency so uncontrolled, that to attempt operating upon it is the never failing resource of all those orators, who are destitute of every other. I shall conclude this lecture with a few remarks upon them; and with pointing them out to you rather by way of warning, than of recommendation. These passions are jealousy, avarice, and fear.

The deliberative passion is jealousy. The ordinary mode of exciting it is by raising suspicions against the person or character of an opponent; by invidious reflections; by insinuations against his integrity, and imputations upon his motives. This species of oratory is generally suggested by the virulence of party spirit. It is forbidden by the rules of order in all deliberative assemblies; but is always practised upon the discussion of questions, which rouse the spirit of faction. It is the natural resort of those, who are unable to support by reason or argument the opinions, to which they adhere. Its efficacy is proportioned to the prejudices and ignorance of the hearers, to whom it is addressed, and the frequency of its use in our legislative assemblies for many years is not the most honorable feature in our national character. It is also not uncommon in the demonstrative discourses of our public anniversaries, which are thus made the engines of envy and slander. It is not to be denied, that these are weapons of formidable power; but a sound understanding will disdain, and a generous heart will abhor the use of them.

The judicial passion is avarice. I have heretofore shown, that the occasions, upon which any address to the passions is admissible in our courts of justice, are rare; and that they must of necessity imply a discretionary power in the persons, who are to decide upon the issue. There are certain cases, in which our judges possess certain discretionary powers; but they always presuppose the offender tried and convicted. The discretion of the court extends only to the degree of punishment. Here is not much scope for eloquence of any kind. The mercy of the court usually forestalls the need of the culprit, and there is scarcely ever a disposition or an opportunity to urge their severity. There are other cases, when the exercise of discretionary powers is allotted to juries. These are mostly upon trials for personal injuries, where juries have to settle the amount of damages. Such as actions for assault and battery, slander, libels, and other wrongs if possible of a still more atrocious complexion; which, from the comparative purity of our manners, are happily almost unknown among us. In these cases however the only sympathies of the jury, which an orator can attempt to move, are their love of money; for, by a gross imperfection in our codes of law, the only reparation attainable for all the bodily pain, mental affliction, or laceration of fame, which the villany of one man can inflict upon the feelings of another, is a compensation in money. The only powers of a jury, in the most atrocious outrages of these kinds, are to strike an arithmetical rule of three between the pecuniary means of the offender and the moral and physical sufferings of the injured party. There is, it must be confessed, not much delicacy of sentiment in this tariff of moral feelings, this scale of depreciation for honor and fame. A ruffian has crippled you for life; a seducer has murdered your domestic peace; a slanderer has blasted your good name; and for wrongs thus enormous, thus inexpiable, you are compelled to ask of your country's justice a beggarly retribution of dollars and cents; to solicit the equivalent for affliction, the premium for pain, the indemnity for shame, cast up correctly to a mill in regular federal currency. A fiend in human shape has trampled under foot honor, humanity, friendship, the rights of nature, and the ties of connubial society; but a check upon the bank atones for all his crime; a scrap of silk paper spunges up the whole blot of his infamy. It is not here the place to inquire, whether a system of juris-prudence might not be devised, which should secure a more honorable pro-tection to personal rights; but it is manifest that the maxim, which affixes to personal sufferings their stated price in current coin, which estimates honor and shame by troy weight, which balances so many pangs of body with so many ounces of silver, and so much anguish of mind with so many penny-weights of gold, makes avarice the unresisted umpire of the soul. It adminis-ters money as the universal potion for healing all the bruises of the mind; and makes extortion the only standard for measuring the merits of virtue.

The passion of the pulpit orator is fear. As the exhortations of the divine have reference principally to the interests of a future existence, it is natural and proper, that he should often draw from the same source his materials of argument or of persuasion. And as the doctrines of religion are not aided among us by the weapons of secular power, the terrors of futurity are the only instruments, by which numerous classes of people are retained stead-fast in their faith, or regulated, in their practice. The vengeance of an offend-ed Deity is to many preachers of many denominations the only fountain of motives or of reasoning; and their eloquence can never kindle without re-sorting to the flames of hell. I would not be understood, my friends, to treat this subject with a trifling hand. It is a serious concern to us all. But mere ter-ror is a base and servile passion; nor should I value at a straw the religion or the morality, which hinges upon nothing else. Let me hope that you, and those who may hereafter enjoy the benefits of your ministry, will ever feel the force and efficacy of some nobler, some more generous stimulus to piety and virtue, than the mere selfishness even of eternity, and the shivering hor-rors of hell fire.

We have now gone through the first great division of the rhetorical science. We have successively treated of the state of the controversy, the oratorical topics, the arguments peculiarly adapted to the demonstrative, deliberative, judicial, and religious class of discourses. We have endeavoured to trace the address and character suitable to an orator, and to point out the true use and proper means of exciting and directing the passions. The subject is copious; and, although it has occupied so large a portion of our time, is very far from being exhausted. My duties have been to collect and present to your view the materials for the plastic hands of genius to fashion into shape. For the em-ployment of these materials you will naturally look not to me, but to yourselves; not to the lessons of a teacher, but to the fertility of your own invention.

Lecture Seventeen - Disposition. Exordium.

IT will be remembered, that, in making the general distribution of the science of rhetoric into its primary divisions, they were stated to be five; invention, disposition, elocution, memory, and pronunciation or action.

To the first of these divisions, invention, my ten last lectures have been devoted; containing a general view of every thing, which the rhetoricians of antiquity considered as constituting the materials of an oratorical discourse. The formation of these materials was the proper and exclusive function of invention; which was analogous only to the state of chaos in the creation of the world. To shape this chaos into form, to give the original mass of mingled elements an existence for use or beauty, the principle of order must be introduced; as the creation of light immediately succeeded that of matter; and the division of light from darkness was the first thing, which the Supreme Creator saw to be good. This principle of order in rhetoric is termed disposition; and it is that, upon which I am now to discourse.

Disposition, according to the definition of Cicero, to which I formerly referred you, is "the orderly arrangement of the things invented." And I then suggested to you some considerations for estimating its importance. They will the more especially merit your attention, inasmuch as this part of the oratorical talent is more indebted to study, than to nature; rather to be acquired by the assiduous toils of industry, than communicated by the gratuitous bounties of genius. The power of invention is distributed with the same capricious partiality, which marks all the endowments of nature to the superficial mind of man. In the views of a wise and beneficent Providence there must be some great and regular principle, upon which the energies of genius are bestowed in their relative proportions, as they appear among mankind; but to our contracted capacity of observation that principle is not discoverable. Invention is the child of genius, and genius is not to be imparted by tuition. But if genius be heaven's best gift, "order is heaven's first law;" and the power of giving effect and execution to this law is placed within the reach of our own assiduity. In contemplating that stupendous system of physical being, which hangs upon the unvarying laws of matter and the regular motions of unnumbered worlds, the human mind shrinks from the vastness of its own conceptions. Of the power of creation it is incapable of forming a distinct idea. But it sees, it comprehends, it calculates the operations of a Supreme Disposer; and in the act of arrangement or disposition alone are the works of man capable of imitating the laws of the Deity. The system of the universe itself is maintained only by its perfect and immutable order. Suppose that order but for one instant suspended, and the innumerable host of heaven,

143

those fixed or wandering stars, which through the regions of unbounded space, "still choiring to the young eyed cherubim," sing the omnipotence of their Maker, would rush together in hideous ruin, and chaos return again.

In the comparative estimate of the two faculties, as they are susceptible of being possessed by the human understanding, we shall perceive, that invention is an attribute of the imagination, and disposition an exercise of the judgment. Invention soars on the pinions of fancy; disposition plods in the path of reason. Yet are they mutually dependent upon each other. Invention without order is chaos before the creation of light. Order without invention is a mere unintelligent operation of mechanical power. And widely as the characters of these co-ordinate agents differ from each other, there are points of contact between them, which assimilate and almost identify them together. Some invention is indispensable to conceive and combine any complicated system of arrangement, and some rule of order no less essential to embody the visions of fancy.

Disposition, as applied to rhetoric, is but another word for method. According to Quinctilian it is "a useful distribution of things, or of parts; assigning to each its proper place and station." It is obvious then, that no general rule of disposition can be given for the various classes of public speaking. The same disposition, which would be suitable to a deliberative speech, would be utterly inapplicable for the management of a cause in a judicial court. That, which would be proper for a demonstrative oration or a sermon, would again differ from both the others, and even with regard to discourses of the same kind it must be admitted, that from the creation of the world to this hour no two occasions of public speaking have been in every respect alike. The speaker therefore must exercise his own discernment. He must study his subject, examine its bearings, measure its capacities, and use his own ingenuity according to his opportunities.

The ancient rhetoricians are not all agreed either in the subjects, which they comprehend under the article of disposition, or in the number and denominations of the distinct parts, which are combined in the composition of a regular discourse. Under the head of disposition Quinctilian treats solely and exclusively of judicial causes; and teaches how and when the several states of conjecture, of definition, of quantity, of quality, are to be assumed, together with the various questions, which may put in issue the jurisdiction of the court, or the meaning and construction of the law; while Aristotle and Cicero include in their ideas of disposition the several component parts of an oration; a subject likewise copiously handled by Quinctilian, but which he ranges under the first general head of invention.

The distinct parts of a discourse, enumerated by Aristotle, are only four; introduction, proposition, proof, and conclusion; and even of these four he pronounces the second and third only to be indispensable; since a discourse may be complete without the formality of an exordium or of a peroration. To these four parts Quinctilian adds a fifth, with some difference in the denomination of the parts. He distinguishes the introduction, narration, proof, refutation, and conclusion. But the distribution of Cicero is still further extended, and recognises six parts under the names of introduction, narration, proposition, proof, refutation, and conclusion.

In examining particularly into this diversity of technical divisions we perceive, that it arises in both instances from that rage of minute and subtle subdivisions, which we have noticed on former occasions. Thus Quinctilian gains a point upon Aristotle by subdividing his proof into two parts, which he calls confirmation and refutation; by the first of which he understands proof, adduced m support of a proposition, without reference to an adversary; and by the second, proof in reply to objections. A similar minuteness of analysis forms the sixth head of division, assumed by Cicero. Under the name of proposition Aristotle included the narration. Quinctilian changes the name, and under the head of narration includes the proposition. Cicero separates them entirely, and treats each of them as a distinct general division. Other rhetoricians have multiplied them still further; but microscopic researches into trivial distinctions will never teach us genuine rhetoric; much less will they ever form an eloquent orator. The line of distinction between the parts assigned by Aristotle is strong and clear. It will suit every class of discourses, and adapt itself to every form of eloquence. The divisions of Cicero and Quinctilian are more peculiarly applicable to the practice of the bar. It is not very material which of these arrangements is pursued; but I shall follow that of Cicero, because it has been prescribed to me, and shall successively treat of the properties and uses of the introduction, narration, proposition, confirmation, confutation, and conclusion, as distinct parts of a regular discourse; and to these I shall add, as occasion may require, remarks on the subordinate and incidental topics of transition, digression, and amplification.

It will scarcely be necessary to detain you long with a definition or explanation of the terms, which of themselves are sufficiently understood. They mean only, that in the composition of an elaborate oration the most easy and proper course you can adopt is to begin with an exordium; then proceed to relate the facts, upon which you mean to rely; after which you are to unfold the proposition, constituting the subject of your discourse, and support it by such proof, as you are able to adduce for its confirmation. When the objections of your antagonist have been heard, you are to reinforce your proof by confuting them; and close the whole by a peroration, or conclusion.

Of all these parts you are to bear in mind, that the proposition and the proof are alone of absolute necessity to every public discourse. Although in real life it is not unexampled to hear a man speaking in public without purpose and without proof, yet the case is not admissible in theory, and there is no speculative system of rhetoric, to which such harrangues are reducible. But the exordium and peroration are ornamental, rather than vital parts. Narration and refutation are incidental, and not always necessary or proper. In elucidating however the properties and uses of these several parts, it will be most useful to consider them in the order, which they themselves take in the discourses where they all find a place, rather than in that of their relative importance. Let us begin then with the exordium.

The exordium is defined by Cicero "a discourse to prepare the minds of the audience for the favorable reception of the remainder." Hence you will observe it is not inherent in the subject; but a mere preliminary to conciliate the favor of the hearer. Though not always indispensable, it is often necessary; and when not improper should never be omitted. It is not peculiar to the scenes of public oratory; it is equally habitual to every species of written composition, and its use is analogous to that of the common salutations among men, which under some form or other in every state of society precede their entrance upon the transaction of business. The universal propensity to some sort of prefatory introduction, at the threshold of all intercourse between men, may perhaps be traced to the constitution of human nature, independent of any state of society. It has been a question among philosophers whether the natural state of man is that of peace or of war. Different solutions have with great and rival ingenuity been drawn from different speculative views of human nature. If we judge however from the experience we have of mankind in the state, approaching nearest to that of nature, in which men have ever been found, or from the nature and character of human wants and human passions, or by analogy from the state of other wild beasts among themselves, I think we shall conclude, that the state of nature, like the state of society, is in itself not uniformly a state either of peace or war; but alternately of either. Stimulated by the necessities or the passions, implanted in his nature for the preservation of the individual or of the species, man would be at war with any of his fellow creatures, from whom he could wrest the object of his immediate wants. Satiated and satisfied, he would be at peace with the whole creation. In hunger he would be active and violent; in fullness indolent and cowardly. A natural result of this variation of temper would be, that, in the accidental meeting of two human creatures, a reciprocal uncertainty would exist in the bosom of each with regard to the disposition of the other; and one of the first steps towards association would be the concert of some sign or indication, which might be understood as a pledge of peace at such occurrences. A manifestation of amity would thus become habitual, as introductory to every transaction of a peaceable nature between men; and passing from speculation to experience, we find some usage of this kind practised by every tribe of savages, as well as among all the civilized nations, with which we are acquainted. When by the progress of society the original motive for exhibiting these banners of benevolence disappears, the courtesies of civilized life assume its place, and adopt, as a customary formality, what was in its origin a promise of kindness. In all civilized society professions of friendship are multiplied in proportion as its realities diminish. Salutations, embraces, the joining of hands, are lavished as tokens of mutual regard, even when it is not felt; and wherever man meets man in the attitude of peace, be it for objects of pleasure, of business, or of devotion, some introduction to every purpose is held to be not less necessary, than the purpose itself. From the common forms of personal intercourse the usage was transferred to the silent communications, introduced by the art of writing, and all literary discourse, from the familiar letter to the epic poem, announces itself with more or less formality of introduction, according to the nature of the subject and the genius of the writer.

The general purpose of an oratorical exordium then is to prepare the minds of the hearers for receiving the rest of the discourse; or in other words to engage their good will, their attention, and their docility; to interest them in favor of the speaker; to rivet their attention to his speech; and to enlist their feelings in behalf of his cause. These are distinct objects, and are to be promoted by different means. The skill of the orator consists in combining them judiciously, and pointing them with effect to the same end.

The good will of the audience towards the speaker is the first object of consideration. To estimate its importance we need only place ourselves in the situation of hearers, and consult our own breasts. How much more readily do we believe those, whom we love, than those, against whom we feel disgust or aversion. Confidence is the natural companion of affection, and distrust is almost inseparable from dislike. In a former lecture I suggested this to you, as one of the most powerful motives, which should urge a public Speaker to lay the foundations of confidence in the general excellence of his personal character. But a speaker may be unknown to most of his audience, and therefore an object of their indifference; or he may have had prejudices excited against him, and have evil impressions to remove. We are now inquiring what aids he can derive for this purpose from his exordium.

He may bespeak favor by allusions, direct or indirect, to himself; by explanations of his own motives; by professions of honor and virtue; by disproving or extenuating charges or inculpations, which may have been alleged against him; by leading the mind of his hearers to recollections of his services or good deeds; by enlarging upon the difficulties, obstacles, and dangers, with which he has contended; or by express and open solicitation. This is an easy but a dangerous topic. There are few men, possessed of any talent for public speaking, but can display great eloquence upon so favorite a subject, as themselves. But the danger is of overrating its importance; of dwelling upon it with too much emphasis; of provoking the censure of the hearer by self-applause, or his derision by self-admiration. He may bespeak favor by stimulating an opposite sentiment against his adversary; an expedient of frequent resort in all controversial causes; but which, like the last, requires great delicacy of hand to be properly managed. It is not difficult at any time to stir up sentiments of hatred, envy, and contempt in the human heart. But, as I have heretofore observed to you, these are poisoned arrows, which the improved morality of modern ages rejects, as unlawful weapons of war. There are indeed vices, which even charity cannot rescue from the scourge of scorn; and crimes, which even mercy would doom to the rack of indignation. If the detection or exposure of these should at any time become the duty of a public orator, he may draw the kindness of his audience to himself in proportion to the odium he pours upon them; but he must above all things be cautious not to mistake the cry of his own passions for the voice of virtue; and remember that profound admonition of the wisest of men, wrath is cruel, and anger is outrageous; but who is able to stand before envy? The favor of an auditory may be induced by the expression of confidence in them; by the manifestation of an ardent zeal for their welfare, of respect for their opinions, of reliance upon their wisdom, their fortitude, their magnanimity. It has been remarked by accurate observers of human nature, that for conciliating kindness praise is a more efficacious instrument, than beneficence; and perhaps it may be added, that a multitude is still more susceptible of being influenced by praise, than an individual. Direct praise to a single man is more liable to the suspicion of flattery. To an assemblage of men it may be offered in bolder nakedness, as they are generally less scrupulous in receiving it. Yet in administering these sweetmeats of persuasion the speaker should be cautious to guard at once against the profusion, which must cloy the receiver, and that officiousness, which would degrade himself.

The favor of an auditory may finally be engaged by an exordium, borrowed from the subject itself; for which purpose the orator must prepare himself by a careful and impartial examination of its character, with reference to the previous dispositions of his hearers. And in this point of view there are five different shades of complexion, which the subject may bear. It may be popular, obnoxious, equivocal, trivial, or obscure.

The popular subject is that, which, being already possessed of the public favor, calls for no exertion on the part of the orator to bespeak kindness. The obnoxious subject is that, against which the hearers come forearmed with strong prepossessions. The equivocal subject is that, which presents a doubtful aspect; a mixture of favorable and of unpropitious circumstances. The trivial subject is that, which, involving no important interest or engaging no strong sensation, is considered by the hearer as insignificant, and deserving little attention. And the obscure subject is that, which, by embracing a multitude of intricate and entangled facts or principles, perplexes the understanding of the auditory.

To suit these various descriptions of subjects introductions are divided into two general classes, the first direct, and the second oblique; which the Roman rhetoricians distinguish by the names of principium or beginning, and insinuation. The direct introduction is always to be employed upon popular subjects, if any exordium is expedient; and it is the most suitable for the trivial and the obscure subjects. But in equivocal cases for the most part, and in obnoxious subjects generally, a skilful orator will begin with insinuation. The name is sufficiently indicative of the thing. It arises from the necessity of the case and the most common propensities of mankind. For directly to solicit their good will in the moment of their animosity, instead of conciliating their kindness only exasperates their indignation. On such occasions the only possible chance of success, of which the speaker can avail himself, is to begin by diverting his hearers from their own thoughts. He must appease them with excuses; soothe them with apologies. He must allure the attention of their minds from objects of their aversion to images, in which they take delight; from characters, whom they despise or hate, to those, whom they love and revere. The real purpose of his discourse must sometimes be concealed; sometimes even disguised. An occasional incident occurring at the moment; a humorous anecdote, ingeniously pointed to the purpose; a smart retort or repartee, arising from the opponent's recent conclusion; an allusion to some object of sympathy to the audience; an address to the natural love of novelty, or to the taste for satire; all these may furnish the variety of expedients, which the speaker must seize with the suddenness of instinct, to commence a discourse by insinuation.

The introduction, whether direct or oblique, should be simple and unassuming in its language; avoiding all appearance of brilliancy, wit, or polished elegance. These are graces, the display of which tend rather to prepossess the audience against a speaker, than in his favor. They raise that sort of temper, with which we observe a handsome person admiring himself before a glass. The natural kindness towards beauty is lost in the natural disgust at vanity. To excite the admiration of his audience the speaker must cautiously forbear to discover his own. But he may throw into it the whole powers of his mind, by energy of thought and dignity of sentiment; for nothing can so forcibly propitiate his healer both to himself and to his discourse, as the exhibition of ideas, which command respect without the appearance of a solicitude to obtain it.

The introduction should avoid vulgarity; that is, a character, which would render it equally suitable for many other occasions, as for that, upon which it is used. It should not be common nor convertible; that is, capable of being employed with little or no variation to the purpose of the speaker's antagonist, as usefully as to his own. It should not be too long; charged with no heavy redundancies; incumbered with no superfluous repetitions. It should shun all appearance of incongruity or of transposition; that is of tendencies opposite or even obviously variant from those of the discourse, which it precedes. Most of all should it beware of such a violation of these rules, as to spend itself upon purposes different from those of engaging the attention, the confidence, and the kindness of the hearer. To say that it ought to avoid exciting contrary emotions in his mind would be to suppose the speaker had lost his senses.

In all cases where the speaker and his subject arc both fully known, as most frequently happens in our judicial courts, and in our deliberative assemblies, a formal exordium is generally unnecessary, and often improper. On some occasions of great urgency the omission of all introduction becomes itself a beauty of a high order, as you see exemplified in a distinguished manner by the first of Cicero's orations against Catiline. To this example the sublimest of poets must have alluded in that passage, where he compares the arch enemy, Satan, practising in his temptation of Eve the arts of an orator of ancient times.

As when of old some orator renown'd
In Athens, or free Rome, where eloquence
Flourish'd (since mute) to some great cause addrest,
Stood in himself collected, while each part,
Motion, each act won audience, ere the tongue.
Sometimes in height began, as no delay
Of preface brooking, through his zeal of right.
So standing, moving, or to height up grown,
The tempter all impassion'd, thus began.

P. L. IX. 670.

As the magnitude of the cause, and the crisis of the moment point the judgment of the speaker to the cases, which exclude a regular exordium, they serve to indicate, that an elaborate introduction is most peculiarly adapted to demonstrative and pulpit discourses. The speaker stands alone. His subject generally depends upon his choice, and until announced by himself is generally unknown to his audience. There is something new to introduce, and no sudden or unexpected pressure of circumstance can lop away the preliminaries of custom. Indeed in the practice of modern oratory it may be laid down as a general rule, that extemporaneous speeches seldom can require, and written orations as seldom can forbear the formalities of a rhetorical exordium.

Lecture Eighteen - Narration

In the composition of a formal oratorical discourse the narration is the part, which immediately succeeds the exordium. The object of the introduction being, as in my last lecture I explained, to conciliate the attention, the kindness, and the docility of the audience, when that has been accomplished, or at least attempted, so far as the situation and circumstances of the speaker have rendered it expedient, his next object must obviously be to give a general exposition of the facts, upon which he purposes to raise his argument.

The term itself, narration, is doubtless so well understood by you all, that it would derive no additional clearness or precision in your minds from a definition. But, in considering its application to the several classes of oratory we shall find its character and uses to differ materially on different occasions, when it may be employed.

It has sometimes been questioned whether narration belonged at all to discourses of the deliberative class; because deliberation, relating always to future time, can furnish no materials for a narrative. Indeed it is of judicial orations alone upon the state of conjecture, or, to speak in reference to our own modern practice, it is of trials at the bar upon issues of fact, questions for the decision of juries, that narration forms a principal and indispensable ingredient; and therefore most of the rhetorical precepts for the conduct of this part of a discourse are adapted especially to occasions of that nature. But to every other mode of public speaking narration is incidental. The utility of any measure, which is the subject of deliberative discussion, generally depends upon a previously existing state of things; often upon a particular disclosure of facts, which the purpose of the deliberative orator requires him to make before his auditory. No question upon the imposition of a tax, the collection of a revenue, the sale of lands, or the subscription to a loan, a declaration of war, or the ratification of a treaty, can arise, in a public assembly, in a state of abstraction. These great topics of debate must always be connected with a series of great public events; and the expediency, upon which the issue of the deliberation will turn, must lean upon the basis of the public affairs at the time of deliberation. The policy of the future is interwoven with the history of the past; and every deliberative orator, whose views of a proposed measure are directed by facts within his own knowledge, must lay before his hearers, in justification of his opinions, as well the facts themselves, as their connexion with the benefits or disadvantages of the measure, which he recommends or dissuades.

In demonstrative oratory, so far as this is made the vehicle of panegyric or of censure, narration is equally necessary. A character can be justly commended or reprobated only on account of the deeds, by which it has been distinguished; and these deeds can be emblazoned only by means of a narrative.

But in all such cases, when the narrative does not contain the whole proposition within itself, there is no necessity, nor even would there be any propriety in confining this part of the discourse to a separate location, immediately subsequent to the introduction. It should be introduced occasionally in any part of the speech, intermingled with discussion, diversified by argument, assumed, laid aside, and again renewed, as may serve the purpose of the speaker.

The Manilian law was an act of the Roman people, proposed by the tribune, Manilius, giving the command of the army by an extraordinary commission, and with unusual powers, to Pompey, for the purpose of finishing the war against Mithridates. The celebrated oration of Cicero upon that subject was delivered with a view to prevail upon the people to bestow this unprecedented favor, and to place this uncommon trust in Pompey. The expediency of the act was to be proved by arguments, drawn from the nature of the war and the character of the proposed commander. This oration therefore partook both of the deliberative and of the demonstrative class; and a distinct narrative was necessary to both. The nature of the war was to be manifested by a narrative of the most important events, which had marked its progress. The character of Pompey was to be recommended by a narrative of his prior achievements. It was the first occasion, upon which Cicero ever addressed the assembly of the people, and he labored his discourse with more than ordinary solicitude; stimulated at once by the treble motive of serving his friend, of maintaining his own influence with the people, and of obtaining a general adequate to the exigences of the war. The narration is double; one part detailing the disasters of the war, and the other extolling the exploits of Pompey. They both contribute essentially to the object of the discourse, but neither of them contains it entirely. They are indeed placed in strict conformity to the rules, in immediate connexion together, and follow directly after the introduction. But, as they were narrations merely destined to illustrate particular arguments, they might have been produced in any other part of the discourse. This distinction it is proper to make even upon jury trials, where the narration, entitled immediately to succeed the introduction, can only be that, which embraces the facts in issue, and upon which the verdict is to be pronounced.

There are likewise cases, when the narration even of judicial causes should be postponed for the consideration of other preliminaries besides the introduction. This is especially the case, when the orator has to combat strong prejudices against himself or his cause. The removal of such obstacles naturally belongs to the head of confutation; but it will sometimes be advisable to transfer them to an earlier stage of his discourse, and connect them immediately with his exordium. For the effect of unfavorable prejudice is to make the auditor unwilling to hear; and very little indeed can be expected either of attention, benevolence, or docility, from that, against which the person addressed has barred his ears.

But wheresoever the narration is introduced, whether in regular form immediately after the exordium, or at any subsequent stage of the discourse; whether in one connected train, or in frequent and occasional recurrences, there are certain peculiar characters, by which it should be distinguished. The most essential of these are brevity, perspicuity, probability. The brevity of a narration must however be a relative, rather than a positive quality; and always bear reference to the nature of the speaker's subject. That narrative is always sufficiently short, which is not overcharged with any superfluous circumstances. Hence Aristotle, whose precision of intellect never suffered him to admit the use of general, indefinite terms, expressly denies that brevity can be included among the essentials of a narration. Its length, he contends, must be measured by the complication or the simplicity of the transactions to be told; and he says that the rhetoricians, who require that every narration should be short, may be answered like the baker, who asked his customer whether he should make his bread hard or soft. "Pray sir, cannot you make my bread good?"

This reasoning is obviously just. But some rule is as obviously necessary for curtailing superfluities of narration; nor is it impossible in prescribing brevity to indicate some criterion, by which the looseness of this general precept may be circumscribed. What is the use of the narration? It is to lay the foundation for the speaker's argument; and the end, for which it is introduced, is the best measure for marking its limits. Narration, adduced as the basis of reasoning, comprises three periods of time, and three distinct links, chained in succession together; the important facts, the causes in which they

152

originated, and the consequences which flowed from them. The facts are composed of various incidents, the selection of which should be diversified according to the purpose, for which they are alleged. The same events are susceptible of very various narratives, all strictly conformable to the truth; and the same assemblage of circumstances, which would constitute a concise narrative for the purpose of illustrating an important argument, would be tediously long if the position, which gives them pith and moment, were removed.

Take for example the narration of Milo's departure from Rome, the day of the encounter, which terminated in the death of Clodius. "Milo," says the orator, "had attended that day in the senate, and after their adjournment went home, changed his shoes and garments, waited a little, as usual, for his wife to get ready, and finally left his house at a time, when Clodius, had he meant to return that day to Rome, must have been arrived. Clodius meets him on horseback, without carriage, without baggage, without his usual train of effeminate Greeks, nay without his wife, which was almost unexampled; while this supposed assassin, who is represented as having taken that road for the express purpose of murder, was travelling in his carriage, muffled up in his cloak, encumbered with a load of baggage, and surrounded by a delicate and timorous train of women and children,"

Suppose that the defence of Milo upon that trial had been like that in the case of Roscius of Ameria. Suppose the murder had been committed at Rome, and the object of Cicero had been to show, that it was not and could not be committed by Milo, because he was, at the time of its commission, in the country. The material fact of his departure from Rome would have been precisely the same; but the narration must have been altogether different. The selection of incidents would have been varied, or omitted. The purpose being merely to show that he was not at Rome, it would have been useless and impertinent to tell of his attendance in the senate; of his change of clothing; of his wife's adjustment of cap and ribbons; of his cloak, his maid-servants, and his boys. In such a state of the cause those very incidents, which in the oration, as it now appears, are selected with such consummate address, would have been tedious and ridiculous. In that case the absence from the city would alone have been material, and the narration might have been comprised in half a line. But here the object was to exhibit Milo in a certain state of mind, for the purpose of convincing the judges, that his meeting with Clodius was on his part unpremeditated. What an admirable grouping of incidents to produce this effect! In Shakespeare's tragedy of Julius Caesar, the poet makes the principal conspirator of Caesar's death describe the state of mind, which in the human constitution precedes the commission of such unnatural deeds.

"Between the acting of a dreadful thing
And the first motion, all the interim is
Like a phantasma, or a hideous dream;

153

The genius and the mortal instruments
Are then in council; and the state of man,
Like to a little kingdom, suffers then
The nature of an insurrection."

Cicero does not precisely say this; but the whole tenor of his narration is founded upon the presumption, that the judges would feel what extreme agitation of deportment, and what a fearful conflict of the passions accompanies in the human breast the premeditation of murder. Milo was a senator. He had on the same day, when Clodius was killed, attended the meeting of the senate, and had not left that assembly until after their adjournment. To a superficial observer of human nature it were perhaps impossible to select an incident less entitled to notice in a narrative than this. Why, no doubt Milo, like the other senators, habitually attended the meetings of the senate, and waited for the adjournment to go home. True; but this regular recurrence to his ordinary daily occupation has a tendency to show, that he was not in the convulsive agitations of a laboring crime. The settled intent of murder would have produced a deviation from the common round of business. He would not have attended at the senate at all; or he would have left the assembly before its adjournment, had the bloody purpose been teeming in his soul. A purpose of murder would have absorbed all his faculties. He could not have enjoyed the composure of spirit, nor the coolness of recollection to go home and change his clothes, and wait for the lingering arrangements of a lady's dress. Still less would he have thought of taking her with her chambermaids and boys in his retinue. This is the argument, which Cicero intends to raise from the facts, thus recapitulated; and the bare notice of circumstances, thus trifling in themselves, prepares the minds of the judges for the reception of his defence. By turning to the subsequent argumentative part of the same oration, you will see with what earnestness and force he dwells upon these incidents seemingly so slight, as affording the clearest demonstration of Milo's innocence.

To comply then with the requisition, that the narration should be short, it will be sufficient to remember that you must begin precisely with that incident, which is material to the argument you intend to urge; and, as you proceed, to suppress every circumstance, which has no relation to it. For the purpose of brevity you must exclude likewise every part of a transaction, necessarily implied in the statement of the fact itself. Suppose in the narrative of a journey you should say, we came to the river, inquired the rate of ferriage, entered the boat, were rowed across, and landed on the opposite shore; every part of this relation, considered separately, is as short as it could be made; but "we crossed the river" would tell the same fact in four words.

The rule of brevity is not necessary for the purpose of proscribing repetitions and tautology. For however allowable it might be to protract the narration, these would still be inadmissible. But, in the endeavour to avoid these faults, we must be no less careful to avoid those of confusion and obscurity. This was the caution of Horace to the poets, "brevis esse laboro, obscurus tio." And the danger is still more incident to an orator, over anxious of brevity in his narration. The danger of redundancy too is not of such vital importance, as that of obscurity. By saying too much the speaker may become tedious. But in saying too little he puts in jeopardy the very justice of his Cause. So that the precept of brevity must be relative, not only with regard to the character of the cause, but also with regard to that of the audience. Nothing, already known to all his hearers, can be essential to the narration of a speaker. To a very select and intelligent body a concise summary will fully answer the end of a narrative, when to a numerous, popular assembly, or to an ordinary jury a circumstantial detail might be indispensable to make them understand your subject. If the narrative comprehends events so multifarious and complicated, that it must be positively long, it will be most advisable to divide it into several distinct periods, and mark the divisions either by formal enumeration, or as the relation proceeds, so that the mind of your hearer may dwell upon them, as resting stages for his attention. Nor let the love of brevity preclude the seasoning of occasional ornament. As you lead your hearer along, scatter fragrance in his path. Spread the smiling landscape around. With the attractive charm of fancy make all nature beauty to his eye and music to his ear. The road will then never be long.

The second of the qualities essential to a good narration is clearness or perspicuity; to obtain which the speaker must use plain, intelligible language, never descending to vulgarity; never soaring into affectation. He must mark with obvious distinctions the things, persons, times, places, and motives, of which he discourses; and observe a due conformity of voice, action, and delivery, to the substance of his speech. He must fasten the attention of his hearers altogether upon the facts, which he is relating; and, instead of attracting it, use his most strenuous endeavours to withdraw it from the manner, in which he tells the story. Let him relate so that every hearer may seem to have been present at the scene, and may fancy that he could himself have told it exactly so. If the orator labors here for admiration, he must earn it at the expense of his credit. He will be applauded, and not understood, or not believed.

The same principle dictates the rule of probability. The facts are to constitute the foundation for the reasoning; of course the great object of the narration is to obtain belief. In the other parts of the discourse the speaker may plead some excuse for aiming to attract some of the hearer's attention to himself. The success of the orator might not be lost, though his audience should sometimes think that he reasons forcibly, or deeply feels his subject. But once give your hearer time, while your story is telling, to think, this man tells his story well, and ten to one but your cause is lost. He had much better think you tell it ill. Art and labor may naturally be expected elsewhere; but in the narration they must not even be suspected. You want the acquiescence of your hearer's mind not to the goodness, but to the truth of what you say. You may perhaps inquire, why then the precept is not that the narrative should be true? It is undoubtedly of great importance to an orator that his statement of facts should be true; but this is not included among the precepts of his art, for two reasons; first because the truth of his statement does not always depend upon himself. His narrative must generally be founded upon the testimony of others, and he cannot be responsible for its truth. And secondly because the truth is not by itself sufficient to obtain the hearer's belief. there is a natural connexion between truth and probability; and so strong is this connexion, that an audience is seldom willing to admit any other test of that truth, which they cannot certainly know, but that probability, of which all can judge. Hence it follows, that an improbable truth is less adapted to obtain belief, than a probable falsehood. And hence the rhetorical instruction to an orator is not "make your narration true;" but make your narration probable.

To observe the rule of probability, you must in the first place, by a severe and impartial scrutiny and comparison of incidents, exert your faculties to discover the truth; and lay it down as a maxim of rhetoric no less than of morality, never to give for truth what you know to be false. You must then trace and exhibit a natural connexion between your facts, their causes, and the motives, in which they originated. You should give intimations of character, which may account for the acts of persons, which form a part of your relation. You should observe all the conformities of time, place, and circumstance; and as there is in all human transactions a sort of homogeneous congruity of facts, you must be attentive to give your narrative that natural air of truth, which forms the first excellence of dramatic representation. If the first part of the story be properly told, it will prepare the hearer for the sequel, and even for the substance of the argument. As the narrative is the foundation, upon which the proof or confirmation is to be built, whatsoever is there to be enlarged upon, the characters, time, place, motives, and occasions, are to be first sketched in the narration.

In addition to these rules some rhetorical teachers consider the narration as requiring peculiar dignity of language, and loftiness of expression. A more judicious rule will be to diversify the style according to the nature of the subject to be related. Digressions should here seldom be indulged, and always be short. Exclamations, figures of the high poetical character, personifications, formal arguments, and forceful appeals to the passions, have no place here; for they would extend the narrative to unnecessary length, or veil it with obscurity, or impair its credibility. But of all the parts of an oration the narrative is that, which calls for the profoundest art, for that art, which disguises itself, for that "callidissima simplicitatis imitatio," which belongs only to the most eloquent of men. It is the part, which requires graces of the most delicate refinement, beauties of the most exquisite polish. But the speaker must cling to the character of his subject. In causes of a private character and of minor importance, he must present only those modest, unassuming graces, which attain distinction by flying from notice. Every word should be selected for its meaning, and bear the sterling stamp of significancy. Yet his simplicity

156

must not be plain; his purity must not be barren. The discourse should be seasoned with pleasantry; the language quickened with variety.

The attention of the auditory seldom fixes upon any part of a public speaker's performance so intensely, as upon his narration. There is something in the nature of narrative interesting to all mankind; and it is owing to this propensity, that the most popular of all reading in every stage of society subsequent to the introduction of letters, and at every period of life, is history, real or fictitious. Hence the general fondness for biography. Hence the still more universal attachment to romances, novels, and ballads. But, independent of this passion for hearing stories told, the auditory have a further stimulus to attention in the wish to form their own judgment from the facts. They suppose themselves as able to reason and draw conclusions, as the orator himself; and they give themselves credit for as much feeling, as he can display. There is upon most judicial trials a spirit of pride and of self love in the judge or jury, which gives birth to a professed principle of total disregard to the argument or eloquence of the advocate, and glories in making up the decision exclusively upon the facts. At the narration alone, jealousy, suspicion, and self complacency may be lulled to sleep in exact proportion, as attention is awakened. The pleasure of the hearer imperceptibly ripens into judgment; and, in surrendering entire acquiescence to the narrative of the orator, the judge or juror fancies he has pronounced upon the naked facts, without any bias from the oratory of the pleader.

The credit of a narrative must therefore always depend much upon that of the narrator. An established reputation for veracity is often equivalent to a cloud of witnesses. This reputation it behooves then every public speaker to acquire by the general tenor of his life, and the uniform adherence to truth. This acquisition can be made only by degrees, and in process of time. When once attained, it calls for the same solicitude to be retained; and the public speaker should never forget, that a single detected deviation from truth may forfeit the accumulated confidence of many spotless years.

One of the most powerful arts of narration is to intersperse the relation with such sensible images, as present the scene to the hearer's eye. All narrative is a species of imitation. It is the representation to the mind by the means of speech of events, which have before been the objects of observation. The more picturesque then a narration is made, the closer is its resemblance to the truth, and the better adapted must it be to obtain belief. The preeminence of the eye over the ear, as a judge of imitation, is remarked by Horace, whose principles of taste, though prescribed only for the composition of poetry, are universally applicable to all the fine arts.

Segnius irritant animos demissa per aurem,
Quam quae sunt oculis subjecta fidelibus, et quae
Ipse sibi tradit spectator.

Art. Poet. 180.

A passage, which has been well translated by Roscommon:

But what we hear moves less, than what we see;
Spectators only have their eyes to trust,
But auditors must trust their ears and you.

This talent of picturesque description furnishes one of the surest tests for the genius of an orator. The power of painting by speech cannot, like the expression of sentiments or of passions, be borrowed from others. It requires accuracy of observation, correctness of judgment, and facility of communication; an union of faculties, bestowed only upon the darlings of nature. But as, if attainable at all by exertions of your own, it must be rather by the contemplation of examples, than from the abstraction of precepts, I shall at a future stage of our inquiries invite your attention to some of those imperishable models, which have commanded the admiration of ages, and survived the revolutions of empires; which may teach you what to do, by showing you what has been done.